Is Jazz Dead?

Is

Jazz

Dead?

(Or has it moved
to a new address)

STUART NICHOLSON

Routledge
Taylor & Francis Group

New York   London

All citations are from the author's personal interviews and/or email conversations, unless otherwise noted.

Published in 2005 by
Routledge
Taylor & Francis Group
270 Madison Avenue
New York, NY 10016

Published in Great Britain by
Routledge
Taylor & Francis Group
2 Park Square
Milton Park, Abingdon
Oxon OX14 4RN

© 2005 by Taylor & Francis Group, LLC
Routledge is an imprint of Taylor & Francis Group

Printed in the United States of America on acid-free paper
10 9 8 7 6 5 4 3 2 1

International Standard Book Number-10: 0-415-96708-2 (Hardcover) 0-415-97583-2 (Softcover)
International Standard Book Number-13: 978-0-415-96708-2 (Hardcover) 978-0-415-97583-4 (Softcover)
Library of Congress Card Number 2005024395

Library of Congress Cataloging-in-Publication Data

Nicholson, Stuart.
    Is jazz dead? : (or has it moved to a new address) / by Stuart Nicholson.
        p. cm.
    ISBN 0-415-96708-2 (hardback : alk. paper) -- ISBN 0-415-97583-2 (pbk. : alk. paper)
    1. Jazz--History and criticism. I. Title.

ML3506.N5 2005
781.65'09'051--dc22   2005024395

Taylor & Francis Group
is the Academic Division of T&F Informa plc.

Visit the Taylor & Francis Web site at
http://www.taylorandfrancis.com

and the Routledge Web site at
http://www.routledge-ny.com

To Dr. Elizabeth Peterson

Contents

Introduction

The globalization of jazz is not just another engaging story, another sign of the music's growing acceptance. To my mind it is the main story, the overwhelming trend, the key evolutionary thread taking us to the music's future.

Ted Gioia, musician and author of *The History of Jazz*
and *West Coast Jazz*

Jazz in the new millennium is in a very different world than that which was so lovingly re-created in the Ken Burns television retrospective *Jazz*. The reason is simple: It is competing for the leisure dollar in a highly competitive marketplace. Pop music, promoted with ruthless efficiency by the major corporations, dominates the cultural spaces. Jazz's voice is struggling to be heard.

So what's new? Hasn't jazz always jostled with consumer and popular culture for the public's attention throughout its history? Of course it has, but the early millennium years presented a very different music marketplace than that of the 1980s or even the 1990s. A once chaotic music industry, with an ever-changing array of music labels with names like Chess, Motown, Island, and Creation that were once as anarchic as the music itself, has hardened into an immovable oligarchy of EMI, Time-Warner, Universal, and Sony/BMG. As the number of "majors" shrank to these four players, the number of international superstars was also downsized, enabling the corporations to focus their efforts on promoting a smaller number of people more effectively. Their success can be measured by the ubiquity of these stars on the record charts and in the media, television, radio, and the Internet, and is a triumph of the corporate marketing machine. The increasing, homogenizing effect of the majors was reinforced by the deregulation of the airwaves that allowed companies like Clear Channel Communications, with more than 1,200 stations, to dominate the airwaves, which critics claim contributes to the growing blandness of broadcast music.

So where does an art form like jazz figure in a corporate jungle like this? Unprotected from market forces in the United States by public subsidy, it is fighting an unequal battle for survival. Jazz is at the mercy of a market that exerts its own disciplines, which can result in the music being shaped by commercial imperatives rather than aesthetic logic. This can take many forms, from an innocent request by a record producer to include a track by a jazz vocalist on an otherwise instrumental album to a kind of natural selection where promoters and club owners stick with a specific style they think the public wants (which is often an idealized representation of jazz from the 1950s or 1960s) to the exclusion of more experimental styles. If musicians don't want to play by the rules of supply and demand, then there is no shortage of those who will. A music that was founded in spontaneity and self-expression is in danger of ending up at the core of an ever more standardized world.

The inevitable homogenizing effects of the market take many forms, which I have tried to explore in this book, and they have contributed to the rise of an American mainstream that dominates current jazz practice. Those who do not broadly adhere to its conventions risk claims they are not playing "jazz" at all — the "real" jazz that swings and alludes to the blues. This overwhelming legacy of the music exerts a powerful influence on how the music is shaped today, as exemplified in the music of Wynton Marsalis and in the ethos of Jazz at Lincoln Center. Meanwhile, a group of retro-styled singers have gained increasing popularity by imitating the sounds and styles of the great pop vocalists of the past. In the minds of many members of the public at large, and even some musicians, jazz today has come to represent the past rather than the present. This has been the cause of considerable controversy within the music. "The terms of this debate pit the so-called neo-classicists, who insist on the priority of tradition and draw their inspiration and identity from a sense of connectedness with the historical jazz past, against both the continuous revolution of the avant-garde and the commercial orientation of fusion," wrote educator

Scott DeVaux in his essay "Constructing the Jazz Tradition." I suggest this debate goes even further, to include styles influenced by so-called World Music and "glocalized" styles of music from around the world.

A continuing theme throughout jazz history has been the use of appropriation that reveals a continuing dialogue not only with popular culture but other musical forms to broaden the scope of jazz expression. The culture of jazz is based on change because that is the culture of American: If a product or enterprise does not keep reinventing itself, it is swept aside by something that does. That is why it is vital for jazz musicians, as they have in the past, to keep their lines of input open to appropriate whatever is around them today, whether it be computer technology, sound processing tools and so on, or whatever, in order to continue the historic task of broadening the expressive base of the music. Some musicians are reinvigorating the music and keeping it relevant to today's audiences, but they are struggling to be heard. Because little has been written about these developments, the time seemed right to attempt to contextualize these new innovators within the continuing narrative of jazz history.

This book attempts to examine some of the tensions in today's jazz scene. Reading through the drafts, I realize that I have made a recurring argument for public subsidy to support the music. I am more than ever convinced that the music cannot survive without the injection of public money to a greater or lesser degree. If this sounds like a plea to governments of all stripes everywhere to support this valuable art form, then you are right; it is. Art and commerce seldom mix, and at this point in the history of the music, the need for funding has never been more acute. "It's pretty rough here, there's no 'jazz middle class,' you either play at Lincoln Center or the Iridium for people dining, or you play at Tonic for the door," said drummer and composer Bobby Previte told me in 2003. "I think it's really harder for younger people than it was when I first came to New York [in the early 1980s], and it was hard then! I don't know how they do it." The issue of the elimination of the midrange gig is something that is explored in the broader context of jazz funding in the United States.

With the jazz economy under pressure in the United States and jobs for musicians contracting rather than expanding, I try to illustrate how public subsidy could rejuvenate the U.S. jazz scene by showing how it is working effectively and producing thriving jazz scenes in Europe, where most professional U.S. jazz musicians now derive a significant portion of their income stream. Equally, subsidy is vital to shelter jazz from the homogenizing effects of the marketplace by giving artists space to develop their music away from commercial pressures. But in an age when the most salient political event has been the rise of the conservatism and the retreat of liberalism, the notion of a healthy public realm subsidized by taxes has come under attack in the United States. The idea of central government and regional government funding jazz in the United States seems remote — but that should not stop the debate from going to the top of the agenda.

The phenomenon known as globalization and its impact on jazz is the key subtext of this book. The globalization of jazz is seldom written about, yet its effects are profound and far reaching. When the recording machine caught jazz's first stirrings as a provincial Southern music in the second decade of the twentieth century, the music was immediately exported around the globe courtesy of the phonograph record. When masters like Armstrong, Ellington, Goodman, Parker, Coltrane, and Davis roamed the earth, the development of alternative forms of jazz outside of the American scene commanded little attention. But times are changing. Those towering figures are no longer with us, and distances are collapsing with cheap air travel, the Internet, and the effects of the global marketplace. Today, it is in countries outside the United States where the most profound changes in the music are occurring. The globalization of jazz is now yielding the most significant evolutionary change in the music in decades, and I try to examine what this actually means and the effects that flow from it.

Jazz may be an international language, but away from home it is either spoken in its overarching hegemonic styles (so that walking into a jazz club in London, Rome or Paris can sometimes seem like walking into a jazz club in New York) are often spoken in "local" dialects, and it is these latter developments I explore in the context of jazz in Europe. For a long while, these homegrown hybridized (or "glocalized") versions of the music tended to be regarded not for what they were, but for what they were not — American jazz. But since the 1960s, there has been a gradual realization, more outside the United States than in it, that jazz does not have to be American, or even sound American, to be jazz. As jazz has spread around the world, it has acquired other histories in other countries; some countries have jazz histories that almost stretch back to the beginnings of jazz itself. One of the strongest centers for contemporary jazz is in the Scandinavian countries. Here, jazz had time to develop and evolve against a very different cultural backdrop to that of the United States and has produced the phenomenon known as the "Nordic tone" in jazz, a greatly misunderstood yet widely influential approach to jazz improvisation.

I have concentrated on the effects on globalization in Europe since that is where I come from. But the basic principle underlying the key musical changes that are occurring in jazz outside the United States — that of "glocalization" — can of course apply anywhere around the globe, and is doing so, in Brazil, South Africa, Russia, India and, well, just about everywhere. To chart these developments would take several volumes and is obviously impossible in a text such as this. As the twenty-first century develops, we will see the increasing "multidialectism" of jazz through the glocalization process, which is primarily a response to identity. Glocalization in jazz has been occurring for decades but has often been largely ignored because events in the United States have proved more compelling. But since the death of Miles Davis in 1991, there have been no significant developments in American jazz, while many glocalized styles of the music have become so strong they can no longer be ignored. As E. Taylor Atkins, associate professor of history at Northern Illinois University, points out in his chapter "Toward a Global History of Jazz":

> Jazz, both as a sociocultural force and as a musical idiom is significantly impaired by construing it as a narrowly national art, expressive of uniquely American experiences and characteristics and splendidly autonomous from consideration of global politics, cultural power and national identity. . . . At the very least, it is important [to] acknowledge that the evolution of jazz as an art did not occur solely within the borders of the United States, but rather in a global context in which musicians from a variety of musical traditions exchanged information and inspiration.

This book has taken me far longer to complete than I (or my editor) ever envisaged; I have traveled extensively over a period of almost four years to many European countries to research and speak to many kinds of people involved in the jazz economy, including musicians, jazz educators, writers, and critics; departments of culture for European governments; and animators from festival producers to venue managers. It seemed to me that many people in Europe had been thinking along the same lines as me for several years now, and this book attempts to connect the dots, and to make sense of the tensions flowing through the music in the new millennium years. In attempting to achieve this, I owe a debt of gratitude to Dr. Elizabeth Peterson, formerly a linguistics lecturer at Indiana University, a sociolinguist at the Center for Applied Linguistics in Washington D.C., and in 2005 pursing a career in academia in Finland, who brought to bear her formidable intellect on several chapters in this book. She was of enormous help and inspiration to me, and it is to her this book is dedicated. I am also very grateful to those who reviewed drafts of individual chapters and shared their thoughts and insights with me: Steen Meier, chairman of the Nordic Music Council and Copenhagen's famous Jazzhouse; Dr. Tony Whyton, assistant head of Higher Education (Research & Postgraduate Studies) at Leeds College of Music; Erling Aksdal, head of the jazz department at the Norwegian University of Science and Technology in Trondheim (and for our many long and detailed and enjoyable conversations); Frank Griffith, course leader for the B.A. Music Degree in Jazz Performance at the School of Arts, Brunel University in Uxbridge (with whom I have enjoyed many long and valuable conversations); Caspar Llewellyn-Smith, editor of *The Observer Music Monthly* and author of *Poplife: A Journey by Sofa* for his help, advice, and corrections in matters of pop music; musicologist Lars Westin of the Swedish Rikskonserter; the Italian musicologists Marcello Piras and Francesco Martinelli; Marty Khan, a long time jazz professional and author of *Straight Ahead: A Comprehensive Guide to the Business of Jazz*; and to the musicians Bob Brookmeyer, Brad Mheldau, Steve Marcus, Iain Ballamy, Lennart Aberg, Bob Belden, and Bugge Weseltoft.

My thanks and gratitude to John Cumming, director of the London Jazz Festival and Serious Music Productions, for our long (and enjoyable) conversations and for acting as conduit to the European Jazz Odyssey, which gave me the opportunity to meet and get to know some 40 major European jazz promoters. I am especially grateful to Bo Grønningsaeter, former director of the Molde Jazz Festival and the Nattjazz Festival and now chief executive of the West Norway Jazz Center and general secretary of the Europe Jazz Odyssey for his unfailing help, generosity, and support. The Europe Jazz Odyssey is a platform for cultural cooperation involving over 15 European countries to further European jazz, formed with financial support from the European Commission under the aegis of its "Culture 2000" program. I am very grateful to all its members with whom I spoke about the "jazz business" and the winds of change running through the music. Thanks also to Gerry Godley, director of the Improvised Music Company in Dublin (funded by the Irish government to provide festival programming, concert promotion, touring, recording, education, and audience development, plus the promotion of the critically acclaimed Dublin Jazz Festival), for valuable conversations, his comments for the book, and a wonderful craic in Dublin.

Grateful thanks also to Chris Hodgkins of Jazz Services in London; Dr. Wolfram Knauer, director of the Jazzinstitut Darmstadt; Jarmo Savolainen of the jazz course at Helsinki's prestigious Sibelius Academy; Wouter Turkenburg, chairman of the Jazz Department of the Royal Conservatory, The Hague for being so forthcoming; Gast Waltzing, professor of trumpet and head of Jazz Studies at the Conservatory of Luxembourg for his impeccable gastronomical taste and stimulating conversation (which dovetailed perfectly); Jacques Panisset, director of the Grenoble Jazz Festival; Peter Shultze, director of the Berlin Jazz Festival; Tore Flesjø, director of the Norsk Jazz Forum; Jan Granlie, editor of *Jazznytt*; Paul Gompes of the Dutch Jazz Connection; Pawel Brodowski, editor of Poland's *Jazz Forum*; Nod Knowles, head of Music for the Scottish Arts Council and director of the Bath Jazz Festival; Simon Purcell, professor of Jazz Improvisation and Piano at the Guildhall School, London, for letting me quote from his valuable study *Musical Patchwork: The Threads of Teaching and Learning in a Conservatoire*; Anne Ulset of the Royal Norwegian Embassy in London; Paul Wilson of the British Library for his valuable help in research, helpful comments, and thoughts along the way; Minna Huuskonen of the Finnish Music Center; Markus Partannen of Radio YLE in Helsinki; Annamaija Saarela, director of the UMO Jazz Orchestra; Tapio Korjus of Rockadillo Records; Jouni Jarvella for his wonderful solo on "Enkelin Kannel," which numbers among the finest in contemporary jazz; Adrian Jackson, director of the Wangaratta Jazz Festival, for enabling me to gain valuable insight into the Australian jazz scene; Paul Grabowsky, director of the Australian Art Orchestra; Kevin Jones and John Shand, fine Australian journalists, for a great time in Melbourne; Peter Margasak at the *Chicago Reader*; Sten Nilsen of Jazzland Records; Saxophonist Gilad Atzmon for our conversations about the issue of identity in jazz; trumpeter Randy Sandke, author of *Harmony for a New Millennium*; Bengt Strokirk of the Swedish Rikskonserter; Ola Bengtsson, director of jazz studies at the Royal College of Music in Stockholm, for his detailed e-mail responses to my persistent

questions; and Erice Horpestad Berthelsen, venue manager of the Club
Bla, Oslo.

A special vote of thanks to the folks at *Jazzwise* — Charles Alexander,
Jon Newey, and Stephen Graham — for their support and for allowing
me to work through many ideas in their pages, which in expanded form
appear in this book. Also grateful thanks to Odd Sneeggen of Svensk
Musik for commissioning several essays for the *Swedish Jazz Handbook*,
which later evolved into chapters; and to Chris Porter, Cim Meyer, Wulf
Muller, Nathan Grave, Florence Halfon, and Adam Seiff. Behind the
scenes, my editor Richard Carlin has been a model of forbearance, and his
suggestions following various drafts of each chapter were both well
observed and timely, and were key to shaping the final form of this book.
It has been a pleasure working with him on this project, and I hope he
found the time, trouble, frustrations, and gray hairs he has accumulated
over this project worth it. Thanks to Glenon Butler Jr., for his profession-
alism, patience and unfailing courtesy. Finally, my thanks and love to my
family — my mother, brother, and his family, my in-laws Eileen and Jim,
and my dear wife Kath — for their encouragement, and for understanding
the basic truth about writing a book: You can't be in two places at once.

Stuart Nicholson
Woodlands St. Mary
Berkshire, England

1

WHERE DO WE GO FROM HERE? THE JAZZ MAINSTREAM 1990 TO 2005

Jazz is radical music, but it's now practiced by conservative people.

John Coxon, Spring Heel Jack

When Miles Davis died on September 28, 1991, at St. Johns Hospital and Health Center in Santa Monica, jazz was plunged into a crisis of confidence as much as conscience.

Jazz's only surviving bona fide superstar was suddenly gone. The passing of such a legendary and charismatic figure served to underline the fact that there was no one of comparable stature to step into the jazz canon and continue the teleological "great man" model of jazz history. Subsequently, jazz seemed to be in a state of waiting for Godot, with no single musician providentially appearing, as had happened in the past, to become emblematic of a new direction, like a Louis Armstrong, Benny Goodman, Charlie Parker, John Coltrane, Ornette Coleman, or, indeed, another Miles Davis around whom history could be constructed. "Jazz was already short of marquee names when the '90s began," wrote critic Francis Davis in July 1996 in his *Atlantic Monthly* column. "The loss of [Davis] threatened to become a permanent void at the top of the bill."

Davis had been an omnipresent figure in the music from the time he played Hal to Charlie Parker's Hotspur in the 1940s to his final recordings with rap artist Easy Mo Bee in 1991. When he returned to the performing stage following almost six years of inactivity in 1981, his "comeback" concert on July 5 at Lincoln Center sold out within two hours. It was the most publicized event in jazz history, with almost every major newspaper in the world devoting column inches to the event. Davis's subsequent eight-show tour through Japan that October grossed over $700,000. Although he suffered a stroke in February 1982, he and his group toured Sweden, Denmark, Germany, England, Italy, Holland, France, and Belgium in April and May. Big tours such as these would become a feature of Davis's postfurlough comeback as he became *the* major draw in jazz during the 1980s.

As guitarist John Scofield, a sideman for Davis between 1982 and 1985, observed to a reporter from *Wire* magazine in 1991, "Nobody else could do big long tours every summer and fall and sell out stadiums all over Europe. And these people were not jazz snobs, they just dug Miles. He could make a believer out of a non-jazz person with the beauty of his sound and the rhythm of his notes. That's pretty heavy." Audiences came in droves; box offices frequently could have sold out three and four times over. The reason was simple: fans wanted to consume the aura of the physical presence of one of the great and enduring legends of twentieth-century music and to acknowledge a musical giant during his lifetime. In many ways the music, paradoxically, was less important than "the event."

While Davis's past musical achievements may have overshadowed his current musical aspiration during the final decade of his life — his legacy comprises some of the best-performed and most adventurously crafted albums in all of jazz — what may have been lacking in trailblazing innovation was made up with charisma. Miles's whole career had been one of constantly reinventing himself by deftly changing the backdrop that framed the fragile lyricism of his playing, his regular feats of musical prestidigitation keeping him ahead of the game for almost forty years. The distinction in his music was how the varied settings he created for himself often influenced events within jazz itself.

Although his prolific creativity ceased during a furlough from jazz that lasted from 1975 to 1981, his career on records continued unabated during this period as his record company delved into their vaults to draw on previously unreleased material. "When he was not playing, his career went on — thanks to me," Teo Macero, his long-time record producer at

Columbia, told writer Gene Santoro in his book *Dancing in Your Head*, "working in the studio with tapes we'd amassed. Without that he would've been in the soup." When Davis made his 1981 comeback concert at Avery Fisher Hall, in terms of record releases at least, it was as if he had never been away.

After his death in 1991, there was a distinct feeling of déjà vu as Davis albums, often with previously unissued material, continued to appear at regular intervals. In 1997 Columbia produced a brochure of Davis albums currently in print, detailing forty-three album reissues, twelve compilations, and five box sets, the latter including his ground-breaking studio collaborations with Gil Evans in their entirety and his marvelous mid-1960s acoustic quintet with Wayne Shorter, Herbie Hancock, Ron Carter, and Tony Williams. On release, these scrupulously packaged sets were given considerable prominence in newspapers around the world; in 1997, for example, a new Davis box set was worthy of a full-page review in the *New York Times*. Indeed, twelve years after his death, in October 2003, Davis was still figuring prominently on *The Billboard* Jazz Chart, reaching number 4 with *The Complete Jack Johnson Sessions*. When Charlie Parker died in 1955, graffiti across New York proclaimed "Bird Lives." In the musically conservative 1990s, there was no graffiti for Davis; had there been, "Miles Smiles" might have been appropriate.

Davis's most effusive obituaries grew noticeably ambiguous about the last twenty years of his career and especially about the last ten. The reason was that a standardized, some may say homogenized, version of an American jazz mainstream had emerged — the term "mainstream" for the purposes of this book meaning "main stream," the favored style of the majority. In jazz, the prevailing orthodoxy was based on the certainties of the acoustic hard-bop–post-bop nexus of the late 1950s and early 1960s. Electric jazz — which Davis had championed in the late 1960s, most notably through the album *Bitches Brew* (1970) — and experimental free jazz styles — originally pioneered in the late 1950s and 1960s by the likes of Ornette Coleman, Albert Ayler, John Coltrane in his final period, Cecil Taylor, and others — had become marginalized. Acoustic jazz had become the standard; as Christopher Porter, editor of *Jazz Times*, pointed out in his April 2003 editorial: "The status quo in jazz is music that sounds like it was made between the 1940s and the 1960s." Somehow a remarkable reversal of values had taken place. Where once it had been possible to characterize jazz as a flight from the status quo, it could now be defined as a flight back to it.

The term "mainstream" was first coined by writer and chronicler Stanley Dance in the 1950s. He was describing a group of ex–Count Basie sidemen, still plying their craft within the conventions of the swing era despite the changing musical climate around them. During the 1950s and 1960s, the mainstream was an alternative attraction to the main events going on elsewhere: John Coltrane at the Village Vanguard, Miles Davis at the Blackhawk, a Mingus imbroglio at the Café Bohemia, Albert Ayler with Gary Peacock and Sunny Murray at the Village Gate. By the end of the 1990s, however, the mainstream had become, to all intents and purposes, the main event.

Even during the late 1980s, the kind of pluralistic scene that had characterized jazz in the past had seemed set to continue. Steve Coleman and his M-Base experiments into arty rococo funk was, as *Downbeat* noted, "The p.r. coup of 1988 — the jazz critics flavor of the month for, well, months." Elsewhere, electric jazz was undergoing something of a renaissance prompted by Miles Davis's comeback, with John Scofield's Blue Matter band enjoying worldwide critical acclaim and bands led by Pat Metheny, Chick Corea, and Mike Brecker touring the major circuits. Musicians like Dave Holland, Charles Lloyd, Joe Henderson, and McCoy Tyner saw their careers rejuvenated, while Sonny Rollins and Keith Jarrett could still sell out almost any venue around the world.

In February 1987, Michael Dorf had opened the door of the Knitting Factory in New York and by April that year was booking improvisers every night of the week. "The Knitting Factory, a club on 47 East Houston Street, had almost singlehandedly revived New York's downtown arts scene in the first six months of operation," noted the *New York Times*. "The downtown scene quickly became trendy and marketable," observed pianist Brad Mehldau. "It used precisely that 'Other' status, that appearance of marginalization, to sell itself. Many more 'straight ahead' players would say that they have felt marginalized by the modishness of the downtown scene — if you just show up with an acoustic band, playing tunes, you're not 'avant-garde' enough."

The Knitting Factory plugged into a niche market for experimental music, with its own record label, web events, T-shirts, and even a West Coast branch as the term "downtown jazz" gradually became descriptive of, it seemed, almost any kind of experimental music. "There was a thriving (every way except economically) Downtown scene, [where] a night at the Knitting Factory was usually for the door," observed trumpeter Randy Sandke, author of *Harmony for a New Millennium*. Marketing strategies as much as canon formation helped create the concept of a succession of "schools" of jazz, beginning with "New Orleans" and moving through "Chicago," "swing," "bop," "cool" or "West Coast," "hard bop," "free," "jazz-rock," and so on. But unlike the collective force these communities of similarly oriented and competing artists playing within a single coherent style generated, downtown music embraced a myriad of highly personal styles and came to mean many things to many people. As a brand, downtown jazz was stronger than the recognition an individual player might achieve. Consequently, several artists became keen to shed the downtown sobriquet after its first flush of success because they felt it deflected attention from their music. Some felt it made it more difficult to "sell" to a consuming public, compared with the more traditional hierarchy of competing performers found in the more distinct genres marked out by the young lions or smooth jazz musicians.

Experimentation continued, however, as a niche music within a niche music; indeed, any self-respecting critic can recite a shopping list of experimenters laboring in relative obscurity at the music's margins. From the mid-1990s, there was a resurgence of loft-style jazz at New York's Vision Festival, while the Blue Series Continuum directed by pianist Matthew Shipp for the Thirsty Ear label and the more understated warping of mainstream expectation by some Palmetto label artists attracted critical acclaim, as did improvisers in the rugged mien of late period Coltrane, Albert Ayler, and others, such as David S. Ware, David Murray, and Charles Gayle. The Chicago scene also enjoyed recognition as a vibrant center of, at times, exciting musical anarchy, particularly at the hands of musicians such as Ken Vandermark, Rob Mazurek, Jeff Parker, Hamid Drake, Fred Anderson, and Tortoise. "No one interested in the future of jazz can afford to ignore them," said the *New York Times*.

Yet, ultimately, experimental jazz remained an interesting sideshow to the main event, the omnipresent jazz mainstream. Even by the early millennium years, no artists seemed to have had the impact of the first wave of downtown experimenters in the 1980s, who seemed, for a time at least, capable of mounting a serious challenge to the current jazz propriety of the day. Some of these players included Bobby Previte, Wayne Horvitz, Tim Berne, and especially John Zorn, whose career, as Ajay Heble observed in his book *Landing on the Wrong Note*, has "been marked by an extraordinary ability to cut across the high art/popular culture divide by popularizing music that's edgy, dissonant and inaccessible."

As interest began to wane in the M-Base experimenters and the myriad of styles contained under the downtown umbrella, the influence of the American jazz mainstream increased. By the end of the 1990s, those not performing within its shadow invited doubt by some as to whether they were playing jazz at all. There were several reasons for this, which individually might not have had a powerful impact on the music, but collectively had the effect of shaping a mainstream that had gradually become resistant to the kind of change, innovation, and invention that had swept through the music in the past. "I don't feel like there has been much by way of radical change," the clarinetist and composer Don Byron told me. "Just a few younger players who weren't around a few years ago, a few people who were around a few years ago are leaders now, but that's not a radical change to me!" By 2000 — in retrospective documentaries like Ken Burns's ten-part series on jazz — the jazz mainstream had become so self-contained it even denied the contemporary in the narrative of jazz history. But why did this renascent mood descend on jazz and what was its effect?

In 1981, Wynton Marsalis (b. 1961) became the first person to win simultaneous Grammys for a classical recording, *Trumpet Concertos* (a collection of trumpet concertos by Haydn, Hummel, and Leopold Mozart), and a jazz recording (his quintet's recording of *Think of One*). A trumpet player with a sure sense of identity — in 1991 he told me, "I know what my position is, Art Blakey told me what my position is, I know when I talk to Dizzy Gillespie. I know when I talk to Sweets Edison, I know when I was talking to Miles Davis" — he seemed destined for great things, and by the time he was twenty-five, he was a prominent figure in jazz.

Columbia's success in marketing Marsalis encouraged record companies to sign similar *wunderkinder*, who had the effect of partly demystifying the aura jazz had acquired among a potential audience of their peers. "I thought if I went after young artists at least that would pique the interest of kids," George Butler, the Columbia executive who signed Marsalis, told *Newsweek*. These young musicians — products of a jazz-education system that was producing graduates fluent in bebop and postbebop styles in such numbers it was regarded by some critics as a "phenomenon" — aspired to the high musical standards set by Marsalis, often copied his visual signature of sartorial elegance, and played in the adopted voices of some of jazz's older and often posthumous heroes. Critic Gary Giddins, in the introduction to his well-known 1985 collection *Rhythm-a-Ning*, noted that with this latest development, "Jazz turns neoclassical." This was indeed an apposite term because as a neoclassicist, Stravinsky became more interested in narrowing and refining the range of sonority than expanding it. So too the emerging young neoclassicists in jazz. Nevertheless, this style represented a major area of recording activity in jazz during the 1980s and well into the 1990s. Thanks largely to Marsalis, jazz was now undergoing a renaissance, but as historian Eric Hobsbawm pointed out in *Uncommon People*, "There was something strange about this revival . . . jazz of the early '90s looked back."

The product the neoconservatives offered can be stated simply as a return to the harmonic and melodic values of the hard-bop and postbop improvisers of the 1950s and early 1960s, and, in Marsalis's case, back to Ellington and Armstrong as well. Like F. R. Leavis codifying the literary tradition along narrow and intolerantly proscriptive lines, Marsalis espoused 4/4 swing and the blues as basic ingredients without which, he believed, there could be no jazz. It was a reassertion of what the neoconservatives considered to be the very value system of jazz itself and an attack on jazz for having lost touch with its audience (in the case of free jazz) and for losing touch with the acoustic "tradition" (in the case of jazz–rock fusion). In essence, neoconservatism presented a return to internalist principles of unity and coherence or a post-Romantic concept of thematic and organic unity. By the late 1980s, musicians playing in the so-called neoclassical style had become known as the "young lions," a sobriquet taken from the name of the famous collaborative LP by Lee Morgan, Wayne Shorter, Frank Strozier, and Bobby Timmons from April 25, 1960, and given contemporary relevance by a concert of the same name at the Kool Jazz Festival in New York on June 30, 1982. Performed by "seventeen exceptional young musicians" including Marsalis, James Newton, Chico Freeman, John Blake, Anthony Davis, John Purcell, and Paquito D'Rivera, it set the tone in jazz for almost two decades.

In 1990, Marsalis was featured on the cover of *Time* magazine, which announced the dawn of "The New Jazz Age." The neoconservatives were now central to the major recording companies' commitment to jazz, and as they jostled to sign young musicians, it had the welcome effect of focusing media attention on jazz and raising its public profile. "Because of the Young Lions era, the quote–unquote 'phenomenon' they had in the early 1990s, any jazz musician under the age of 25 got offered a recording contract," bassist Christian McBride, one of the leading young musicians of his generation, told me in late 2002. "I turned one down. I got offered a recording contract from Blue Note when I was 20 or 21, but I knew I wasn't ready. Yes, sure, I would probably play okay, but it wouldn't be much of an overall statement, so I decided I would hold off for a little while. I always felt like something that frivolous would kind of destroy the reputation or the foundation of what jazz is all about. You don't give somebody a recording contract because of their *age* — not in jazz! I mean, that is what pop is about, but you don't do that in jazz." In his *Atlantic Monthly* column, Francis Davis pithily commented, "There have always been young jazz musicians, but only lately has anyone made a fuss over them just for *being* young — instead of auguring for change."

The demands of the marketplace meant some young musicians had record contracts thrust upon them in advance of artistic maturity. "We sign people when they are too young," said Yves Beauvais in late 2002 when he was vice president of A&R for jazz at Columbia, after having held a similar post at Warner Bros. "They don't have the experience of fifteen years on the road with various bands before making their own statement." It was a point that saxophonist Branford Marsalis was quite frank about. "I was given contract too early, I admit. But if you win the lottery you're not going to say, 'Ohh, it's too much!' So I had to deal with it and people had to deal with it," he told me. However, some young musicians did not handle their newly found prestige as wisely as Marsalis, as master trumpeter Jon Faddis observed in 1993: "A lot of time, a young musician doesn't feel he's got to go out there and pay his dues. It's good for them but a little dangerous for jazz."

Competition was intense; as sales of one young artist's recordings began to falter, they were replaced with a new young signing who played within the same stylistic parameters of the previous "star," so that the music stayed the same, only the faces changed. "When you are basically a nobody with no experience and you're put in the position to make a major record and you blow, the record companies don't care," tenor saxophonist Javon Jackson told *Downbeat* in 1992. "They're going to drop you and you'll go from the top to the bottom just that quickly."

The influence of the major recording companies on jazz through the promotion of their talented young photogenic signings was profound. "The major labels were at this time seized with the idea that their marketing departments could create instant jazz stars as they had done for decades in the pop field," observed Randy Sandke, "So, as a good friend once said, bebop and modal jazz became the Dixieland of the 1990's. Only this time many of our foremost critics took it much more seriously than those of the 1940s and 1950s took the trad revival. Maybe because they hadn't heard it the first time around?" "I think part of the problem with jazz of the 1980s and 1990s was that there was a sea change in the way the business of jazz was conducted," continued Sandke.

> Of course you could say the same thing for just about any decade of jazz history, but this time these changes mitigated against the creation and propagation of new music. Jazz clubs in New York became so expensive that they relied heavily on tourists to fill their seats. God bless the tourists for helping to keep jazz alive in NY, but there was also a downside. Most tourists want to see the New York of their jazz fantasies: one that resembles the halcyon days of Birdland and Bop City. The concurrent marketing of the "Young Lions" fitted right into the wishes of this market, but as far as I'm concerned it kept the music for the most part stale and unadventurous. Clubs were no longer a haven for research and development but primarily a showcase for slick imitations of jazz's former glories. New York threatened to become a less retro version of New Orleans, where jazz is little more than part of the local folklore show. No wonder Europeans became skeptical about new musical advances coming out of the States.

The way the majors promoted these young musicians in the New York clubs to celebrate a new signing or launch an album also caused tensions in the beleaguered business infrastructure of jazz. "From the mid-1980s, the major New York clubs began to rely on money from record companies," points out Sandke. "It became policy for clubs to hire musicians only if their label would either pay for the band, guarantee a minimum of seats, pay for advertising, sponsor a press party or all of the above. Needless to say musicians who didn't enjoy this level of support were mostly shut out."

This tended to reinforce a narrowing of the perceived mainstream to the extent that the casual jazz follower in the late 1980s and for most of the 1990s could be forgiven for thinking the only show in town was the young lions. Those squeezed out of the main New York clubs found their out-of-town fees were affected. With New York viewed by many American promoters, club owners, and festival organizers as the "jazz capital of the world," exposure at its leading clubs had a bearing on a musician's asking price, both nationally and internationally. "Since the mid-1980s there's grown a whole class of musicians who have numerous CDs out, tour regularly, even get named in the polls, yet can't get into the New York clubs. I think this is a new phenomenon," Sandke asserts.

Musicians too old to be young lions, yet too young to be elder statesmen, were bypassed by the big recording companies in favor of the new, young breed of retro-boppers. Some middle-aged musicians, who were at their peak artistically, found themselves unable to find adequate exposure on records or in New York's big clubs, and slipped into a kind of second-class jazz citizenship. In 1993 Jon Faddis spoke to me of two internationally respected musicians who were unfashionably close to their fortieth birthdays. He said neither had a recording contract but were giving lessons to two musicians in their early twenties who did. Perhaps unsurprisingly, some older musicians, feeling excluded, harbored resentment toward the younger players. "A lot of older cats are so bitter that they miss a lot of opportunities because they hold a grudge against us," pianist Stephen Scott told *Downbeat* in 1992. This situation was reflected in a feature by Tom Masland in *Newsweek* called "Between Lions and Legends," which highlighted the fate of middle-aged musicians earning less money than young lions with fewer credentials, "They served their apprenticeships long ago," he wrote:

> Without pandering to popular tastes they have survived. And while the latest young lions work to master earlier idioms of acoustic, straight ahead jazz, these older players stand at the cutting edge of its evolution. This should be their time, and they know it. Says bass player Ray Drummond, 45, "There are some guys my age who feel not just cheated, but betrayed."

Parallel to the young lions renaissance was the rise of smooth jazz, which emerged from the commercial homogenization of late 1960s to early 1970s jazz–rock. By 1975 the dominant nonjazz elements of the jazz–rock equation were no longer coming from the creative side of rock music, but from pop music with simple melodic hooks and currently fashionable dance beats. Now known as "fusion," record companies discovered there was a demand for immaculately recorded concoctions of flawlessly executed pop–jazz. In the 1980s Los Angeles's radio station KTWV coined a new name for this kind of music: smooth jazz. By 1987, Radio KTWV was the city's most popular broadcaster among the twenty-five to fifty-five age group, dubbed "the money demographic" by advertisers, thanks to the station's slick rotation of airplay friendly fusion and instrumental pop music. The music's appeal to this key demographic encouraged other stations to adopt the same format. In a remarkably short time smooth jazz became the fastest growing radio format of the 1990s.

"Several factors led to the emergence of this mix of Quiet Storm ballads and groove-based soft jazz," points out Larry Appelbaum, jazz radio host and producer at WPFW-FM in Washington, D.C.:

> The most important among them was a burgeoning concentration of station ownership combined with sophisticated corporate music marketing techniques. The American radio landscape changed dramatically with the Telecommunications Act of 1996, which in effect deregulated radio and allowed media conglomerates like Clear Channel Communications to buy up unlimited numbers of independent stations in small and medium sized markets across the United States.
>
> This consolidation made radio more corporate and homogenous, and resulted in a heavy reliance on consultant designed play-lists and rotation clocks devised by marketing services like Broadcast Architecture. While traditional, mainstream or straight-ahead jazz became relegated to non-commercial college or public radio, smooth jazz was a cost-effective, market-tested commercial format that appealed to a favorite demographic for advertisers: white and black educated, professional males and (more importantly) females ages 24-36.
>
> In a corporate music environment where a small handful of multinationals own most recorded music, Smooth Jazz is a format that offers its owners a higher return on investment. With a central programming service it minimizes operating and overhead expenses, and its focus group-based marketing research allows them to avoid the risk of "tune-out" factors. Of course that also means less access by new or independent artists without promotional dollars behind them. It also makes listening to such stations much more predictable, and some might say boring. You'll never hear the sound of surprise on a Smooth Jazz station.

The FM radio stations that adopted the smooth jazz format represented an important marketing tool for the major recording companies to promote their signings. In turn, FM radio made specific requirements of the recording companies. The smooth jazz stations demanded music with a catchy melodic hook, a bright and breezy theme, a contagious backbeat, and tunes that lasted no more than four minutes. More traditional "jazz" radio programs typically found on National Public Radio or college stations became a similar tool through which the major labels marketed their neoclassical jazz signings. These programs exerted a similar influence on acoustic jazz, setting parameters for the kind of product they would broadcast: the overall characteristics of the music had to be acoustic, it had to "swing," and it could not venture too far "outside." These requirements, broadly speaking, were imposed by radio stations across the board and made major recording companies wary of signing jazz acts that did not comfortably fall into one of these two categories.

"The majors chose to bank on two styles of music," commented Yves Beauvais. "Acoustic straight ahead bebop revivalists, the Wynton Marsalis school on the one hand — Marcus Roberts, Wynton Marsalis, Cyrus Chestnut, James Carter, Jeff 'Tain' Watts, David Sanchez — a very conservative musical current where virtuosity is prime, that compositionally is not really inventing the wheel, but keeping alive a form of music that is inherently American and I for one would hate to see die. Then, on the other hand Smooth Jazz, which is mostly radio and record driven. This is not really jazz by my definition, but still a very vital, very visible music that is perceived by some as being jazz — going around in circles, it does what it does — it's instrumental pop music that outsells jazz 10 to 1. This leaves very little room for the more cutting edge Downtown players."

Categorizing tends to be an after-the-fact rationalization to define music in its market used by the music industry to organize the sales process and thus target potential consumers. Jazz had to pay its way, and there was a reluctance on the part of the major recording companies and many independents to take chances with any kind of music that did not fit comfortably within a specific genre. Adventurous jazz that pushed the envelope presented the major recording companies with both a commercial and a marketing problem. What do you call it? To whom are you going to sell it? How will it get exposure on the radio (thus affecting potential sales)? Beset by declining music sales in all music markets in the 1990s and early millennium years, the major recording companies were reluctant to go beyond a well-defined product — the young lions styles or smooth jazz — that could be sold into an established market (consumers who had bought similar product in the past) through traditional channels of retail distribution.

Yet getting *any* form of instrumental jazz into retail outlets was becoming increasingly difficult. The stresses and strains felt within the American economy through the 1990s and into the millennium years deeply wounded all forms of American music. In the recording business, the five (now four) international corporate music labels increasingly centralized production and narrowed distribution, gradually attempting to freeze new instrumental jazz releases (reissues continued apace) out of the traditional music marketplace. "The real issue is distribution," said the distinguished jazz observer Will Friedwald in *The Future of Jazz*. "It seems that 90 percent of records are retailed through chain stores in malls that have precious little shelf space for jazz." Large distribution companies were becoming less and less interested in the kind of profits yielded by the relatively small sales enjoyed by newer jazz artists and small independent labels, while computerized stock control enabled retail outlets to analyze more precisely the speed of turnover of goods, judging the success of cultural products such as albums, books, and DVDs on the basis of their performance in the marketplace during the first six weeks or so of release. "The big stores have got the supermarket ethic," observed Jon Newey, editor and publisher of *Jazzwise*, the United Kingdom's leading jazz magazine. "They're concerned with profit per square meter so the possibility of lesser known instrumental jazz hanging around in the racks is small. The only other route is if the record company do[es] a deal with the shop to take the album, which usually means paying for co-op advertising, an 'in house' chart position which the record company pays for, or an end-cap rack deal. What jazz label [other than a major] can afford that?"

The major label's focus on smooth jazz and the young lions — which would be broadened to include vocalists in the late 1990s and early millennium years — was partly driven by their high production and marketing costs. "Speaking in terms of US sales . . . if I don't sell 10,000 copies of a record I'm losing money, no matter how cheaply it is made for," explained Yves Beauvais. "So you sell 10,000 in the US another 10 or 15 thousand in the rest of the world and Japan and Europe you're OK — and this is in the first year of release."

Amid ruthlessly efficient corporate consolidation, the major labels periodically "rationalized" their portfolio of signings, a word in corporate circles synonymous with a hard look at profitability usually followed by "downsizing" (or eliminating less profitable acts). Thus the highly respected pianist Geri Allen, for example, with a strong individual style difficult to pigeonhole, was one artist "downsized" by Verve's American operation. She was typical of the kind of artist that the major labels believed did not fit into a specific, marketable style and so was considered an uncommercial proposition. By 2004, Universal's Verve label had become a shadow of its past glories. Underneath a patina of jazz respectably afforded them by a small roster of what the company calls "heritage" signings — Wayne Shorter, Shirley Horn, and Mike Brecker — whose artistic standing was intended to lend the label credibility to the media community and established customers, their real marketing priorities had become personable, young jazz-lite singers like Diana Krall, Lizz Wright, Gwyneth Herbert, and Jamie Cullum.

Universal had enjoyed increasing commercial success with singer–pianist Diana Krall since signing her in 1994 from the Canadian Justin Time Records label. After an aggressive promotion campaign in 2001, Krall's album *The Look of Love* saw sales in excess of 2 million worldwide. It prompted EMI/Blue Note to sign easy listening singer–pianist Norah Jones, daughter of the legendary sitar player Ravi Shankar. Her major label debut from 2002, *Come Away with Me,* eventually reached sales of over 17 million worldwide and swept the 45th Grammy ceremony in New York in February 2003, picking up five awards, including Album of the Year, Best New Artist, and Best Female Pop Vocal performance. Jones's transformation from an arty jazz-house favorite to global pop star prompted a rush by the majors to sign similar jazz-styled singers. However, with the major's commitment to jazz now being focused on singers post–Norah Jones, instrumental jazz was becoming, according to one major recording company executive, a low priority.

Yet a curious paradox existed in jazz. While it accounted for only per-cent of total music sales in 2002, according to figures from the Recording Industry Association of America (RIAA), it was a business overwhelmed by new releases. Quite simply, the supply of CDs exceeded demand and quality was becoming diluted. "There were records being marketed by record companies that didn't seem to have any purpose," observed Adam Seiff, Sony's Director of Jazz, United Kingdom and Europe. Jon Newey, the editor and publisher of *Jazzwise,* observed that there was far more product than consumers could reasonably purchase or jazz magazines, the press, and radio could ever hope to review:

> We're receiving more CDs for review than we ever have before, hun-dreds a week worldwide. A lot from small indie labels, often from single artist labels. Cheaper recording costs have made all this possible. You can produce an album at home with professional quality recording equipment, which in relative terms is not expensive today. Musicians can get small quantities pressed up at low cost bulk CD prices, and the artwork is now cheaper than it has ever been. There's no barriers to doing all this, the problem is getting them into the stores, which for instrumental jazz is getting increasingly more difficult by the day, so most artists sell them at gigs — a signed CD which you can't get in the shops — or through web sites.

Every artist wanted their own CD, and if they had to pay the costs themselves, they did. A CD was a valuable publicity tool essential to attracting the attention of concert promoters, club owners, festival producers, and record producers, or to get that much needed puff in the press.

While new releases were flooding the market, jazz fans were also confronted with even greater choice at the point of sale by back catalog "reissues" that were in direct competition with new artists. In 1989, record company executive Steve Backer speculated to me that every worthwhile jazz record would probably be rereleased on CD by the year 2000, a prediction that in retrospect does not seem too wide of the mark. "The abundance of reissues on the market cannot help but hurt the new issues," wrote Fred Kaplan in the *Boston Globe* in September 2002. "One jazz publicist recalls asking a few years ago why pianist Danilio Perez's *Panamonk*, a lively and highly praised Latinized album of Thelonious Monk tunes, was selling so poorly. 'Look,' one distributor told him, 'you've got Danilio Perez in one bin selling for $16.99. You've got a reissue by Monk himself right next to it selling for $10.99. Which one would you buy?'"

It was an unusual and unprecedented paradox in jazz. Once the recordings of the young lions reached the retailer's racks, their version of the hard bop style was placed in direct competition with jazz's posthumous heroes who created and shaped the style in the 1950s and 1960s. Jazz has always been in competition with its past — after all, jazz reissues began in the United Kingdom in 1930s — but never like this. Not only did it have the effect of reinforcing the feeling of *mode retro*, but it also prompted a gradual realization among the major recording companies that there was little point in competing with their own back catalogs. "Why make a record that would cost sometimes the same price as putting out three classic jazz albums, for the price of breaking a new saxophonist: A&R costs, recording costs, promotion and so on?" said Adam Seiff. "What you're finding is the jazz audience is going back and buying the classics rather than listening and buying records by the new artists." Clearly it made more sense to repackage albums from their vaults paid for decades earlier than sign and promote new artists. By the end of the 1990s, it had become clear that the young lions phenomena unwittingly contained the seeds of its own demise. "In paying homage to the greats," said former record company executive Jeff Levenson in the *Atlantic Monthly* in 2003, "Wynton and his peers have gotten supplanted by them in the minds of the populace. They've gotten supplanted by dead people."

The 1990s and the early millennium years was a period when audiences for all forms of cultural production generally found the past a more comfortable place to be, a period when, as critic Larry Kart observed, in his book, *Jazz in Search of Itself*, "American society seems to be thinking along conservative lines," allowing a *mode retro* to flourish that was reflected in most areas of the entertainment business. In Hollywood, for example, which for generations has set fashion and established taste, producers increasingly began looking over their shoulder with big budget films of 1960s hit movies, such as *Alfie*, *The Italian Job*, *Psycho*, *Cape Fear*, and *The Stepford Wives*; 1930s to 1950s comic heroes like Superman, Dick Tracy, Spiderman, and Spiderwoman; 1960s spoofs with Austin Powers; and remakes of long running 1970s TV series such as Charlie's Angels, Starsky and Hutch, and the Incredible Hulk.

But it was not just Hollywood that had a foot in the past. This was a period when all forms of music felt more comfortable looking backward than addressing the future. In 2000, James Jolly, the editor of *Gramophone* magazine, warned how an infatuation with "endless recreations" of the established classical repertoire was stifling opportunities for the current crop of composers. "Our delight in new interpretations of old favorites shouldn't obscure exploration of the new and original," he cautioned. Indeed, Joan Jeanrenaud of the Kronos Quartet said that when, in the early days of the group, they wanted to concentrate on contemporary classical music, "No manager wanted us. 'Contemporary music?' they said. 'Who's going to come to your concerts?'" The composer Ned Rorem, in expanding on this problem, made an observation that coincidentally had a strong resonance in jazz. "In the 19th century, they played Liszt, Chopin, and the composer and performer were the same person," he said. "But the performer has become the star — *the re-creator is more important than the creator*" (my italics).

Equally, in pop music, Simon Frith in the *Village Voice* expressed the opinion that the perceived "postmodern condition" of fragmentation and breakdown of "master narratives" in popular music had led to recyclings and pastiches (sampling) of earlier forms of pop music, "a culture of margins around a collapsed center." In their end-of-year surveys in 1987, rock critics on both sides of the Atlantic pointed to the extraordinary number of reissues and old records on the charts. By the 1990s and early millennium years, new versions of old hits were producing huge sales. Yet amid all the uncertainty in the music marketplace, one certainty prevailed: the past sold. At almost any given time from the mid-1990s you could find several cover versions of 1960s and 1970s hits in the charts, creating the unusual paradox where "older" music became contemporary for today's younger audiences. One 1975 hit, "Lady Marmalade" by LaBelle, was covered not once but twice. Some bands even built careers out of covers (Boyzone) and others from writing songs that resonated with the past, such as Oasis, Supergrass (who have often sounded overtly Beatles-esque and did at least one video aping the style of the Beatles 1960's film clips), and Suede (modeled on the Glam sound of early 1970's David Bowie).

An important aspect of the repackaging phenomenon in pop was the use of pastiche or sampling, which first became prominent at the end of the 1970s with Sugarhill Gang's "Rapper's Delight," the first hip-hop single to have chart success and that used a sample of Chic's "Good Times." Initially record companies were against sampling and viewed it as a threat to their copyright interests, but once they realized the potential to revive interest in their back catalogs, while simultaneously collecting copyright payments for the samples, they began actively promoting their publishing catalogs to would-be samplers. Initially samples took the form of brief snatches of (usually) distorted riffs played on turntables, but later large chunks of old hits were used as the basis of "new" songs (an example of this was the Robbie Williams's 1998 hit "Millennium" that relied entirely on the theme from John Barry's 1967 score for *You Only Live Twice*). In 1989, the British pop act M/A/R/R/S enjoyed huge international success with the hit single "Pump Up the Volume," a record that was made up largely of pieces of about thirty other records. The trend for sampling has extended into most areas of contemporary dance music in the new millennium and also sparked a craze for remixes. The word "remix" covers a multitude of sins that extends from a dull ripoff to fresh creativity, but was principally a marketing ploy, a way of squeezing extra commercial nectar from an earlier hit. Cover versions, samples, and remixes were all variations of pop music revisiting (and recycling) its past.

It was in this broader cultural context of popular music, classical music, and cinema revisiting the past that the young lions trend, emphasizing the primacy of the tradition, flourished in jazz, particularly during the late 1980s to 1990s. This feeling of *mode retro* in jazz was also reinforced by jazz repertory and concerts and albums "celebrating" the music of an icon from the golden age of jazz. In a competitive marketplace for all forms of cultural production, conventional marketing wisdom now said that if you wanted to boost sales in jazz, you did it through evoking a "great name" from jazz's hall of fame: a Duke Ellington or a Louis Armstrong or a recently deceased giant like Tommy Flanagan (who died in 2001), or even compelling also-rans such as a Herbie Nichols or a Fred Katz. Reflecting this trend, the jazz Grammy Awards in 2002, for example, included a "tribute" to Count Basie and a "tribute" to Louis Armstrong.

As Burton W. Peretti noted in his essay *Epilogue: Jazz as American History*, "The popularity of the 'classicism' of Wynton Marsalis have shown some players' and fans' resistance to change and their nostalgia. Like the heroin some bebop musicians took to escape the pain of the present, nostalgia has been a narcotic of choice for people terrified by the unfamiliarity of the ever-changing present. Almost regularly in the twentieth century, Americans have expressed disgust with the present and yearned for the imagined 'normalcy' of yesteryear."

This conservative music climate was reinforced in jazz by the unforeseen and often unacknowledged consequences of jazz education. "There's a lot of gifted young musicians coming out of music schools who haven't had any experience of life — they can play the instruments, they've got the chops, but they don't seem to have anything to *say*," observed Adam Seiff. The inevitable homogenization effect of jazz education was leading to individuality becoming less important than technique. "We're at a point now with so many great young players, it's a little like there's a thousand channels on cable but there's nothing to watch," says guitarist Pat Metheny. "There's so many really good players who play really good and you listen to them and you say, 'Man, you play good, that's great!' But it's sort of like outside of the context of the culture in a way, it's in reference to something else, it doesn't come *embodied in a conception*, it's 'just' good playing." Familiarity with the harmonic and rhythmic conventions of past styles and the huge repertoire of standards and original compositions associated with the jazz tradition presented a challenge that, pianist Brad Mehldau has noted, created "a sort of post-modern haze that turns [young musicians] into chameleons with no identity."

Steen Meier, chairman of the Nordic Music Council and Copenhagen's JazzHouse, a club that regularly promotes visiting American musicians, expressed frustration at the numbers of musicians "able to imitate all the previous idols to perfection. Typically we admire them," he wrote in *Spontaneous Combustion*, a history of the JazzHouse:

They are considered clever. The question is, do they really concern us? Do we need somebody to tell the same old story over and over again? Are these musicians mere custodians in a historical museum of music?"

Where the music once evolved in the clubs and after-hours joints in New Orleans, Chicago, Kansas City, and Harlem, today the sound of the contemporary jazz mainstream is, as saxophonist and arranger Bob Belden put it to me in 2001, "The sound of the practice rooms at Berklee or North Texas State. All it says is they've spent a lot of time in the practice room and listened to this record or that record from the 1950s or 1960s.

As music sales continued to drop — "The music business went from bad to worse in 2002, as overall sales declined by more 10% year over year," reported *Billboard* — jazz became cocooned in establishment paranoia, disguised, as are many elements in our society, as "tradition." Whereas in the past definitions of jazz styles had been after-the-fact rationalizations, now definitions of what jazz was, and what it was not, began to fill the air, often excluding the possibility of future change. Usually, whoever did the defining put themselves at the center of the music. With technical and mechanical prolixity becoming commonplace in an age of college-educated jazz musicians, new concerns emerged such as whether the music "swung" or had "a blues sensibility" in order for it to be considered "jazz." These competing claims of what constituted "jazz" were beginning to sound a little like Humpty Dumpty in *Alice through the Looking Glass*. "When I use a word," he said, "It means just what I choose it to mean." The problem was that usually the people doing the defining wanted jazz to be what it used to be, not what it was becoming.

Many argued that those musicians who identified so much with its past were in danger of losing sight of the future. Gradually, as Adam Shatz suggested in the *New York Times* (2000), there was, "a sense of boredom with the classical polish of mainstream jazz." This was beginning to be felt most acutely in Europe, crucially a major market for American jazz, where there was both impatience and disenchantment at current developments. "Europeans, at any rate, will be nonplussed by the deliberate attempt to 'play by numbers' and follow a predefined canon of jazz," wrote Konrad Heidkamp, the music critic of the German newspaper *Die Zeit*. "The USA has slithered into musical provinciality. It produces great instrumentalists but no new approaches." It was a theme echoed by many European commentators. "It's easy to despair at the state of US jazz," wrote columnist John L. Walters in *The Guardian*. "You might pick up a few albums at random and

conclude that bandleaders have little to say that hasn't been said, a generation or two earlier, by more charismatic leaders — heroes you can call by a
single name: Duke, Cannonball, Lady Day, Trane." There was sadness too
at the turn of events, as expressed by Geoff Dyer, author of *But Beautiful*,
writing in *The Observer*: "A little less than a decade ago, going to hear
McCoy Tyner or Elvin Jones at Ronnie Scott's seemed to me a pleasure
supreme. I loved jazz so much that I even went to live in New York so that
I could go to jazz clubs every night and write about it on site. I didn't just
love jazz, I pitied anyone who didn't . . . . Now, when I go to a jazz gig I
often feel like I'm in an improvised mausoleum."

Equally, many European jazz musicians no longer looked across the
Atlantic for inspiration, as they had during jazz's golden years. "I'm influenced by bands such as Radiohead and Wilco," Swedish pianist Esbjörn
Svenssön told *Downbeat* in 2004, "I don't see much creativity in jazz at the
moment, so that's not where I get my inspiration. I find a lot of it boring
and not creative at all, with many bands just repeating what has already
been done."

With change now occurring at "a glacial pace," in Geoff Dyer's words,
almost imperceptibly over the years historians, writers, critics, and the
music press lowered the bar of critical expectation in line with the narrowing paradigm of jazz. As one disgruntled fan complained to the music
pages of *The Guardian* in 2003, "According to the bland reviews in the
press, no jazz record is ever less than good, a stance that is of no use what-
soever to the customers. Whatever the reason it doesn't help the music,
and it doesn't make for good reading." With more and more albums in the
tradition, or a synthesis of earlier styles, it was becoming clear that many
were often without the value many critics claimed for them. "Throughout
these two decades [the 1980s and 1990s] a bewildering deluge of recordings were issued," observed Randy Sandke. "A lot of good stuff got lost in
the shuffle so it may take some time to really make sense of this period. As
usual, though, most of it was pretty run-of-the-mill."

Those who felt the essence of jazz had been realized in the process of
change itself, were increasingly seen to be out of step with the prevailing
mode retro. "Newness — as in music that has never been heard before —
is a very tricky idea," wrote Ben Ratliff of the *New York Times*. "I don't
trust it anymore. . . . The problem with the 'you're not playing anything
new!' argument is that it's only half right. Yes, jazz has depended on lots
of very individual voices to evolve it. But — in case we hadn't noticed —
it also has a delicious side to it and that is about refinement of tradition."

The key for any art form, however, is how it negotiates with its tradition to adapt to changing times. Larry Kart, in *Jazz in Search of Itself*, observed that never before had a return to selected aspects of the jazz past been presented — and to a remarkable degree accepted — as an event of central aesthetic importance. "That it was not such an event . . . but that it could be regarded as one at all is significant," he wrote. "Not quite a sign that jazz was dead or dying . . . but evidence that the weight of the music's past, relative to its present and possible futures, was something that jazz was grappling with as never before."

As jazz found itself weighed down by the high expectations of the people who knew its history, it was adapting less to changing times, more to the tradition oriented currents flowing through the music. For some musicians, it meant a radical change of musical direction to adapt to the times. For example, Michael Brecker, acclaimed for his postfusion work with Steps Ahead in the 1980s and with his own group with Mike Stern following the release of *Michael Brecker* in 1987, reinvented himself as a tradition oriented player on *Tales from the Hudson* (1996), *Two Blocks from the Edge* (1998), and *Time is of the Essence* (1999).

Alan MacFarlane, a historian and Professor of Anthropology at Cambridge, points out that history shows very few civilizations have avoided the tendency towards conservation for more than a few hundred years. Increasing complexity is one cause of this and has occured in all forms of knowledge and culture including secular processes, religion and politics. The task becomes to preserve the "traditional" way of doing things, "which is the opposite of innovation and invention which deliberately force us to forget superceeding knowledge, making it 'out-of-date' and irrelevant."

If art is meant to be a reflection of life, then in America, by instinct a conservative nation, the main area of jazz activity had become conservative because there was a growing realization there was much to conserve.

2
Between Image and Artistry: The Wynton Marsalis Phenomenon

Is jazz being transformed beyond redemption into another version of classical music: an accepted cultural treasure, consisting of a repertoire of mostly dead styles, performed live by artists — some of them young — for a financially comfortable middle class public, black and white, and the Japanese tourist?

Eric Hobsbawm, historian, author, and a fellow of the British Academy and the American Academy of Arts

Mention the name Wynton Marsalis to any jazz fan and you are sure to spark off a debate. From whatever angle you choose to view him, there's no shortage of controversy when it comes to his role in shaping recent jazz history.

On the one hand, there's the glowing view of his achievements in the press and mainstream media, who have come to refer to him as "the most famous living jazz musician," citing him as an ideal role model for youth. In this version, the jazz trumpeter is portrayed as nothing short of an American cultural icon, with over thirty albums to his credit, nine Grammy awards, a Pulitzer Prize, and countless honors from around the globe including the Grand Prix du Disque of France, the Edison Award of the Netherlands, and honorary membership of England's Royal Academy of Music. Marsalis's supporters point to the many hours he has contributed to music education, community organizations, and charities, the keys to cities across America he's received, and a congressional citation. A tireless worker on behalf of jazz education, from master classes at Juilliard to informal talks to youngsters in primary schools, Marsalis is known to generously supply trumpets to needy students. "I'm a grassroots worker," he said. "My father was a teacher. I love kids." In his role as artistic director of the Jazz at Lincoln Center program in New York City, he's been lauded for his tireless presentation of concerts, for defining a "classical jazz" canon, for the funding and profile he's attracted for jazz, and for rescuing a complex musical tradition from dumbing-down and pop opportunism. According to saxophonist and bandleader Loren Schoenberg, who is also executive director of the Jazz Museum in Harlem, he has "turned around jazz's absence from American cultural life."

Yet Marsalis has his share of critics who paint a less rosy view of his achievements, questioning whether the cost of increasing the prestige of jazz within American cultural institutions has been too high, placing the future of the music in jeopardy. They portray Marsalis as a musician more secure in jazz's past than its future, playing what saxophonist Greg Osby once referred to as "Model T music," early styles of jazz, such as — to quote from Marsalis's publicity material — "the classic big band sounds of Count Basie, Chick Webb, Jimmie Lunceford and Duke Ellington." They complain that Marsalis is guilty of stifling innovation through his championing of earlier styles of jazz, and that by focusing on historical repertoire — or his own original compositions *ad modum* — he is turning jazz into a mausoleum of picturesque relics, exemplified by his 1999 recording of Jelly Roll Morton's "Tom Cat Blues" using the old, scratchy acoustic 78 recording technology at the Edison Studios in West Orange, New Jersey. As writer Richard Williams acerbically noted in the pages of *The Guardian*, "If Wynton Marsalis is its creative Figure head, then jazz is probably really dead this time."

From wherever you view Wynton Marsalis, one thing seems certain: the former trumpet prodigy from New Orleans seems to have had a polarizing effect on jazz.

By the time he was twenty-five, Marsalis already numbered among the most famous jazz musicians in the world, and so he has remained. As is usual with jazz heroes, his popularity has waxed and waned; what is not usual with heroes is that his artistry, uniquely in jazz, has come to play a secondary role to his image. For writer Stanley Crouch, quoted by Mya Jaggi in *The Guardian*, Marsalis is, "The greatest trumpet player since Booker Little, Don Cherry, Freddie Hubbard and Woody Shaw, and the most rhythmically intricate and original since Dizzy Gillespie." But, perhaps surprisingly for a hero, there is no settled consensus about Crouch's claims; in fact, there are many dissenting voices who question Marsalis's musical gifts. "If Wynton died tomorrow he wouldn't leave us one note on paper or on record that's worth anything," says trombonist, composer, and educator Bob Brookmeyer.

In 2002, saxophonist and composer Wayne Shorter commented about Marsalis in an interview with Adam Sweeting published in *The Guardian:*

> I remember back in the Seventies, when people had been hearing about this new trumpet player, he showed up at my house by surprise. He introduced himself and I said, "Come on in." He wanted to listen to a little bit of the [Miles] Davis Plugged Nickel album [a 1965 live recording made by the Davis quintet including Shorter] and he said he wanted to watch me while he was listening to it. That means, to me, that he recognized at that time he was in a position to grasp the profundity of what was going on then at those Plugged Nickel dates. Somewhere after that, between when he left my house and now, that grasping process is on vacation — quite a long vacation.

Pianist Joe Zawinul was unequivocal. "To me he is more of a teacher, as an artist he really can't carry the stick. He's been put on pedestal, which is a high one, but he doesn't call the tune, sorry to say that," he told me. And pianist Keith Jarrett, in an interview in the *New York Times Magazine*, said, "Wynton imitates other people's styles too well. . . . I've never heard anything Wynton played sound like it meant anything at all. Wynton has no voice and no presence." This is harsh criticism indeed, especially from some of jazz's most respected musicians.

Clearly then, Marsalis provokes strong opinions, indeed, when the *Daily Telegraph*, the U.K.'s largest circulation broadsheet, ran a feature on him in their arts pages in 2003, it was bylined, "A Talent For Making Music and Enemies." But who are these "enemies"? They are nothing less than the "jazz establishment" whom, he has said, are "racist, ignorant and disrespectful of musicians." Race is an important issue for Marsalis, one that appears to underpin his ideology and his musical aesthetic. Indeed, it is often at the heart of the controversies that swirl around him. In one of his first interviews in 1981, given to *Downbeat* magazine shortly after he recorded his debut album for the Columbia label, writer Mitchell Seidel observed, "Marsalis believes it is the conscious recognition in the minds of most white jazz players that they are not black that limits their ability and prevents them from 'getting into the meat of the music.'"

As his fame grew, Marsalis consolidated a vision of jazz in conjunction with the writers Albert Murray — usually referred to as a novelist but celebrated more for his nonfiction works — and Stanley Crouch — a recipient in 1993 of the Jean Stein Award from the American Academy of Arts and Letters and a MacArthur Foundation grant. Their interpretation of jazz was as much musical as it was ideological; Marsalis, through his celebrity, lent it authority, advancing it to both controversy and success. By 1997, the *New York Times Magazine* observed that, "Over the past decade, in large part because of Wynton Marsalis's efforts, jazz has been widely celebrated as an essential element of the African-American cultural heritage and white practitioners have been seen increasingly as interlopers." Marsalis's aesthetic of jazz, shaped by how the music was acknowledged during its golden years, a period of indisputable African American exceptionalism in jazz, was then applied to contemporary jazz. It was a unique moment in the history of the music: a musician, in conjunction with two writers, were seeking to influence the future course of the music through an idealized representation of the past. But can any art form be regulated in this way?

Born October 18, 1961, Wynton Marsalis began studying trumpet seriously at the age of twelve. During high school he performed in local marching bands, jazz bands, funk bands, and classical orchestras, and at age eighteen he moved to New York to attend the Juilliard School of Music. In the summer of 1980, he became a member of Art Blakey's Jazz Messengers and signed with Columbia Records. Following the 1982 release of *Wynton Marsalis*, his first album as a leader, which sold a remarkable 100,000 copies, Columbia assigned him to high-powered publicist Marilyn Laverty, whose clients included rock star Bruce Springsteen, who she famously got onto the covers of *Time* and *Newsweek*. With the full weight of a corporate promotional budget behind him, Marsalis became, according to Eric Porter in *What Is This Thing Called Jazz?* "one of the most promoted jazz artists in the history of the idiom," appearing on television and radio, in Sunday color supplements, style magazines, and the music press.

Marsalis's success prompted recording companies to sign similar young musicians; in turn, their PR departments began promoting these artists to the mass media, providing an irresistible hook for arts editors of newspapers and magazines: here, surely, was a "jazz renaissance," and at its head was Wynton Marsalis. Marsalis was portrayed in several newspaper and magazine features, including a major piece in *Time* magazine in 1990, as a cynosure for born-again jazz, who had saved the music from the sirens of fusion and the "apostasy" of the free jazz players. "When I first came to New York in 1979, everybody was talking about fusion," he told critic Francis Davis in 1983. "Everyone was saying jazz was dead because no young black musicians wanted to play it anymore. . . so when people heard me, they knew it was time to start takin' care of business again." In 1991, Marsalis expanded on this point to me: "Everything I did was new. The blues was new, in my generation. Which is all you can relate to, dealing with standards was new, dealing with jazz was new, because people were bullshitting, playing fusion and saying it was jazz. All these critics were following Miles Davis, he was playing rock music — they didn't realize the absurdity of their position." Marsalis's heroic role was immortalized in the lengthy Ken Burns documentary *Jazz: A History of America's Music* (2001). Burns, who devoted entire episodes to just two and three years of early jazz history, suggesting the music was more about the past than the present, famously sped through almost a quarter of jazz history, from the 1960s to Marsalis's emergence in the early 1980s, in *one* program — "Masterpiece by Midnight" — thereby failing to acknowledge that anything of significance had happened in the interim.

Yet as drummer Winard Harper pointed out to Larry Birnbaum in *Downbeat*, "Even before Wynton there were young musicians trying to play this music — Bobby Watson, James Williams, Donald Brown, Kenny Washington, Curtis Lundy, Bill Saxton." And it was not just younger musicians. In the same January 1982 edition of *Downbeat* that first profiled the then 20-year-old Marsalis, Phil Woods, one of the keepers of the bebop flame, was the cover feature. Woods's group had remained steadfast to the bebop tradition throughout the 1970s; indeed, Woods's *Live from the Showboat* earned him a Grammy in 1977, an album that remains a superb example of consummate bebop playing, exemplified by the track "Cheek to Cheek."

"If jazz was dead in 1978, it was a surprise to many of us in New York," said Bob Brookmeyer. "I had just returned from California and my rehabilitation from alcoholism and found a whole new world waiting for me — had to get back on board, learn some new chromatic language and try to be up to the players around the city. The music had also become widely spread across Europe, and their influence was affecting us, as it should." In fact, a brief snapshot of jazz activity as the 1970s gave way to the 1980s presents a quite different scene to that painted by Marsalis. Roy Haynes and Sonny Rollins had continued leading groups through the 1970s. Rollins toured with the Milestone Jazzstars in 1978, where his playing was "essentially true to the bop tradition" according to *The New Grove Dictionary of Jazz*, while also producing several excellent albums under his own name. The Miles Davis rhythm section of Herbie Hancock, Ron Carter, and Tony Williams, plus Wayne Shorter on tenor, reunited and with the addition of Freddie Hubbard on trumpet made several critically acclaimed albums as VSOP, while a live album of duets by Chick Corea and Gary Burton on the ECM label garnered several awards, including a Grammy for "Best Instrumental Jazz Performance." Art Blakey and Horace Silver were touring regularly, trumpeter Woody Shaw was making fine albums for the Columbia label (1977 to 1981), and the Art Ensemble of Chicago were reaching the height of their creativity. Bill Evans had continued to tour with his trio throughout the 1970s making a number of excellent albums until his death in September 1980, and at the end of the 1970s McCoy Tyner was leading a widely acclaimed acoustic ensemble, his earlier albums from the decade such as *Atlantis* and *Enlightenment*, together with *Horizon* (1979), among the finest of his distinguished career.

In October 1981 the Modern Jazz Quartet re-formed, while Columbia's other main jazz signing alongside Marsalis, alto saxophonist Arthur Blythe, could look back on a series of excellent, critically acclaimed albums for the label such as *Lenox Avenue Breakdown* (1979) with James Newton, Cecil McBee, and Jack DeJohnette. DeJohnette's own group, Special Edition, and the quartet Old and New Dreams (with Don Cherry, Dewey Redman, Charlie Haden, and Ed Blackwell) were being actively promoted by the ECM label to considerable success; DeJohnette's album *Special Edition* was voted "Album of the Year" in the *Downbeat* Reader's Poll in 1980. That same year, as Art Pepper and Dexter Gordon were enjoying highly successful comebacks, a young bebop phenomenon named Richie Cole was featured on the covers of *Downbeat*, *Jazz Times*, and the Japanese *Swing Journal*. The big bands of Lionel Hampton (directed by a talented young alto saxophonist in the bebop tradition called Thomas Chapin), Count Basie, Woody Herman, and Buddy Rich were maintaining year-round touring schedules. At the same time, the Mel Lewis Jazz Orchestra, resident on Monday nights at the Village Vanguard, recorded the critically acclaimed *Bob Brookmeyer Composer, Arranger* with Brookmeyer and guest star Clark Terry, who was then, like his fellow trumpeter Dizzy Gillespie, enjoying huge popularity at jazz festivals around the world.

In 1977, the recently formed Concord Records was enjoying success with a live album of jazz repertory by the Frankie Capp and Nat Pierce big band called *Juggernaut*, with exhilarating performances of numbers like "Avenue 'C,'" "Moten Swing," "Dickie's Dream," and "Wee Baby Blues." The same year the label also released *A Good Wind Who Is Blowing Us No Ill*, the debut of tenor saxophonist Scott Hamilton, a player whose style emerged from swing era models such as Coleman Hawkins, Ben Webster, Flip Phillips, and Paul Gonsalves. After he and fellow swing era traveler Warren Vaché on trumpet were invited to tour with Benny Goodman, they attracted considerable attention and controversy, years before Marsalis, for championing earlier styles of jazz. Under the media spotlight, they also brought attention to players such as Howard Alden and Ken Peplowski, and helped rejuvenate the careers of old masters such as Ruby Braff, Flip Phillips, John Bunch, and Dave McKenna, all of whom appeared on the Concord label, to the delight of audiences around the world.

As David Hajdu pointed out in the pages of *Atlantic Monthly*, when Marsalis appeared at the club Seventh Avenue South in the last week of January 1982 to showcase his debut album on Columbia, nearly every jazz room in New York was presenting bebop or older styles of jazz: Kai Winding was at the Village Vanguard, Anita O'Day was at the Blue Note, Dizzy Gillespie at Fat Tuesday's, George Shearing at Michael's Pub, and Archie Shepp was at Sweet Basil. "There was a whole lot of jazz in New York then, and it was straight ahead bebop, by and large," pianist Barry Harris told Hajdu. "You had all the work you could do [as a bebop musician], and nobody was doing fusion but the kids. Now they made festivals and whatnot for the younger crowd. That was where that was at. It was no big thing. That was a good time for straight ahead [music] in New York."

Although Marsalis's dedication to the jazz idiom was beyond question, his initial releases, including *Think of One* from 1983, *Hot House Flowers* from 1984, and *Black Codes (From the Underground)* from 1985, were perhaps too scrupulous at the expense of emotion, contrasting the sparkle and *joie de vivre* he demonstrated during his solo on "Wilpan's Walk" while sitting in with Chico Freeman on the 1981 album *Destiny's Dance*. Even so, the first Marsalis group achieved considerable fluency and internal cohesion, incorporating metric modulation with ease, and in live performance, suggested they had the potential to become a major force in jazz. However, in March 1985, this talented ensemble broke up after the decision of Marsalis's brother Branford, the group's tenor saxophonist, and pianist Kenny Kirkland, to tour with rock star Sting. Their departure was a blow to Marsalis; "Man, if you lost your whole band to go play rock music and you're out there saying jazz music is not rock music and the guys in your band decide to cosign some shit that's being called jazz, and that's the exact opposite of what you're preaching, would it be a problem with you?" he rhetorically asked *Wire* magazine in 1991. "Yeah it would! It wasn't a crime or nothing. I mean nobody got killed. It was just another stab at the culture, the Afro-American culture."

Three months later Marsalis formed a new group with young piano virtuoso Marcus Roberts and, from his former group, Robert Hurst on bass and Jeff Watts on drums, all still in their early to mid-twenties. Their first album together, *J-Mood*, came in December 1985. "On *J Mood* I was trying to slow it down, play blues," Marsalis explained. "That kind of got lost in my generation." A year later came *Live at Blues Alley*; at last Marsalis appeared to have reconciled his virtuosity with an altogether more exuberant musical vision that did not smack of the intricate, almost painstaking search for perfection of his earlier work on record. These live performances capture a feeling of genuine risk-taking that adds a humanizing factor to his playing that seemed less apparent on many of his previous albums. The album was a key point in his career. "For me, *Live at Blues Alley* was about the whole chance-taking aspect of improvisation in the truest sense," he told writer Bill Milkowski in *Rockers, Jazzbos & Visionaries*. "That's a type of very advanced rhythmic improvisation, the kind you hear with the Coltrane quartet or the classic Miles quintets."

However, this promising direction was not one that Marsalis pursued. He came to believe that jazz's prestige suffered from "the fallacy that it was a product of emotion and not intellect," preferring a somewhat austere precision in his playing. On recordings at least, Marsalis increasingly gave the impression to some listeners of someone who failed to acknowledge great music could be produced through tension between the irrational, mysterious apprehensions that make people delight in being surprised, outraged, or otherwise shaken up, and the need to know and master the way in which music is created. He did not appear to accept the contradictory — yet compelling — idea that the perfection of the jazz solo often includes imperfections. "The beauty of it is regrouping after a mistake," observed saxophonist Greg Osby in *Downbeat*, "Some of the baddest stuff that's been thought was accidental."

On one number from *Live at Blues Alley*, "Do You Know What It Means to Miss New Orleans," Marsalis gave notice that he was about to turn his back on the conspicuous advances his music had made to confront and explore jazz from its "golden age." It is interesting to note that Marcus Roberts, his pianist at this time and perhaps the finest young player to emerge from the Marsalis orbit whose playing throughout *Live at Blues Alley* was every bit as exciting as his leader, would also explore the past as he developed his own career on the Novus/BMG label. By his sixth album, *If I Could Be with You*, Roberts was confronting the methods of the Harlem "stride" pianists of the 1920s on "Carolina Shout," and ragtime with Scott Joplin's "Maple Leaf Rag."

By the mid-1980s, Marsalis felt he had to make a choice of continuing his classical concerts or concentrating entirely on jazz. He chose the latter, saying, "I couldn't find the time to keep my classical technique up. Finally, given the choice, I had to take jazz, because that's what attracted me to music in the first place." In 1987 came the Grammy-winning *Marsalis Standard Time Vol. 1* that in part was intended to assert certain enduring musical values from jazz's past, paralleling Albert Murray's aesthetic of a "style for living" with "a standard for performance." As Stanley Crouch noted in the liner notes, the challenge was to "learn how to redefine the fundamentals while maintaining the essences that give art its scope and grandeur." Between 1987 and 1991 came two further volumes of *Marsalis Standard Time* — *Vol. 2: Intimacy Calling* and *Vol. 3: The Resolution of Romance* recorded with his father, pianist Ellis Marsalis. But, as Gene Santoro observed in *The Nation*, "The discs, despite their subtitles, differed not a whit in tone or approach. Their main problem . . . was their worshipful attitude towards the material. Sacramental reverence isn't necessarily the best approach when a musician is trying to re-roast old chestnuts."

Perhaps unsurprisingly, Marsalis felt his music wasn't being properly "addressed," as he put it, by the "critics." This frustration with jazz critics was a recurring theme in Marsalis's interviews. "I want people to address my music for what it is," he told me in 1991. "They [the critics] know it

represents jazz, they know it. And they know what I represent. What they
hate about it is that they think it's a black/white issue. Because I won't kiss
their ass, it *is* a black/white issue between me and them." A similar assertion, albeit phrased slightly differently, appeared in an interview in *The
Village Voice* in 1994 when he was quoted as saying, "These men's asses
will never have these brown lips graze them."

Marsalis's opinion of the critics seemed to be shaped in part by the
views of Ralph Ellison, who once said jazz critics were entertainment page
journalists residing in the privileged sanctuary of New York publications,
and his long-time friend Albert Murray. In his book *Stomping the Blues*,
Murray wrote, "When these . . . reporter/reviewers give their evaluations
of actual performances, whether live or on records, it is almost always as if
they were writing about the concert music of Europe." In other words,
(white) critics were "outside" the social and ritualistic role of the music —
"the working frame of reference" — or, as Stanley Crouch put it in *Jazz
Times* (April 2003), were "evaluating an art form from which they feel
substantially alienated."

However, in cultural studies, the Gramscian hegemony theory insists
there is a dialectic between the processes of production and the activities
of consumption where the "text" is confronted by consumers who produce
"in use" a range of possible meanings which cannot be read from the
materiality of the text or the means of its production.

Certainly, when music is new and fresh, the music community to whom
it is addressed will judge it in relationship to their immediate context, and
how the conventions of the music fulfill their expectations, needs, and
desires. But history has made it clear certain universal responses to music
are shared by different musical communities who are unaware of any social
or ritualistic functions the music may have originally fulfilled. We can still
be moved by Josquin's *musica reservata* from the sixteenth century, for
example, without any knowledge of the conventions of the court of Duke
Hercules I at Ferrara, even though we know the impact of Italian culture in
general and the taste of Josquin's noble patrons in particular had a profound effect on the composer.

Today, for example, with world music enjoying a considerable following in terms of albums sales and concert attendances, it is worth noting
that the prospect of an audience enjoying songs in languages they do not
understand would hold little promise for them if the melodies, rhythms,
and harmonies did not move or stimulate them in some way. In 2004,
Youssou n'Dour released his best-selling album *Egypt*, a celebration of

Sufism that includes several religious texts of profound socialistic and ritu-alistic function. But as popular culture critic Charlie Gillett, author of the classic rock text *The Sound of the City*, pointed out, "Our appreciation of Youssou's music has never depended on understanding what his songs are about, even though their meaning is paramount to him and to his Wolof audience. We are convinced by his commitment, and gladly surrender to the melodies and rhythms in which he envelops himself."

Equally, audiences need not be acquainted with the ritualistic and social conventions at the Savoy Ballroom in Harlem in 1934 to appreciate Chick Webb's version of "Stomping at the Savoy." Webb's lead alto saxophonist Louis Jordan did not need to be aware of the ritual and social convention of white socialites dancing at London's Savoy Hotel in the 1930s when, after leaving Webb, Jordan called his group the Tympani Five after being impressed by the way the Ambrose Orchestra, then the resident band at the Savoy, incorporated tympani into pieces like "Night Ride" and "Hors d'Oeuvres." What Murray, Crouch, and Marsalis overlook is the ancient paradox of music, that while it appears rich and full of meaning, no com-munity of listeners can agree with any precision on the exact nature of that meaning because all community members are not alike. A community may agree a particular work is "significant" if it moves and interests them, but detailed, specific descriptions of their subjective reactions may differ con-siderably. As pianist and educator Billy Taylor points out in *Jazz Piano: A Jazz History*: "Americans share an understanding of the emotional con-notations of jazz which is based on an Afro-American value system, but the interpretation of the musical symbols varies a great deal because the music has transcended ethnic boundaries."

At a more pragmatic level, Marsalis, who complains that "the levels of complexity" in his music are "not addressed" by the critics, gives every impression of failing to acknowledge the problems of how music *is* "addressed" in the print media today, despite having written many features for newspapers and magazines. Generally, arts editors do not want (and will not accept) pieces that are confined to describing the music in terms that explain the techniques at work in a piece: the form, the use of disso-nance and consonance, modulation from one key to another, metric modulation, changes of tempo, and so on. They see this type of approach (that addresses the "levels of complexity" in music) as one that actually *excludes* the listener's own engagement with the music. If a score were available, they would argue, the critic who employed such methods need never hear a note of music. While this way of discussing music is essential to scholarship, history, and formal description, it can also become a scholastic endeavor devoid of emotional significance.

Most lay listeners are aware of the roles of form, structure, rhythm, and melody without the need for technical language; if they did not, the prospect of listening to music would not offer much pleasure for them. For example, when a piece of music becomes embedded in the memory, so that the listener "knows what's coming next," he or she has already grasped something of its structure. Music seems to create its effects without any mediation or explanation. Lay listeners are not usually aware of any interpretation on their part, of any cognitive process that contributes to their understanding of the music. The music plays, the body moves, and they involve themselves in it by means of empathy, identifying with its expressive aspects and, if the music moves them, allowing themselves to be aroused emotionally. Every culture talks and every culture sings; that is why music lovers, from academics to garage rock bands, talk about music in descriptive terms.

Thus instead of technical explanation, editors want to engage the general reader. What emotions are aroused when listening to an album? What did the listener get out of the experience? In what way were they moved by the music? Would they buy the album themselves? Critics are encouraged to try and circumscribe the effects of music metaphorically, bringing their own experiences to bear in unpacking musical gestures, to try and parallel in words something of how the music feels to them.

The greatest artists are those who appear to reveal certain universal emotions common to all — be it Josquin's *musica reservata*, Youssou n'Dour, or Louis Armstrong — while, in contrast, most seem to agree on music that fails to touch the heart or seems dull and lifeless, regardless of the ingenuity of its construction. The key point here, perhaps, is that the "level of complexity" of a composition does not, in of itself, necessarily evoke an emotional response from an audience. For example, the classical composer and music critic Constant Lambert, an early champion of Duke Ellington, failed to be moved by some of Stravinsky's neoclassical works, because the composer's ideal was to create works in which the personal dimension was eliminated, causing Lambert to condemn them as inhuman and mechanical.

In 1987 and 1988, Marsalis entered a period of intense recording that produced *Majesty of the Blues*, released in 1989, and the three-volume *Soul Gestures in Southern Blue*, released in 1991. Originally Marsalis intended these albums as a trilogy, with Volume 3, *Levee Low Moan* and *Majesty of the Blues,* released as a double album to underline the importance of the blues in his music, because he believed this situated his music at the heart of Afro-American culture. These four albums, Marsalis explained, "came out of a desire to really address the broad range of blues music, because that's what I felt we needed to deal with in our generation, to really get a good centering. But not just to try to play folk blues, but use the elements of the blues and deal with the fundamentals, from a contemporary stand-point."

The significance of the blues in Marsalis's music emerges from the ideas expressed in Albert Murray's book *Stomping the Blues* that celebrated a heroic vision of blues music, its artistry, social function, and ritualistic role that only some musicians are capable of fulfilling. Murray's views have much in common with the writer Ralph Ellison's view of jazz. Ellison — who famously wrote the novel *Invisible Man* in 1952 — and Murray believe there can be no jazz without a blues foundation. Both emphasize the importance of Armstrong and Ellington in the pantheon, the artist as a heroic figure, and the social and ritualistic function of the music. But whereas Ellison, in his letters to Murray, expressed a strong distaste for bebop since the "lyrical ritual elements of folk jazz" had been replaced by "the near themeless technical virtuosity of bebop," thus severing for him the crucial link between bandstand and dance floor, Murray, a younger man, embraced bebop and later, to a degree, Ornette Coleman. Another point of departure was in Ellison's insistence that issues of racial and national power politics were an intrinsic part of the music.

Murray's prose, like Ellison's, is full of allegory and metaphor. Both describe the blues as a celebratory music bringing men and women together, rather than a vehicle of social protest or an expression of sorrow. Jazz is situated within the blues, so it follows that for jazz to be jazz it must contain a blues sensibility. Equally, Ellison and Murray emphasize the link between jazz and dance floor; Ellison, in particular, believed a common culture is celebrated through the jazz dance's combination of instrumentalist, singer, and dancer, producing the physical dimensions of jazz and blues as ritual music. "The blues, the spirituals, the jazz, the dance — was what we had in place of freedom," he said. They believed the "blues" went to the heart of what it meant to be black and American, as the contemporary blues artist Mighty Mo Rogers emphasized to me in 2002:

Blues came about because of race. If it wasn't through slavery there wouldn't be any blues. So race is the issue, as W. E. B. Du Bois said,

"Race is the dividing line of the 20th century." He pointed out in his classic book *Soul of the Black Folks* which was written in 1902 and here we are in 2002 and it's still an issue. It's a profound issue. Blues came from something that was disfigured called slavery which produced something that was transfigured called blues.

In Murray's chapter "The Blues as Dance Music" in *Stomping the Blues*, he describes how the ritualistic function of the blues is achieved through swing. He further underlines its importance in *The Omni-Americans* by asserting Duke Ellington's composition, "It Don't Mean a Thing If It Ain't Got That Swing," is "the definitive statement of the epistemological assumptions that underlie the blues idiom."

Although Murray acknowledges musicians such as John Coltrane and Ornette Coleman, the main thrust of *Stomping the Blues* is primarily concerned with the early years of jazz, when it provided the soundtrack to African American social life, before the likes of Louis Jordan began leading black (and white) audiences toward rhythm and blues, and the emergence of subsequent styles that were increasingly remote from the jazz values he espoused, such as funk, Motown, disco, and eventually rap. A pantheon of jazz greats, a jazz canon, was created to exemplify black artistry and achievement, emphasizing Duke Ellington and Louis Armstrong, who Murray asserted, achieved their artistry through "swing" and, in particular, a "blues sensibility."

For Murray, the heroic cultural symbolism of the blues, its artistry, and social function are rooted in a musical past when jazz had a direct connection with black social and cultural expression. Ellison, too, writes nostalgically of the public jazz dance of his youth, the physicality of musicians and dancers alike, of bodies in motion, "with no 'squares' sitting around just to be entertained." It follows that for jazz to be considered "jazz," it must possess those elements (swing and a blues sensibility) that were present when jazz was a shared culture, an expression of black engagement with modern life and articulated the experience of collective identity based on implicit notions of musical roots, authenticity, and community. This reading of jazz places its core values in its "golden years," ambiguously located somewhere between the birth of jazz and the early 1960s, a period that conforms to conventional notions of a distinct musical culture: By the early 1960s, jazz had a tradition, evolution, history, and an air of permanence. These sociomusical values, as celebrated by Murray and echoed by Marsalis and writer Stanley Crouch, were in turn used to place African

American culture at the center of the broader stream of American cultural life, forcing the majority white mainstream to confront and acknowledge black excellence as an integral part of American life and culture.

But post-1960, as Burton W. Peretti has pointed out in his essay *Epilogue: Jazz as American History*, "The fragmentation of the African-American community . . . was reflected in the breakup of the jazz mainstream. Just as the civil rights movement broke into various conflicting groups, so did jazz — fragmented into modal, 'free,' and 'outside' styles — face a crisis of identity and lose its revolutionary fervor." Facing the breakdown of the "classic jazz" continuum or "master narrative" into a series of fragmented, decentered forms, Murray calls for historical continuity, because he cannot trust the direction these still mobile forms might take, thus defining "the real jazz" in terms of the styles of jazz that reside in its golden years becomes a powerful weapon. As is made plain in the Ken Burns television documentary *Jazz*, Murray and Marsalis achieve this through exclusion, denying contemporary (post-1965) developments in the narrative of jazz history. "What is missing? Or rather: who is missing?" complained Konrad Heidkamp, music critic of the German newspaper *Die Zeit*. "And who will no longer exist or, according to the logic of Minitrue in Orwell's *1984*, will never have existed, if one accepts the insight that historiography determines what really happened in the past: 'He who controls the past controls the future: he who controls the present controls the past.'"

The Murray–Marsalis–Crouch vision of jazz, which underpinned the Ken Burns documentary series, was seen by many critics as an idealization of a musical past, in which music making had a direct and uncomplicated connection with social, cultural, and community expression, unmediated by any other factors. But, as Tony Mitchell points out in *Popular Music and Local Identity: Rock, Pop and Rap in Europe and Oceania*, such essentialist notions of authenticity and musical stability are exemplified by those who:

> criticized Bob Dylan for adopting electric guitars into his folk music in the late 1960s, or Miles Davis for incorporating rock and funk elements into jazz, or Philip Glass for employing minimalist classical music in popular contexts. Such criticisms are usually predicated on notions of musical authenticity which regard a particular form of music as possessing an inherent truth, value, tradition and originality which places obligations on performers not to deviate from implicit rules inherent in these elements. These notions often amount to fixed traditional orthodoxies which fail to account for often radical processes of evolution which musical forms undergo.

Murray's attempts to limit jazz to certain "acceptable" performers, styles, and instrumentation find a parallel in the writings of folk music scholars, notably the father–son team of John and Alan Lomax. Like Murray, the Lomaxes felt that folk music was a true expression of "the people," and that there was a vital connection between its performers and the communities in which they lived and worked. Age-old songs were passed down from generation to generation; while subject to change, the basic forms were relatively fixed. "Authentic" performers were those who were raised within the tradition; all others were, at best, interpreters. Folk music was seen in opposition to popular styles, rather than related to them, so the constant fear of the folklorist was that the "authentic" performer might be "diluted" if he or she achieved popular success — and succumbed to the lure of catering to a larger audience. (John and Alan Lomax were dismayed when their "discovery," the blues performer Lead Belly, began developing skills as a performer and molded his "act" to appeal to his audience.) The net result was that anyone who tried to broaden the style — or introduce elements from pop music (such as rock instrumentation or rhythms) — was accused of turning his back on the "folk." Mitchell's comparison of the reaction of hardcore folk fans to Bob Dylan's "going electric" at the Newport Folk Festival in 1965 with the dismay of the jazz audience when Miles Davis similarly "went electric" is telling in this respect.

The powerful formalist ideology and renascent vision advanced by Murray, Crouch, and Marsalis in claiming jazz of the present should retain certain elements that were central to the ritualistic and social function it played within urban black communities between 1900 and 1960 fails to acknowledge "the radical processes of evolution which musical forms undergo." The necessity to define robs any art form of its potential for growth, because when music — or any art form — becomes a refuge from the present, from facing up to the world today, then its force is diminished; it becomes an embalmed corpse, beautiful to behold but ultimately inert.

Cultural and intellectual trends develop in a constant cycle: When a new style or phenomenon becomes owned by the mainstream, the originating subgroup let go of it. African American culture has long since let go of jazz and moved onto other arenas: rhythm and blues, Motown, funk, disco, rap, hip-hop, and so on. In his book *The Death of Rhythm and Blues*, Nelson George argues, "The black audience's consumerism and restlessness burns out and abandons musical styles, whereas white Americans, in the European tradition of supporting forms and styles for the sake of tradition, seem to hold styles dear long after they have ceased to evolve." This constant process of renewal, of taking a music from the margins and mainstreaming it for popular consumption is the way the music business, for better or worse, has always functioned. "Ten years from now I give you a prediction, there will be nobody black doing hip hop, it'll be all white, it'll be gentrification again," observed Mo Rogers in 2002. "It has to do with marketing, something is in vogue then it goes out of style. When an art form is invented and it's close to the edge it's hot. The more it goes to the center then the people on the edge say it's not hot any more." This cycle has meant the social and ritualistic function jazz played within African American society ceased many years ago.

The paradox was that in returning to the styles of jazz's golden era, these styles were being supported for "the sake of tradition," styles that had quite probably ceased to evolve. But that did not matter; placing swing and blues at the heart of jazz's core values was a means of asserting personal and cultural identity because these elements were central to a period when Murray considered the music had not been "diluted" by outside influences, such as white musicians, whom, he asserted in *Stomping the Blues*, were "*not* native to the idiom [of jazz]" (Murray's italics). Assertions such as these (that Chubby Jackson, Miff Mole, Gene Krupa, Max Kaminsky, George Wettling, Bud Freeman, Marian McPartland, and Gerry Mulligan were "third line" musicians) appeared to be echoed by Stanley Crouch's dismissal of Gil Evans for writing "high level television music" or Bill Evans for being "all Debussy."

Crouch's column in *Jazz Times* (January 2002 to May 2003) became a pulpit for separating the jazz sheep from the jazz goats: "[Dave Douglas] . . . knows he should keep as much distance between himself and trumpet players like Wallace Roney, Terence Blanchard and Nicholas Payton, any one of whom on any kind of material . . . would turn him into a puddle on the bandstand." Such comments prompted John Swenson to note in the *Washington Times* that, "Jazz may well have been the single most important force driving racial justice, integration and minority rights in this country's deeply intolerant history. Blacks and whites have been working together as brothers and sisters in the jazz world for a couple of generations now, and attempting to drive this kind of rhetorical wedge between them is a boorish enterprise." Indeed, pianist and composer Jack Reilly, former chairman of jazz studies at the New England Conservatory and adjunct professor at Rowan University, warns that, "At worst, this sort of thing has the potential to reignite racial tensions and undo whatever progress we've made since the 1960s."

However, Murray's and Crouch's subjective assertions about the need to maintain racial "authenticity" in jazz were at best very shaky. As just one example, in the late 1950s, trumpeter Roy Eldridge made a bet with critic Leonard Feather that he could, in a blindfold test, distinguish white musicians from black. After failing the test when listening to tracks by George Shearing, Miles Davis, and Billy Taylor, he was played a duet by Duke Ellington and Billy Strayhorn to which he responded, "White or colored? It's impossible to tell," adding, "I guess I'll have to go along with you Leonard — you can't tell just from listening from records."

In freeing jazz from the elements perceived to have "diluted" the real jazz, Murray's aesthetic, delineated by "the ritual of the blues" expressed "most eloquently in swing," imposed its own boundaries and, in so doing, refused to acknowledge that jazz has grown beyond its roots, like other arts have done. Opera, for example, was synonymous with Italy from one end of Europe to the other until the middle of the eighteenth century. But, with the rise of Romanticism, Gluck, Haydn, and especially Mozart adapted the Italian operatic conventions to their own expressive needs — Mozart's masterpieces *Cosí Fan Tutte* and *Die Zauberflöte* both broaden the expressive resources of opera with *Singspiel,* which had no antecedent in the Italian form, for example. By the following century, only one of the three greatest operatic composers was Italian — Verdi. Berlioz was French and Wagner was German, and each was approaching the idiom from their own cultural perspective, yet today nobody seriously argues that works such as *Les Troyens* or *Tristan und Isolde* are not somehow opera because they do not sound characteristically "Italian."

In art, once an idea or concept is launched into the world, it is there for people to do what they will with it, for better or for worse. Jazz, a product of African American exceptionalism, spread quickly around the globe, courtesy of the phonograph record, and is universally recognized as one of the great art forms to emerge in the twentieth century. Once the music became captured on recordings, its sounds became available to anyone around the globe to appreciate, imitate, and interpret. Today, wherever jazz is played it is, in effect, a celebration of its great founding fathers, Armstrong, Ellington, Parker, Coltrane et al., whose questing musical curiosity and excellence provides inspiration for the experimenters and innovators of the future.

Pianist Billy Taylor points out in *Jazz Piano* that while jazz emerged from African American culture, it is now no longer solely a black music, having transcended its ethnic boundaries. Bob Brookmeyer is more unequivocal: "Now, to me, the excessive Murray-Crouch-Marsalis emphasis on 'if y'all ain't Negro and can't sing the blues, y'all ain't fit to play OUR music' — is, quite simply, untrue. The music grew from diverse sources, black and white, and being born white has nothing to do with the God-given ability to SWING! Zoot Sims, anyone? My mentors were of both races and no one *ever* told me I didn't swing, blue or green."

The vision of jazz shared by the Murray–Crouch–Marsalis triumvirate created a narrow elitism that encapsulated a circumscribed range of sounds, styles, and attitudes. As in other arts, any return to a past "tradition" usually limits horizons rather than extending them. It also brings the risk of totalitarianism, a regime of semantics, definitions, and boundaries. Movements define themselves by that which they exclude, thus the outsiders — the free jazzers, the jazz-rockers, and nontradition based experimenters — became exponents of "nonjazz." Certainly a lack of consensus greeted the Murray–Crouch–Marsalis form of revisionism. "There are those people who are trying to protect [jazz] or say exactly what it is, and they are destroying it, because it grew from the mere fact it embraced all the things that were available, from the Caribbean, from Spanish music, everything," saxophonist Henry Threadgill told *Jazz Times*. "It was all these things that allowed [jazz] to happen and it has been those types of ideas that have made it progress." Trumpeter Lester Bowie was also troubled by the turn of events, as he told *Downbeat* magazine: "[Marsalis] even accused Miles [Davis] of treason because Miles played a Cyndi Lauper tune ['Time After Time']. In the '50s, 'Surrey With The Fringe On Top' was in the Hit Parade. That's part of the thing, to be contemporary, to express yourself. Wynton's trying to tamper with the music's development and I see some kind of evil overlay on that."

History has shown that imposing restrictions on music tends to marginalize it. Shortly after 1560, the Council of Trent decreed that sacred composition should abstain from secular practices, a key moment in the history of Western music. The result of the decree was that sacred music virtually stopping evolving. Hitherto church music had been a part of people's lives; now it continued in a limited role as composers moved out of the church and thought in terms of the motet rather than the mass and became increasingly aware of their individuality — one of the main characteristics of the Renaissance outlook — wanting to exploit their talents to the full. It is an illustration of how music goes where musicians want to take it, irrespective of strictures imposed upon it. After the seventeenth century, church music became a separate community with its musical conventions endlessly repeated for its true believers while secular music continued to evolve elsewhere. By imposing similar strictures on jazz — that it should refrain from secular practices like free jazz or electric jazz, for example — it is in danger of ending up like church music and not evolving at all. Indeed, there is a danger of this already happening: "I teach my students 'You can't move jazz anywhere: settle for first class musicianship,'" asserts Marsalis.

"'Why does everything always have to be new?' comes the friendly question from our Wynton Marsalis from across the garden fence, 'Some things are worth repeating.' Who could refute this statement?" wrote Konrad Heidkamp. "It is this combination of simplistic philosophy and praise of proficiency which suffocates every living art and uses up its energy in the musty basement of belabored explanations."

Jazz — once famously dubbed "The Sound of Surprise" by writer Whitney Balliett in 1959 — was now no longer sounding very surprising, "This is the new day you [the critics] are always searching for," wrote Marsalis in *National Jazz Service Organization Jazz Journal 5*. "The 'sound of surprise' that you all so often claim to want to hear will be the sound of accuracy." This kind of philosophy was answered by the Austrian trumpet player and composer Franz Koglmann. "To me, Marsalis is something like Gombrich on a trumpet," he told Klaus Nüchtern:

> That is to say, an art theory which advocates the primacy of mastery and maintains "anyone can be original." I don't have anything against mastery, I just think it should not suffocate originality, it should encourage it. There is a nice line by Bazon Brock . . . "That which is well made is bad, but so is the unaccomplished." And Marsalis is always about the well made.

This déjà vu jazz, in essence virtuostic recapitulation — however accurate — was curiously unmoving; indeed, Balliett himself wrote Marsalis "fails to stir the feelings, to jar the heart." It was a complaint shared by many of Marsalis's critics, such as the late Miles Davis, who noted in his autobiography: "I knew he could play the hell out of classical music and that he had great technical skills on the trumpet, technique and all of that. But you need more than that to play great jazz music." Others point to the legacy of jazz's great posthumous trumpet heroes that seemed to crowd out Marsalis's originality, such as jazz scholar and educator Dr. Lewis Porter, who noted in his book *Jazz: A Century of Change*, "[Marsalis] pays tribute to such past masters as Louis Armstrong and Duke Ellington's mute specialist, Cootie Williams, in solos that sound, to these ears, like patchworks rather than coherent musical statements. His work is always technically astounding however." It was a view supported by the German scholar and jazz commentator Ekkehard Jost, who adds, "It is hard within [an] impressive repertoire of technical and expressive resources to discover the person Wynton Marsalis, hard to identify a singular musical ego with him. Instead one gets the impression that trumpeter tries to remind one constantly of someone else. We recognize Rex Stewart, Bubber Miley, Clark Terry, Clifford Brown, Miles Davis (of pre-fusion time). We experience a 'brilliant juggling with many masks' (Stéphane Olivier), an 'endless series of hat's off and an urge for recognition' (Yannick Séité)." A good example of Porter and Jost's observations comes during Marsalis's solos on Ted Nash's 2003 album, *Still Evolved*, where a suave, impeccably executed solo reminiscent of 1960s Miles Davis gives way to "brilliant juggling with many masks," utilizing growl effects associated with Ellington brassmen.

"Anyone who thinks that mastering the history of jazz styles is a prerequisite for playing, will be a much admired mimic, but not an artist," asserts Konrad Heidkamp. "What a nightmare if the only writers, painters and sculptors to be accepted were those who were accomplished in all styles; how horrible if writers had to create samples in the styles of Nestroy, Bernhard and Jandl in order to write like Handke."

Ultimately, however, because jazz no longer provides the soundtrack to African American life in the way it did in its golden years, Marsalis's own engagement with jazz from this period has been like anyone else's of his age, through recordings and by playing with and talking to musicians who experienced this era at first hand. Indeed, he has pointed out in interviews when growing up in New Orleans how he thought "jazz was for old people." At thirteen he joined a funk band with his brother Branford called the Creators. "Then our popular music of the time was not blues based," he told Ben Sidran in 1986. "I didn't know any of those recordings, like Trane's recordings in the 1960s, or Miles recordings in the 1960s. Those serious group-interaction recordings. I never listened to Louis Armstrong. I never listened to Ornette Coleman."

However, Marsalis is quick to refute his playing lacks authenticity. "My music has architecture to it," he told me:

There's no random shit in it — now that's attacked in jazz now, because it goes against emotion, that's pure bullshit. If you're talking I don't play with soul, and all that, man, one thing I want to make clear about that is I'm from the neighborhood and I represent Afro-American culture much more than these buffoons they think are authentic negroes. It's something they don't understand 'cos they're outside it, because I won't act in this cliché fashion because I play classical music, and I represent the culture on a high level of sophistication that they think I have any problems with the level of soul I'm on or the level of negroidity — I'm not insecure about that at all. All them attacks, that was a complete waste of time. You know what I'm saying? It didn't make me run away from my technique. . . . So I mean my whole position, man, I *know* it's a position of heroism.

Marsalis's references to technique and heroism again reflect the writings of Ralph Ellison and Albert Murray. Technique, as Professor Robert O'Meally of Columbia University has pointed out, is "One of the key terms in the Ellison aesthetic lexicon. Avoiding the classicist's traditional bias in favor of defining technique as *classical* training, nothing else, Ellison sees it as the 'Artist's very stern discipline.'" Developing artistic technique is a step toward freedom, expressed, for example, in Ellison's *Invisible Man*. Technique is a route toward self-discovery, a rite of passage on the path toward a leader of communal rites (or community leader) echoing the writings of the Italian theorist Antonio Gramsci in the 1970s whose "intellectuals" organize moral and intellectual life. Jazz players were important role models for the young Ellison and heroic figures to Murray. In a lecture at Wesleyan University in May 1985, Murray gave an address on "The Function of the Heroic Image," explaining why this theme was central to his work: "The hero projects or represents a picture of conduct for us to emulate. And he's got to have in his character qualities that will enable him to confront problems with enough confidence in his technique to take on adversaries that might seem to have advantage over him."

Marsalis quickly and easily assumed the mantle of Ellison's and Murray's role model or heroic figure, a task whose responsibility he took with the utmost gravity as he became increasingly called upon to become a spokesperson for jazz and African American culture. In this respect, he had become Ellison's and Murray's "community leader," and as such was well aware of the responsibility vested in him; eloquent, ever gracious, yet firm and uncompromising, he saw the duty as a jazz musician, "and particularly the African-American jazz musician . . . to reintroduce cultural standards into American culture to counteract the relativizing effects of the mass media." He was nevertheless conscious of the paradox that existed in jazz, in that it was now remote from the experience of much of the African American community in America as a whole — as he confirmed to me in 2000: "In terms of Afro-Americans, under no circumstances do they support jazz music at any level."

Marsalis was prepared to risk a further fragmentation of black identity because he saw jazz musicians in terms of Ralph Ellison's "ideal artists" whose technical tools were ever ready in service of the "fight to achieve reality." That reality was unequivocal: you were either for him or against him. Marsalis rejected criticism in a way that suggested it was an attack on jazz and thus African American culture itself. Critics were adversaries, one of the dragons that the heroic figure, armed with technique, had to slay. Another enemy was an inclusive definition of jazz, which, as Crouch suggested in the pages of *Jazz Times* (April, 2003), was an attempt to create an "alternative order of significance." But things are not as simple as battles between moral extremes with nothing in between.

Jazz is a musical language with its own vocabulary, grammar, etymology, morphology, and syntax, and has, like language itself, evolved naturally so that it continues to have relevance to its "language community" (or in the case of jazz, music community). Change in language occurs all the time; for example, the words "talkie" and "wireless" have all but disappeared, while Shakespearean plays illustrate how words and their meanings have changed since the sixteenth century. New words enter the vocabulary and become absorbed by common usage almost unnoticed, yet every time a new edition of a dictionary appears it includes hundreds of new words. One way in which vocabulary is expanded is through borrowing from other language communities (in the same way jazz has broadened its expressive resources by borrowing from other musical communities). In 2004, a host of Hindi words were added to the *Collins English Dictionary*, such as "Angrez" (English person) and "badmash" (naughty), through the influence of second generation Asian immigrants in the United Kingdom. Those who complain about the loss of purity of the language are simply misguided, according to the experts; "English is a mongrel language and always has been," Jeremy Butterfield, editor in chief of the Collins dictionaries, told *The Observer* newspaper.

Like English, jazz is a mongrel, a music that drew together several strands of vernacular music including spirituals, work and folk songs, ragtime, minstrel music, brass band music, and blues that were freely mixed with elements from hymns, popular songs, and popular classics of the day. The whole history of jazz is dotted with examples of appropriation, resulting in a steady broadening of the jazz vocabulary by borrowing from other "languages" such as the Broadway show tune, as Louis Armstrong so eloquently demonstrated, even though it was completely alien to the jazz of his formative years. Music, like language, evolves to suit the culture that uses it and speaks on behalf of the society that spawns it; when it cannot do that or when society fails to hear what it is saying, the future for it becomes bleak. Despite the resistance of the cultural organizations like the Académie Française in France in forbidding English and Americanisms in the French language, the adoption of foreign words is a part of the natural growth of any language, and if language fails to adapt to people's needs, it is abandoned, like Latin. If we fix our attention on what is permanent, we cannot explain what has obviously been transformed, unless we believe that there can be no historical change but only combination and variation. This seems to be precisely the Murray–Crouch–Marsalis line of thinking; for example, in the first of his monthly columns Crouch wrote for *Jazz Times* between 2002 and 2003, he asserted that, "The jazz tradition is not innovation."

By the early 1990s, the young lions phenomenon was at its height, and so too was Marsalis's influence. "More and more musicians are at home doing the work of honing, sharpening and preparing to take the field by addressing the fundamentals of this music — swing, blues, grooves and at least the same level of technical skill serious musicians had over forty years ago," Marsalis told *Downbeat* in 1987. "On trumpet you have Wallace Roney, Terence Blanchard, Roy Hargrove, Marlon Jordan. On saxophone James Carter, Todd Williams, Wes Anderson, Branford [Marsalis], Ralph Moore, Sam Newsome, Gary Thomas. On bass, Reginald Veal, Peter Washington, Christian McBride, Delbert Felix and Charnet Moffett. On piano, Cyrus Chestnut, Peter Martin, Benny Green, Mulgrew Miller, Kenny Kirkland. On drums, Lewis Nash, [Jeff] Tain [Watts], Kenny Washington, Smitty Smith, Winard Harper, and, regardless of how it sounds, my little brother Jason." These musicians, and others, enjoyed the cachet of the young lions sobriquet and had profile in the world of jazz, some with major label recording contracts, and remained true to the values espoused by Marsalis of blues and swing.

But, privately many young musicians bridled under Marsalis's strictures. "I think why a lot of us did what we did, I think some of us were kind of scared to do other things, because we were scared that Wynton

Marsalis or Stanley Crouch would do a big interview in *The New York Times* and blast us, you know?" said bassist Christian McBride, one of the most universally respected musicians of all the young lions. "I try to say this with absolutely no malice — but you know, a lot of the Wynton Marsalis entourage feel that way." McBride continues:

> When I was around those guys and they get to bad mouthing fusion, and pop and a lot of music that was current at that time, of course a little sixteen or seventeen year old is going to take that stuff to heart. But I was always fortunate that — and this is the reason why I wanted to stick around a lot of different musicians because I always thought it interesting that Wynton Marsalis would say something like, er, "Miles Davis sold out after *Bitches Brew*." Then I would go back to another musician I would respect, somebody like Herbie Hancock, who would say, "Some of Miles Davis's greatest work was after *Bitches Brew*." So here I am getting these two completely different concepts, these outlooks on the same subject, so I always took that as, "Okay, at some point I'm going to have to draw my own conclusion and just feel how I feel." For a short time I probably did have that prejudice, acoustic bass players should never use amplifiers, fusion is bad, yeah — all of Miles's records after *Bitches Brew* were pretty bad. But I don't know, just one day I said, "That's really not how I feel, I love Miles's records after *Bitches Brew*, I love Weather Report, I love Return to Forever, I love all the M-Base records with Steve Coleman and everybody, I love that stuff." So why should I negate that kind music into my own music? And what I find most of the time is most of the musicians in my generation *do* love that kind of music, but they are too scared to kind of really show, in a really obvious way, how that fits into their music.

"Marsalism not only leads to the exclusion of certain artists," wrote Konrad Heidkamp, "it also, and this is a far graver matter, leads to a loss of vision, to an endless celebration of the status quo. Beauty becomes manifest within the framework of the traditional form, in the pleasure it takes in itself."

"It's awful, it really is awful," said saxophonist David Murray. "It got so bad when these guys came into power that Freddie Hubbard said, 'I'm glad he likes me!' A lot of jazz musicians are totally intimidated during this period." But it was not only musicians who were affected; critics and writers were confronted if their opinions did not fit the prevailing *mood retro*. "Marsalis now inspires fear, and his letters-to-editors when he is offended, or is even questioned, show why," wrote the author Gene Lees in 1994. Equally, Stanley Crouch, according to Richard B. Woodward in the *Village Voice*, "has menaced more than one writer with whom he has disagreed and was fired from the *Voice* in 1988 after assaulting a young black critic during an argument about hip-hop. You don't converse with Crouch; he stands at the lectern with his pointer and orates."

Professor Paul Gilroy, chair of the department of African American Studies at Yale, saw this problem as systemic, telling *The Guardian* that it was the inevitable product of "turning jazz into a classical music. The idea that culture progresses from a folk to a classical form comes from Goethe and Hegel. The effect is a disciplinary force policing creativity." In 1991, bassist Anthony Jackson argued that, in effect, this was what was happening in jazz:

> Why, then, do we find Mr. Marsalis and his congress of wanna-bes extolling the virtues of "pure" jazz taking upon themselves the twin mantles of protector and rejuvenator? . . . We are, in my opinion, witnessing no less than a modern cultural parallel to Germany in the 1930s, with a megalomaniacal "arbiter of good taste" undertaking a redefinition and reclassification of a country's expressive potential, ostensibly to weed out contaminating influences.

As the millennium approached, the effect of a decade dominated by Marsalis and the young lions was becoming clear. "New York is a very conservative scene now," observed saxophonist and educator Dave Liebman told me in 2000:

> America it's pretty much up and down the line. It's wonderful jazz playing but not that creative to my mind. . . . Young musicians coming up had only the view that to play "safe" and historical was the right thing to do. For them to conform was the rule, whereas earlier jazz generations had as a credo, to upset and go against. In other words, these young people really had no idea of anything different because their world view is stifled by the context they grew up in. Add to this the Marsalis movement . . . and this atmosphere becomes stronger.

Some musicians were prepared to state the case a little more strongly. "This is the most non-creative period in the whole history of jazz," said David Murray. "It's catch up time for people who want to play what's been done before. They've stopped the clock and gone back again, to the 1950s and 1960s, to define jazz." As the novelist and literary critic U. S. Pritchett pointed out, "We only have to glance at the second rate novelists to see how they differ in this sense (of contemporaneity) from the masters. The seond rate are rarely of their time. They are not on the tip of the wave. They are born out of date and out of touch and are rooted not in life but literary convention.

In 1999, Sony Jazz announced its "Swinging Into The 21st Century Series," saying, "While recording artists and creative persons in every field will attempt to end the millennium with works to ensure their place in history, none will equal the recordings and creative output of Wynton Marsalis in 1999 . . . [who] will release an unprecedented eight albums and a six CD box set on Sony Jazz and Sony Classical." But as John Fordham, jazz critic of *The Guardian* observed, Marsalis's concerts seemed to be "turning into musical seminars." Some listeners felt they should be taking notes rather than tapping their toes.

Columbia Records, which had groomed Marsalis for stardom when they signed him in 1980, "dropped him from the roster" in 2001, according to the *Boston Globe*. Apparently the label found "the prestige of his presence far outweighed by the hefty fees he had been demanding. Record company insiders say Marsalis shopped himself around to other labels but was turned down because he wanted too much money, in one case asking $1 million per album." In 2003, he signed with Blue Note records. "This marks the beginning of a vital new creative relationship between one of the great musical artists of our time and the world's premier jazz label," said Blue Note President Bruce Lundvall, in a press release. "I believe that Wynton is on the cusp of an innovative new creative period musically. Blue Note will share a pivotal contributing role in the next phase of his already astounding career."

In 2004, *Magic Hour*, Marsalis's debut on the Blue Note label, was released, with an evangelical liner note encomium by Stanley Crouch: "Jazz accepts no divisions in the realm of understanding. It makes the moment better because, if the moment is an empty bag, jazz fills it with the gifts of feeling and artistry, offered to all, received by any." In a thoughtful and perceptive review in *Jazz Times*, writer Thomas Conrad suggested the album sounded less like music born of the creative process, more born of a thought process. "It is not Marsalis' allusions to the past, in themselves, that give rise to the accusation that he fails to meet the overriding imperative in the jazz aesthetic, innovation," he wrote. "It is not even recognition, in the staccato 'Free To Be,' that Miles Davis has preceded him. Rather, it is a subtle deflation of expectation in so much of Marsalis' music. It is an intimation that it comes from a highly erudite process of assembly from the literature, rather than from inner necessity."

Only time will tell what judgment posterity visits on Wynton Marsalis. As Steve Hahn noted on the *Bird Lives* website, "Isn't it enough that he's the richest and most recognized jazz musician of the day? Must we [all] agree that Wynton Marsalis is the greatest musical genius of the late 20th century?" What seems certain is his artistic and ideological project has been both a blessing and a burden for jazz in America. On the one hand, as a result of Marsalis's influence, jazz has gained considerable prestige and profile in American cultural institutions, opening the door to corporate funding for certain areas of jazz activity. But, as Richard Williams pointed out in *The Guardian*, this has been at the expense of the music: "There had been revivalists in jazz before Marsalis, but he was the first to succeed in reversing the forward momentum that had carried the music through its first century."

Marsalis's response to charges that his vision of jazz is dominated by the past was typically robust. "It's not a matter of the past, jazz is always present," he said. "New Orleans is the most modern style of jazz, nobody has seemed to have recognized that, but that's what the truth is," he said. Expanding on this theme, he continued:

> First of all, New Orleans jazz is still modern. Jazz doesn't have to move forward. The only point I want to make is the development of jazz is not tied to the development of European music in any way. . . . We have to understand jazz music is half African, there's African components, and when I say African I don't mean in the generic sense, I'm talking about the fundamental rule and philosophy of the music and that gives it its functional and ritualistic component. And that component does not have to change because it addresses mythology, that's why New Orleans music always sounds modern, always sounds like something totally new.

Dancing around jazz history like this brings to mind boxer Mohammed Ali in his prime. But as Marsalis bobs and weaves around the "tradition," he boxes himself into a corner, a corner so small there is little room for maneuver. His polemical line often tended to outplay his music, because the "neoclassical effect" was to drain what was once a subversive music of its distinctive energy and truth by framing it within tried and tested methods of articulation and presentation, causing the late Eric Nisenson to note in his book *Blue: The Murder of Jazz*, how "this once continually innovative music has become so reactionary and staid."

If the Marsalis view prevails, that the jazz tradition is "not a tradition of innovation," then apprentice musicians will have to acknowledge the same sort of searching questions students of literature and of pop music have to confront, that the novel and the pop song may well have long since reached their ideal form. This has prompted pianist Keith Jarrett to argue in the pages of the *New York Times* that there can be no future for jazz if there is no present. "It is personal narrative we're losing, personal awareness: players with something to say," he claimed. "If that thread is broken (and it may well be), we're not going to write our way into the jazz future without important improvisatory voices because the narrative that is jazz will have died. The spirit of jazz is the spirit of personal freedom . . . jazz needs these acts of freedom to reconfirm itself in every era."

3

PROPHETS LOOKING BACKWARD: JAZZ AT LINCOLN CENTER

I think controversy in any way was the best thing that ever happened to Jazz at Lincoln Center because it brought so much attention to the program and to what we were trying to do, not just at a local, a regional and a national level but an international level.

Rob Gibson, former Executive Producer and Director of Jazz at Lincoln Center.

When New York's Lincoln Center for the Performing Arts appointed Wynton Marsalis artistic director of the Jazz at Lincoln Center program, he was presented with a high-profile position within the world of jazz. "Lincoln Center is a great institution," he said. "And with the support of the institution we can have the kind of national and international impact for jazz that would be very difficult for us to have on our own." It meant that Marsalis was seldom out of the limelight with concerts, tours, educational programs, TV, and radio appearances, and newspaper and magazine features. But, as *The Oxford Companion to Jazz* points out, to the dismay of many musicians, critics, and jazz fans "who favored a more open minded approach, Marsalis used his Lincoln Center pulpit to make rather autocratic proclamations about what did or didn't deserve to be called jazz." This placed him and his Jazz at Lincoln Center program at the heart of what has been described by Paul Erickson in his 1997 article Black and White, Black and Blue: The Controversy over the Jazz Series at Lincoln Center," as "some of the most acrimonious debates in the jazz community for years, debates which have led to name calling, fistfights and broken friendships."

Beneath what the *Village Voice* called "The Jazz Wars" lurked fiercely antagonistic assessments of the situation facing black America since the setbacks of the Reagan years as accounts of jazz's rise from bordello to the art houses of the world became a political battleground. The controversy over what styles of jazz Marsalis chose to present at Lincoln Center and the cultural issues that flowed from it received considerable profile because it was largely, but not exclusively, fought out in the pages of the nation's leading newspapers, journals, and magazines. The debate it sparked in the late 1980s and 1990s was in essence a struggle, to use educator Scott DeVeaux's words, "over the *possession* of [jazz] history, and the legitimacy that it confers." With significant amounts of money and cultural authority involved, Jazz at Lincoln Center frequently appeared in the eye of a storm amid, what Paul Erickson called, "charges of racism, age discrimination, artistic closed-mindedness, and elitism."

From relatively humble beginnings, Jazz at Lincoln Center grew into a multimillion dollar enterprise. As befits such an organization, the man at the top had an annual salary commensurate with a captain of industry. Wynton Marsalis, once described as "the first CEO in jazz" by the critic Whitney Balliett, received an income of $980,024 from Jazz at Lincoln Center for the tax year 1998–1999. By fiscal year 2003, the center's operating budget had risen to $12 million to pursue its declared aim to "educate the public about jazz music through concerts, national and international tours, weekly broadcasts on National Public Radio, records, lectures and film programs" and "curatorial and archival activities in connection with preserving the music heritage."

In 2000, construction on a new home for Jazz at Lincoln Center — dubbed "The New Center of the Jazz Universe" in its publicity brochures — began at the former site of the Coliseum on Columbus Circle on the southwest corner of Central Park in New York City. A part of the huge $1.6 billion, 3.8 million square foot Columbus Center with corporate offices, condominiums, hotel, and retail space, the Jazz at Lincoln Center facility, with its entrance dominating the corner of Broadway and 60th Street, cost — according to a Lincoln Center Fact Sheet — $128 million.

On October 18, 2004, "the world's first performing arts facility designed specifically for jazz, performance education and broadcast" opened. It comprised the 1,100- to 1,220-seat Frederick P. Rose Hall; a 300- to 600-seat performance space called The Allen Room where musicians play against the backdrop of the Manhattan skyline; the 140-seat jazz club called Dizzy's Club Coca-Cola; The Irene Diamond Education Center, a 3,500-square foot space comprising two education-rehearsal studios and a classroom; and The Ertegun Jazz Hall of Fame, a multimedia installation providing an interactive history of jazz.

For the first time in the music's history, jazz now had an institutional base comparable to a major opera company or symphony orchestra. Its opening was perhaps the most important "event" in jazz in over a decade. NPR radio and PBS TV presented "One Family of Jazz," the opening-night gala concerts from the Frederick P. Rose Hall featuring Wynton Marsalis and the Lincoln Center Jazz Orchestra and guest artists including saxophonist Branford Marsalis, trombonist Delfeayo Marsalis, Abbey Lincoln, the Afro-Latin Jazz Orchestra with Arturo O'Farrill, saxophonists Joe Lovano and Paquito D'Rivera, pianist Kenny Barron, percussionist Cyro Baptista, and the Bill Charlap Trio with trumpeter Nicholas Payton. In the world outside Jazz at Lincoln Center, however, celebrations were muted. While incredible sums of money, in jazz terms at least, had been invested in the Jazz at Lincoln Center project, designed in part to enhance jazz's cultural prestige within the arts, many were wondering privately whether it might turn out to be a luxury American jazz could not afford.

In July 1987, a short piece in the Arts and Leisure section of the *New York Times* announced that Lincoln Center for the Performing Arts was to launch its first concert series devoted exclusively to jazz. Initially it took the form of three concerts called "Classical Jazz" with Wynton Marsalis appointed as artistic adviser. The program, initially devised to fill the empty concert halls in August, quickly gained momentum. As it grew in size and ambition, it became clear that "it was filling seats that were often empty and that the people who were coming to hear the music were more affluent and younger than the Lincoln Center's traditional audiences." Plans to expand the "Classical Jazz" series in coming years were quickly developed.

In 1988, Marsalis published what amounted to a mission statement in the *New York Times* regarding his role at Lincoln Center called "What Jazz Is — And Isn't." Policing what he considered the boundaries of jazz, Marsalis defended his musical "purism" against charges of stagnation and attempted to shape a sense of what he believed jazz should be. It was predominantly through an idealized representation of the past — "the tradition" — and the historical narrative bound up in its construction that Jazz at Lincoln Center sought to exemplify jazz. These principles, when applied to the programming at Lincoln Center, resulted in what Paul Erikson called "an almost constant barrage of criticism, from all major New York newspapers and jazz magazines . . . directed against the exclusion of modern music." In *The Nation*, for example, critic and author Gene Santoro cautioned against, "This thing called The Tradition, which was supposed to be the self-evident lineage of all true jazz. Satchmo to Duke to Bird . . . a double-play combo that ignores all the fascinating bounces and odd hops that . . . [makes] jazz so fundamentally American."

In 1991, the Jazz at Lincoln Center program was created following the success of the "Classical Jazz" series, becoming a department in its own right with a year-round schedule underwritten in part by Lincoln Center. The hope was that it would eventually become a full constituent member of the institution, because it now enjoyed the kind of profile needed for fund raising, itself an essential element of constituent status. Marsalis was named as artistic director, the distinguished writers and social commentators Stanley Crouch and Albert Murray were hired as artistic advisers, and Rob Gibson, former director of the Atlanta Jazz Festival where he had made his reputation by booking all kinds of jazz, including the avant garde, was named administrative director (by the mid-1990s he had become executive producer and director).

Despite the criticisms of a historical bias in programming, Gibson claims that the programming was diverse from the start. "We had Don Byron the first year at Jazz at Lincoln Center," he said in 2003. "We had Muhal Richard Abrams, we had Israel Cuchao Lopez, we had Dewey Redman, Charlie Haden, Don Cherry and Ed Blackwell. I know that — I programmed all of that in the first year of Jazz at Lincoln Center. But it was never ever written about, because the criticism was always about how they were 'museum-ify-ing' the music." Indeed, a chorus of criticism was growing that would become ever more strident, but such were the controversies that had so consumed the press about the Jazz at Lincoln Center project that Richard B. Woodward of the *Village Voice* in an article appro-priately titled "Jazz Wars: A Tale of Age, Rage and Hash Brownies" observed in 1994 that:

> There is persistent belligerence from the leadership of the JLC, a dis-missal of anyone who would dare judge their actions, that does not square with the magnanimous ideals professed by their program or with the protocol of a million-dollar arts organization.

At the end of the fifth annual "Classical Jazz" series, critic Whitney Balliett sounded a note that would be revisited in the press again and again over the coming years. "Just six of the fifty-four performers used this week at Lincoln Center were white," he noted. In 1994, race was behind a charge leveled by Peter Watrous of the *New York Times*, who was quoted in the *Village Voice* as saying, "I don't think that the people who run Jazz at Lincoln Center are racist. But I think the program is racialist. They say they have to put on all the important figures before they get to the lesser-knowns and there happen to be more important figures who are black. That's complete bullshit. I'd like to know what Dewey Redman or Gonzalo Rubalcaba has contributed to jazz [each received a concert, the former in 1991, the latter in 1993]."

Public relations again became strained when Jazz at Lincoln Center began commissioning works, and Marsalis awarded the first one to him-self. Critic Gary Giddins noted in *The Village Voice*, "The debut of Marsa-lis's 'In This House/On This Morning,' an under rehearsed and apparently unfinished suite . . . had Lincoln Center's customers fleeing for the exits and journalists pondering the propriety of an institution handing its first commission to its own musical director." Once again, Lincoln Center was navigating itself into controversy. In 1993, Peter Watrous, normally broadly supportive of Jazz at Lincoln Center's endeavors, "charged nepo-tism influenced the awarding of commissions. Three of the four musicians then selected — Roy Hargrove, Marcus Roberts, and Terence Blanchard — were seen as Marsalis friends or disciples." Two years later, the commis-sions controversy still hung in the air, writer Terry Teachout noting in *Commentary* that, "The fact that [Marsalis] has been the frequent recipient of commissions from Jazz at Lincoln Center is little short of scandalous."

In January 1993, conductor David Berger was dismissed in the middle of the Jazz at Lincoln Center Orchestra's second tour, puzzling many commentators. Berger, a prominent contributor to the Classical Jazz Series for six years and who had contributed enormously to the band's repertoire with transcriptions of Duke Ellington recordings, was fired by Gibson in a Pennsylvania hotel room. In an interview in the *Village Voice*, Berger said he learned from a reporter that pianist Marcus Roberts had been hired as musical director for the Lincoln Center Jazz Orchestra's 1993 to 1994 tour. "I asked Gibson about it and he said Marcus would work with small groups, but I would be in charge of the big band," Berger told the paper. "But Marcus was really in charge. He decided what we played and who played what. I transcribed the music and rehearsed the band and that was it." According to the *Village Voice*, "Berger was told by Gibson that Roberts had been secured as a drawing card, a wildly improbable bet to place on this young and overrated pianist. Only one mind [i.e., Marsalis] could be behind this wishful thinking."

Four months later, on May 31, 1993, a further misstep was made by the Marsalis–Gibson regime. Gibson wrote a letter to all the members of the jazz orchestra, which was reproduced in part by the *Village Voice*:

> It is with mixed emotions that I tell you about an experiment we're trying this summer with the Lincoln Jazz Center Orchestra. We're making across the board changes in the orchestra personnel by hiring an entire band of guys under 30. I hope you'll understand that the decision not to utilize your talents this summer has nothing to do with artistic ability or any personal issues, this is simply an attempt on our part to try and get some of the younger musicians to learn more about this music and begin to play it with some authority.

Under the threat of age discrimination lawsuits, the letter was hastily retracted. Looking back on the incident in 2003, Rob Gibson told me:

> The age remark was a mistake I made and I will live with that, and go to the grave living with that mistake. Wynton wanted to get a band that would be able to play — to try a younger band. I could have just not rehired a lot of the older guys, but I tried to be nice and write a letter, and tell them we were going to try and experiment. I made one mistake of one sentence by saying "we'll hire a younger band." And that was totally on me. It had nothing to do with Wynton, or Jazz at Lincoln Center, it had everything to do with Rob Gibson making a mistake as the director of Jazz at Lincoln Center and I paid dearly for that in the press, but that was a mistake.

In any event, the band retained just one senior musician, baritone saxophonist Joe Temperley. "The firing would seem to be a gross betrayal of a principle that Marsalis and his mentors, Murray and Crouch, have always proclaimed," said the *Village Voice*. "A respect for the transmission of wisdom between generations." It denied younger musicians the age-old aural tradition in jazz of learning from experienced older players that had included Britt Woodman and Norris Turney (former Duke Ellington sidemen) and Roland Hanna, leaving Joe Temperley (ex-Woody Herman) to provide for the needs of all.

Yet despite the outcry in the press and charges of ageism, reporter Lara Pellegrinelli pointed out in the *Village Voice* that, "Not a single critic challenged the chauvinistic assumption that only young men could fulfill the requirements of the band." She further noted that unlike the orchestras of the other Lincoln Center constituents — the New York Philharmonic, the Metropolitan Opera, and City Ballet — Jazz at Lincoln Center did not observe a tenure process, advertise job vacancies, have structured auditions observed by a committee, or conduct "blind auditions" behind a screen. Although Marsalis expresses the deepest respect for women as individuals and as performers in *Sweet Swing Blues on the Road*, a book he coauthored with Frank Stewart, he considers that it is the role of men to be carriers of the jazz tradition. The academic Eric Porter in *What Is This Thing Called Jazz?* said this "patriarchal continuum of jazz artistry" created a "gendered construction of the jazz tradition as male and conforms to the ideology of the contemporary anti-feminist backlash." And while Marsalis has pointed out that women often sit in with the band and sometimes deputize for full-time members, in 2003 the Jazz at Lincoln Center Orchestra remained an all-male preserve. "If rehearsals and subbing form paths to potential employment," Pellegrinelli concluded, "Women's J@LC prospects look bleak."

In an attempt at bridge-building following the harsh criticism the ageism incident provoked in the press, Gibson organized a dinner for selected journalists, at which Stanley Crouch was also present, at Gibson's apartment on July 13, 1993. But this degenerated into a clumsy public relations farce, with disagreement as to what was "on the record" (could be reported and attributed to Gibson and Crouch) and what was not, as well as claims that brownies served at the event contained marijuana in order to make the journalists malleable. "We had a dinner at my house, and talked with critics," said Rob Gibson:

> We invited eight to ten guys over just to talk. I actually thought it was a nice dinner and I thought we had a good time. But at the end of the night the publicist at Jazz at Lincoln Center [Marilyn Laverty], who had made dessert, served brownies. Somebody said "What'd you put in the brownies?" and she said, "Wouldn't you like to know!" Two weeks later a cover story appeared on The Village Voice called "A Rage Supreme" where they claimed we had put hash in the brownies — hashish in the brownies — which was of course a total and utter lie . . . this is the kind of stuff that goes on.

The feature Gibson refers to appeared in the August 9, 1994, edition of the *Village Voice*, which charted what it called "the missteps that have dogged Jazz at Lincoln Center," concluding:

> Until the leadership abandons its prickly, vindictive mind-set, humiliating those who don't share all of their dogmatic views, there should be enough intrigue and ill will to keep everyone in the jazz press employed for years to come.

And so it seemed. Squalls of controversy continued to sweep Jazz at Lincoln Center, ranging from critiques of specific concerts (Gary Giddins described some of the concerts as "confused underachievement") to overarching criticisms of the program's mission (Kevin Whitehead argued against the center's perceived narrow definition of jazz). In early August 1993, *New York Daily News* critic Gene Santoro questioned the personnel for an upcoming Thelonious Monk concert at Jazz at Lincoln Center, asking why Steve Lacy and Johnny Griffin, both excellent interpreters on Monk, had not been invited to perform, suggesting the real reason was because pianist Marcus Roberts did not wish to play with them. In such a climate of mutual mistrust, the tension was increased on August 29, 1993, when Stanley Crouch allegedly harassed and threatened Santoro at a concert in Tompkins Square Park following what Santoro describes as "a long series of sniping and complaints about my writings on Jazz at Lincoln Center, which questioned key aspects of the program and its ideology."

The high (or low, depending on your perspective) point of the controversy came in a debate between Marsalis and author James Lincoln Collier. Marsalis was critical of Collier's biographies of Louis Armstrong and Duke Ellington, two artists whom Marsalis revered, while Collier was critical of Marsalis's programming at Lincoln Center. "There may not have been blood on the walls by the end of the showdown," wrote Clive Davis in the *Times* of London:

> but it was a close run thing. . . . Collier faced a largely hostile standing room only audience and a smirking trumpet virtuoso who was intent on administering a thrashing. I would say (and it's probably a minority view) that the encounter ended roughly even. Marsalis pointed out technical errors in Collier's analysis of Ellington's scores; on the other hand, his none-too-subtle attempt to indict Collier as a closet racist appeared to be based on misreading of passages in the Ellington and Armstrong books.

But, as with many unpleasant accusations, the suggestion of racism continued to linger over the Jazz at Lincoln Center's programming long after the Collier–Marsalis debate. It was exacerbated, as Paul Erickson points out, by the racial climate in New York City in the fall of 1993 during a bitterly fought mayoral campaign between Republican Rudy Giuliani and the incumbent Democrat David Dinkins, the first black mayor of New York City. Race became an issue in the press, as did Dinkins's alleged cronyism: the awarding of political appointments to his supporters. This was similar to the kind of charges that were swirling around the directors of Jazz at Lincoln Center. Giuliani won the race, but Erickson noted, "the venomous tenor of the mayoral campaign lingered well into 1994, and fed an atmosphere of racial tension at Lincoln Center where the directors perhaps saw white jazz critics as playing Giuliani to their Dinkins."

"I think a lot of it had to do with the fact that a black guy, namely Wynton Marsalis, got in a position of authority," said Rob Gibson in 2003. "He was controversial with some of the things that he said. I know he has many regrets for certain things he said along the way. I think he is a smarter man now than he was twenty years ago and he said things that a lot of the people didn't want to hear, or if they did, they didn't like it." For Stanley Crouch, however, any alleged animosity displayed by the "critics" had nothing to do with musical issues. For him the answer resided elsewhere, as he told writer David Hajdu in *The Atlantic Monthly*. It was because, "[Marsalis] has access to…a far higher quality of female than any of them could imagine."

On April 1 and 2, 1994, Marsalis and the Lincoln Center Jazz Orchestra debuted *Blood on the Fields* to packed houses at Lincoln Center. This epic jazz oratorio tells the story of two African slaves, Jesse and Leona, from capture to plantation life. *Time* magazine named it one of the top ten music highlights of the year, while the *New York Times Magazine* said the work, "marked the symbolic moment when the full heritage of the line, Ellington through Mingus, was extended into the present." In January 1995 Marsalis reassembled the company in the recording studio, and when the three hour, three CD set was released in 1997 it was awarded a Pulitzer Prize. It was a significant moment, not only in Marsalis's career but in the recognition of jazz within the arts establishment of America. As the social commentator and filmmaker Imruh Bakari points out in his essay "Exploding Silence":

> Blood on the Fields quite deliberately positions the Black presence within the dominant American twentieth century culture. This epic work unmistakably revisits the narrative of slavery in America with a sense of the contemporary, a strategy similar to that of Duke Ellington, whose Black, Brown and Beige suite premiered in 1943. In their respective contexts Duke Ellington…and Wynton Marsalis testify to an insistence on being active modern subjects in very much the same way DuBois wrote of an American context in which, "we have woven ourselves with the very warp and woof of this nation." The differences in these works, however, are a reflection of the way the jazz aesthetic has been expanded, deepened and simultaneously institutionalized over the years.

Stanley Crouch, Marsalis's dedicated proselytizer, enthused in the liner notes that his protégé had, "reached a level of expression arrived at by only the very great artists…the epic length of the piece, nearly three hours, puts it in a category beyond all other jazz composition. Where many had fumbled before him, either out of a lack of compositional skill or a tendency to pretension, Marsalis was showing how well all of the elements of jazz and its antecedents could work together." Opera? Western classical music? "Just listen to the opening track on Blood on the Fields anytime for anybody who wants to know what cutting edge avant-garde music sounds like," asserted Rob Gibson in 2000.

There were, however, dissenting voices. In reviewing the album Larry Birnbaum in *Downbeat* observed, "As a composer, Marsalis is remarkably tuneless, with none of his idol Duke Ellington's gift for catchy melody; as a librettist he's ludicrously pompous and preachy…he keeps his emotions so closely under control, and his ego so prominently on display, that the music scarcely swings. And that, if you accept the gospel according to Wynton, is jazz's cardinal sin." Clearly *Blood on the Fields* represented many things to many people, the *Downbeat* readers in their annual poll voting it tenth in the Album of the Year category. Certainly the orchestral writing contains many moments of unreconstructed Ellington, whose arranging style seems to have been bitten off and swallowed whole by Marsalis—indeed, as Birnbaum noted in his review, *Blood on the Fields* is "evocative more of the Cotton Club than cotton fields."

The following May, The Chamber Music Society of Lincoln Center and Jazz at Lincoln Center collaborated in a program that brought together jazz-inspired classics and improvisations in classic jazz styles. Marsalis debuted his newly commissioned "At The Octoroon Balls," performed by The Orion String Quartet, which the *New York Times* described as the program's centerpiece, "both for those who are attracted to crossover endeavors and for those who find the concept distasteful." The commission, a seven-piece, 38 minute work, was said to "have been completed only two weeks ago," the *New York Times* reviewer noted, adding that "Mr. Marsalis will consider taking the editorial shears to it." Indeed, there has continued to be a lack of consensus about Marsalis's large-scale compositions, "They are unfinished, sometimes frankly amateurish and betray a lack of technique startling in an artist so generously equipped in other areas," Terry Teachout noted in *Commentary* in 1995. Nine years on, however, Larry Kart, former music critic of the *Chicago Tribune*, was able to observe in *Jazz in Search of Itself* that: "It now seems clear that despite the prominence that the engines of cultural politics and publicity have given to Wynton Marsalis, his music (especially his latter day orchestral work) is a nonissue aesthetically and has been for some time."

On December 18, 1995, the Lincoln Center Board awarded Jazz at Lincoln Center equal status with the New York Philharmonic, the Metropolitan Opera, the New York City Ballet, and the other constituents of the center. "Jazz has done very well here," said Nathan Leventhal, the president of Lincoln Center, in making the announcement. "It deserves its place." It was the first time that jazz, an art form born in America, was fully accepted by one of the nation's premier performing arts centers whose programming was normally dominated by European arts. "When we announced a year round program in 1991, we said it was our duty to help the program financially," continued Leventhal. "We set a goal of an endowment of $2.5 million, but the program already has gifts of $3.4 million." The amounts of money earmarked for jazz activity at Lincoln Center, already huge, was set to grow.

Becoming a full constituent member, plans were put in hand to build an endowment of roughly $10 million to support its activities. One of the problems Marsalis had to confront was promoting a black jazz canon from an institution associated with the European arts, because to Murray, Crouch, and Marsalis, so-called Eurocentric associations were antithetical to the spirit of jazz. However, Marsalis eschewed such problems, telling *Downbeat* in 1992, "The belief that a place like Lincoln Center means that the soul is gone from the music or it's going to be like a museum piece or is a repertory band — that's just not true. It's just another setting, and what better setting than a place where the other arts are being celebrated? Like jazz is supposed to stay in Lulu White's house?"

But with programming at Lincoln Center still proving to be a contentious issue, Marsalis not unreasonably pointed out that his appointment as artistic director was on the basis of his musical tastes, saying, "I'm gonna do what I like. That's my job as artistic director. I don't think I'm gonna program the type of avant garde music that sounds a lot like European classical music, which I love, but when the music starts to sound like it's not swinging, that's not a style that I'm personally fond of." Crouch was more unequivocal: "These [free jazz] people are not jazz musicians. They may be improvisers and they may like jazz, but that doesn't make them jazz musicians. A transvestite doesn't become a woman just because he puts on a dress and make-up and walks like a woman."

These exclusionary views were widely seen as taking a felling axe and lopping off large branches of jazz history, causing considerable controversy, not least among the avant-garde musicians themselves. "I have friends who are out of work because of them," claimed saxophonist David Murray, who himself had moved to Paris. "These people have talked about my generation so badly, my generation is scared to say a damn thing. I'm dealing with a whole bunch of scared guys." In 2003, Sholto Byrnes of *The Independent* questioned Marsalis about Murray's remarks and recorded his reaction:

> Marsalis [became] very agitated. His already fast speech speeds up, and he interrupts before I can finish the sentence. "Every four years there's another issue. There's another controversy, but it's never really controversial. What is the controversy?" he demands . . . After stressing his good relations with David Murray (Marsalis plays basketball with Murray's son, Mingus) he concedes the point: "Did some people lose some gigs because I don't like their style of music? Maybe that's true, maybe that's false, I don't know. But that's not controversial to me."

The musical climate in 1994 was such that pianist Cecil Taylor spent $15,000 of his own money (along with Sausages at the Opera, a small production company) to produce his 65th Birthday Concert at Alice Tully Hall. For the two months leading up to the concert, Taylor practiced for up to twelve hours a day, according to *Downbeat*, which noted "the added satisfaction of playing in a hall where he would not otherwise have been invited by the in-house jazz department was too evident for him to conceal. 'What jazz department?' shouted Taylor when asked about Jazz at Lincoln Center." Crouch stated that Taylor did not fit at Jazz at Lincoln Center's definition of jazz, because "even though he improvises, he does not swing." Taylor's response was to describe the Lincoln Center formula of "blues-plus-swing-equals-jazz" as "parochial and retrogressive nonsense. "It's almost the year 2000, for Christ's sake! Dizzy Gillespie used to say, 'The difference between myself and Louis Armstrong is that he improvised on the melody and I improvise on the chord changes.' Well that concept is already 50 years old!" As the writer Gene Lees said of Crouch in 1994, "No critic in the history of America's music has ever had [the] power to censor according to his own biases and limitations."

The Marsalis–Jazz at Lincoln Center line is equally dismissive of electric jazz. Duncan Heining, George Russell's biographer, cites the example where a proposed seventieth birthday concert dedicated to Russell's music foundered due to the triumvirate's opposition to the composer's use of electric instruments to play his classic works such as "All About Rosie" and "Cubana-Be" and "Cubana-Bop." However, Rob Gibson says it was all very amicable; Russell wanted to use his current band, with electronic instruments, to play his early works, which Gibson claimed would not work for Jazz at Lincoln Center. Because Russell refused to have the lineup of his band and how he should play his own music dictated to him by Lincoln Center, there was a parting of the ways. However, according to Heining, Russell was never offered any explanation as to why the intended concert did not go ahead. "Alice Russell is absolutely adamant that George has never had any discussions with Rob Gibson or Stanley Crouch about what material he would play or what instruments would or would not be used," said Heining:

> She told me that she felt the whole business had been handled unprofessionally. The phrase she used was that they were not given "the courtesy of a response." It seems very sad that one of the major figures in jazz history, a guy who knew and worked with people like Dizzy, Miles and

Coltrane should not have been honored with a concert to celebrate his music and his 70th or 80th birthday at Lincoln Center. My impression is that the Russells certainly do not feel that any of this was remotely amicable.

The debate over what constitutes jazz — whether it can include a free jazz musician such as a Cecil Taylor or electrified jazz at the hands of a George Russell, whether it should "swing" and have a "blues" quotient, and so on — goes to the heart of the controversies that surround Jazz at Lincoln Center. As Charley Gerard suggests in her essay "Battling the Black Music Ideology":

> Black music ideologists are correct in their assessment of jazz as a language that black musicians understand in a different way than whites. For whites, jazz is a means of self expression and a means of artistry. For African Americans, jazz is certainly that, but in addition it is an assertion of ethnic identity. The philosopher Kwame Anthony Appiah noted in the context of his study of African culture and philosophy that there was a profound difference between the respective goals of European and African writers that could be summarized as the difference between the search for the self and the search for culture. The same words could be used to distinguish between white and African-American jazz musicians.

It is against this backdrop that the Murray–Crouch–Marsalis aesthetic for the Lincoln Center program must be seen: as a strategic response to both to the state of jazz and to the state of African American society within a predominantly white Anglo-Protestant culture. As Imruh Bakari argued, in the context of Marsalis's epic oratorio *Blood on the Fields*, the Lincoln Center project must be seen "as a part of DuBois's 'double consciousness,' in effect an attempt to overcome an assumed 'lack of identity.'" Between them Murray–Crouch–Marsalis sought to make the dissemination of jazz a vehicle for social change in America, following the social and economic policies of the American right during the Reagan and Bush eras where real wages stagnated or declined along with benefits; working hours increased; and employers were given free rein to ignore protection for labor organizing. Reaganism and the mainstream media (controlled by the major U.S. corporations) celebrated the values of entrepreneurial capitalism while recasting the struggles of the minorities as "reverse discrimination." As Albert Murray stated to Robert S. Boynton in the *New Yorker*: "America's only hope is that the Negroes might save us . . . we're trying to do it with

Wynton and Stanley. That's all we are, just a bunch of Negroes trying to save America."

By using jazz as the basis for projecting a sense of national community, with the emphasis on unity — thus jazz is "America's classical music," or "America's music" — it becomes the means to assert the equal status of African American people in the broader community. By holding true to their beliefs in the face of a constant barrage of criticism, notably in the center's early years, Murray, Crouch, and Marsalis's particular view of what jazz should be achieved what many thought impossible, moving jazz from the margins of American culture and into its mainstream with the highly laudable sociocultural result of forcing the white American mainstream to confront and acknowledge black cultural achievement and excellence.

It is in this context that the ethos of Jazz at Lincoln Center's productions must be seen, emphasizing their sense of connectedness to the jazz tradition. "At stake if the rhetoric is taken at face value," educator Scott DeVeaux, in his chapter "Constructing the Jazz Tradition," suggested, "is nothing less than the music's survival." In fact, what was at stake was keeping alive jazz's core styles of the past to counter the increasing pluralism of post-1960s jazz — its flirtations with rock and funk music, its incorporation of world music influences, and the emergence of jazz styles shaped outside America — which Marsalis, Murray, and Crouch believed was taking the music further and further away from its historic, central core, when jazz had a direct connection with black social and cultural expression. Jazz at Lincoln Center was about preserving the essence of those styles when jazz was at the heart of urban African American social life and culture — effectively those styles that flourished between the turn of the twentieth century to the early 1960s. To achieve this, they defined a jazz canon that matched conventional notions of musical culture — that jazz had a tradition, a long history, and an air of permanence — which established the music as an autonomous art form of substance rather than a fad or an offshoot of pop music. However, texts become cannonical because they meet the needs of the people with cultural power. They are as much about policing knowledge as organizing lines of critical enquiries.

In establishing the depth of the jazz tradition, an unbroken thread going back to the end of the nineteenth century and beyond with a prejazz history in African American forms like the cakewalk, ragtime, and minstrelsy, it belied attempts to portray African Americans as people without a past. Jazz represented a specific musical culture with a long process of maturation that provided powerful examples of black achievement in figures such as Louis Armstrong, Duke Ellington, and John Coltrane. The way the jazz canon quickly assumed importance in American jazz has less to do with the music, more to do with the assertion of American cultural identity. "Many Americans wish they had a long-term, culturally unified history in the sense that a France or a Britain or an Italy does," says Dr. Elizabeth Peterson, a former linguistics lecturer at Indiana University and sociolinguist at the Center for Applied Linguistics in Washington D.C.:

> This is why fourth and fifth generation Irish-Americans, for example, will still say to a person from Ireland, "I'm Irish, too!" For many, perhaps most Americans, being citizens of a country mostly comprised of immigrants there is a sense of something "missing," of no particular history belonging to them thus the pre-American past continues to matter greatly to the majority to provide a sense of identity. This, I think, is one explanation why Americans will cling so possessively to those few things that are considered cultural and yet "American" — baseball and jazz, for example. To me this speaks volumes as to why the American mainstream, then, would need to claim jazz as uniquely American property. However, European Americans are often able to pinpoint a place or a time whence their families came to this continent. "My grandparents came from Italy through Ellis Island in 1906" — or whatever. African Americans can claim no such history. Forced immigration — slavery — would have pretty much annihilated any such sense of connection with a past. Today's African Americans are not likely to know when their forefathers came here, or where they came from so the creation of a sense of history on this continent becomes even more pertinent.

Thus in claiming jazz as an exclusively African American creation it becomes a means of asserting both cultural identity *and* of placing a specifically African American art form at the center of American culture. But the means used to accomplish these goals — the removal of jazz from the rough and tumble of day-to-day life, where it achieves its greatest immediacy, and the importance of an overarching tradition of elite deceased giants and their interpreters — comes with a price tag. In producing nostalgia for a period of history that neither its musicians nor its audiences experienced suggested jazz was now more about America's past than part of its future. "[Wynton's] done a fine job of drawing attention to the music, that's great credit to him and I really respect him for that," pianist and composer Herbie Hancock told me in 2005. "[But there's a caveat] —

unfortunately it's a narrow view and one that largely favors players in history, most of whom have died! And it kinda treats the music, in my view, as one that belongs in a museum."

Jazz at Lincoln Center's "vital mission," according to its fact sheets, "is carried out through three primary objectives, Curatorial, Archival and Educational." These objectives are given shape and definition by the Jazz at Lincoln Center Jazz Orchestra, formed in part to prove that jazz, like classical music, has a canon of masterpieces that merit constant performance. But Konrad Heidkamp, music critic of *Die Zeit*, mischievously questions this kind of composition-as-sacred-endeavor approach, inquiring, "Who would in this day and age rack their brains about new interpretations of Bach, Mozart or Beethoven and fill subsidized concerts with them if we had recordings of their performances, if their sound were documented in audible form and repeatable?" In jazz we do have the recordings of the original jazz masters, so repertory re-creations will always be in competition with them. The paradox in jazz is that its recordings do not nostalgically call up the past, they simply show the past to be real, while in contrast repertory concerts appear as a nostalgic endeavor. "Jazz is a music that constantly renews itself," conductor and scholar Gunther Schuller told the *Village Voice*, "What I've always said is that the repertory idea is an ancillary tradition. It is a small part while the main tradition grows and evolves."

This argument for proportionality in the repertory movement's influence within the current jazz continuum is wholly apposite. However, in the context of the Jazz at Lincoln Center Orchestra, this argument has been reversed. Repertory is not a small ancillary tradition but its main mission, while the Murray–Marsalis–Crouch paradigm of jazz does not acknowledge that the jazz tradition itself can continue to evolve and grow. Instead, repertory provides the means by whose the "swing and blues" definition of jazz can be both articulated and enforced. Marsalis's road tours with the Lincoln Center Jazz Orchestra contained themes using swing, blues, and dance in their titles, such as the "Sweet Swing Blues on the Road" tour or the "For Dancers Only" tour, whose name was taken from a 1937 hit record by the Jimmie Lunceford Orchestra. In a column he wrote for the magazine *Jazz Times* in 2002, Stanley Crouch held unyieldingly to the contention that "swing and blues" provided the authority for the present, and that if the present does not conform to the past, then jazz becomes something else, asserting "anyone was welcome to play jazz...blues and swing are there for you too, *if you want to play jazz*" (my italics). However, imposing such definitions on jazz means setting explicit boundaries and limiting jazz's potential for future growth. Art cannot be regulated in this way; even in the 1920s the international avant-garde in the arts was advancing the notion that art was without limits.

The "swing and blues" mantra clearly arises out of the desire to assign some properties to jazz that make it "jazz." Otherwise, the argument goes, how do we know that it is not R&B, blues, pop, baroque, etc? But as Ludwig Wittgenstein argued, a formal definition of even everyday concepts is probably impossible, as he demonstrated with his famous example of "game." Jazz eludes "definition" in much the same way as there is no "definition" of a beautiful melody. Attempting to define it is probably impossible, and, as Italian musicologist Marcello Piras points out, the Murray–Crouch–Marsalis (M-C-M) definition of jazz is probably ultimately flawed:

> The M-C-M paradigm is what a philosopher would call an "inductive" definition of jazz. It consists—at least in theory—in reviewing all the single occurrences of a given general tag and listing the common traits. There are problems with such definitions. Jazz runs faster than human life. No list of traits compiled in 1920 would have worked in 1950. All such lists are, at best, very imperfect samples of past occurrences, and quickly get outdated. A trick to dodge the problem is choosing a list of traits that include only the jazz you like and leaves out the rest as "non-jazz". The M-C-M definition is just that. Jazz changes and will possibly do again, but what *they* like in jazz doesn't. The trick is possible, once again, because jazz is an area segmented out of a continuum of musical creations. The M-C-M paradigm claims to offer an inductive definition of jazz, but it crops an area called "jazz" *before* defining it, and then finds that all (they say) elements left in fit the definition. Of course! You chose them. How come that Albert Ayler is left out? Because the area to be defined was limited in such a way that he was left out!

Every jazz style shares a set of norms in the same way a language community shares a broad range of phonological, syntactic, semantic, and pragmatic norms. Until M-C-M's ideological definition of the music took hold in America, jazz was generally seen as work in progress, a broad musical form connected to its community in terms of what *audiences* expected from it: be it a bebop, jazz-rock, free jazz, or experimental jazz audience, and so on. As Simon Frith pointed out in his book *Performing Rites*, "Genre is not determined by the form or style of a text itself but by the audience's perception of its style and meaning, defined most importantly at the moment of performance." Like language communities, jazz's users decide the rules of use that the community upholds and understands.

Different modes of expression are used to communicate between different audiences: a free jazz audience will have different expectations to a hard bop audience, a jazz-rock audience will have different expectations to an audience for traditional New Orleans jazz, and so on. If for some reason the rules or values of the musicians or the audience changes, the language or music changes to reflect that. As Frith points out, "Old genres 'fail' when their rules and rituals come to seem silly and restrictive; new genres are born as the transgressions become systematic."

Change in jazz is inevitable because, like language, communities change, provide new contexts that require new expressions, or find new ways of doing things. Language and jazz is constantly being modified into something that works in the here and now for its users. Change occurs when someone wants the language or music to do something it is not doing, at which point the stimulus for change is born. Need causes change but rarely can change be predicted; often it can only be explained in hindsight. The process of change itself is like a form of Darwinism in both language and jazz – ideas are tried with the most successful adapted by imitators, a kind of natural selection that ensures the survival of the idea and ultimately a style.

During the Golden Years of jazz, the dynamic for change stemmed from the Afro-American community, as Amri Baraka asserts in *Blues People*, but this dynamic begins to break down in the 1960s as jazz began to see developments originating beyond the community where it was originally nurtured. Since then its language has been expanded to suit the expectations of a broader, global community. Just like language, jazz is owned by its users, and they make up the rules for how it best works for them; it is not something that can be decided by any one person or interest group. Today jazz is a musical *lingua franca* spoken around the world and is analogous to the English language as a *lingua franca*: in being used by everybody, it is "owned" by nobody.

Jazz's survival has increasingly come to depend on funding, and like the other arts, it had to stand in line for its share. Over the last decade and a half, funding for jazz has primarily flowed into Lincoln Center and other large-scale presenters. Even some attempts to build a jazz touring circuit have tended to focus on these larger venues. In 1996, *The Nation* was initially optimistic that, with funding from the Leila Wallace–Reader's Digest Foundation, a national not-for-profit jazz network with twenty or so centers promoting jazz across the United States would emerge that would greatly benefit the music: "when the dust settles over the next couple of years, the results should look like a coherent national touring circuit . . . whose emphasis will be on non-big-name jazzers who couldn't be heard in small towns and midsized cities."

However, doubt has been expressed whether the impact of this scheme has been as great as it could have been and whether it has fulfilled *The Nation's* optimistic hopes for it. "It's not that Jazz at Lincoln Center has taken money away from other organizations who were getting it before. But rather that all this new income going to them has restructured the industry into big fish and minnows," observes Marty Khan, longtime jazz business professional and author of *Straight Ahead: A Comprehensive Guide to the Business of Jazz*:

> In the mid-1980s, when Jazz at Lincoln Center was first being discussed, my prediction was that it was going to polarize funding, that it would take the lion's share of funding and would essentially undo the work that most grassroots organizations had done in establishing a strong and diverse American scene for jazz. That's exactly what happened, but far beyond even my own expectations. We have seen the virtual elimination of the midrange gig in America. Right now you have fine arts and festival gigs that pay between $15,000-$45,000 and you have lots of gigs that pay between nothing and $1,000 but you have almost nothing in the $3,500- $10,000 range.
>
> When we were operating the Outward Visions Touring Program between 1978-1991, we were able to secure certain $5,000 to $7,500 gigs that we could hang an entire tour on. Using those as an anchor, we would work within various new markets with emerging presenters. We would give them better prices and help them develop a viable marketplace. We did that with the Art Ensemble of Chicago. When we sent them out for their very first US tour in 1978 they went out for 5 ½ weeks for a gross of $22,000. The following year we had them out for 4 weeks for around $40,000 and the following year we had them in 57 cities on two tours that came to around a $175,000 in touring. In many of these situations we were working with promoters whom we had charged $2,000 the first time, got $3,500 the second time, and $5,000 the third

time, $7,500 the fourth time, and everybody made money. We made money and they made money.

So we were developing this in a very intelligent manner and were successful in doing it until we got waylaid by Lincoln Center. Does it really help jazz to raise millions and millions of dollars from the charitable sector at the expense of grassroots organizations to build Jazz at Lincoln Center? It just doesn't make any sense. That's essentially what they've gone ahead and done.

Lincoln Center has spawned a bunch of other Lincoln Center-modeled entities all over the U.S. who have become monoliths — here, the University of Arizona; the NJPAC (New Jersey Performing Arts Center) in Newark; the San Francisco Jazz Festival in San Francisco and so forth — raising huge sums of money for themselves and they essentially wipe out the grassroots organizations. The fees they now pay are lower than the fees we were making 25 years ago when I used to work with Oliver Lake. I was sending Oliver out to the same facilities that are now offering him anywhere from 20 to 30 percent of what they were paying him then. That's what they're offering him now, and these are the organizations that have been getting all these millions of dollars of funding from Leila Wallace and Doris Duke.

They've essentially wiped out the grassroots organizations, and now they pay the grassroots fees except when they're hiring a Herbie Hancock or a Wynton Marsalis or somebody like that, and they're plopping down 25, 30, and 50 thousand dollars. With the exception of some big names like Marsalis, who gets heavy money to enhance their fundraising efforts in the foundation and private sectors, the fees they now pay are lower than the fees we were getting from the grassroots organizations 25 years ago!

Many highly respected artists were making *50% more money* in the same cities that are now part of the heavily funded networks put together by the Leila Wallace and Doris Duke Foundations, *before* any of that funding was put on the table. Well over $20 million has been laid out for these networks — virtually all of it going to presenting institutions in a *trickle-down* economy that never seems to reach most of the working musicians.

So they're cutting the amount of money that is going to the vital artist, to the local artist, to the touring artist not at the height of popularity, and in exchange for that they're basically putting all their money into these higher profile artists who then enable them to generate funding, sell advertising, attract sponsorships, solicit rich white folks, and so forth. A student workshop here, a free concert for a school there, and their "educational programs" satisfy the basically indifferent funders, without actually doing anything to advance or sustain the art form. And the Fine Arts/University circuit is no better.

Here in Tucson, the University of Arizona paid out well over $60,000 for three concerts with Branford Marsalis, Wynton Marsalis, and the Preservation Hall Jazz Band. Outside of those, you can't get a gig here for $1000. I met with the man who runs the program and pointed out the disparity, saying "No economy can thrive in a situation like that." He said, "I believe that a rising tide raises all boats." I said, "That's fine for those of you that have boats. But those of us who live on the shore are drowning in your rising tide." Essentially, this elitist mentality is being replicated all over the country. And that's what we're all facing right now, the virtual elimination of the mid-range gig in America.

The Jazz at Lincoln Center project, however, would argue that it is attempting to create fans of the future through the medium of education and concert tours. "By targeting students at every level of education, from kindergarten to graduate school, Jazz at Lincoln Center aims to make jazz music accessible to young audiences from all walks of life," its publicity brochure stated. "Educational programming currently includes: Jazz for Young People concerts, Jazz in the Schools tours, the *Essentially Ellington* High School Jazz Band and Festival, film programs, lectures, master classes, student and teacher workshops, residencies, open rehearsals and publications," resulting in Jazz at Lincoln Center reaching, "over 100,000 students, teachers and audience members annually." As saxophonist Ted Nash, a member of the Lincoln Center Orchestra, told *Downbeat* magazine, "It's a sort of mission thing. A lot of people are negative about that because they're not getting gigs and I can understand that. But what this band is doing is actually helping everyone, because we're creating an audience that's going to last for generations." However, audience building in this way, even if successful, was no help to jazz musicians in the here and now in need of more employment opportunities.

Gigs, places to play, a touring circuit, and adequate remuneration for musicians have become a serious issue for the survival of jazz in America. In 2002, the *Village Voice* pointed out how the jazz club circuit outside New York had shrunk drastically. "West of the Hudson things drop off pretty quickly," Tom Evered, general manager of Blue Note Records, was quoted as saying. "Where musicians used to make money touring and playing and using CDs as calling cards, that's disappearing."

Against a backdrop of declining audience numbers and venues, the NEA Jazz Masters on Tour was inaugurated in 2004, representing a fresh initiative to set up national jazz touring sponsored by the National Endowment for the Arts in partnership with the Doris Duke Charitable Foundation (which committed $480,000 over a three-year period to help fund the first phase of the scheme). "In a culture overwhelmed by innumerable forms of popular entertainment, we must not allow an art as important as jazz to become lost in the clutter," stated chairman of the NEA Dana Gioia. "Our new touring program will help bring the wealth of jazz talent and experience of our NEA Jazz Masters to audiences and students across the country." Among the celebrated artists who received NEA Jazz Master status were Ornette Coleman, Jim Hall, Abbey Lincoln, Nancy Wilson, Jimmy and Percy Heath, Dave Brubeck, and Chico Hamilton. But while hugely welcome, it did not affect the lives of the majority of working jazz musicians who needed work in the here and now and were forced to find it abroad.

The reason for this can be stated fairly simply: no public money had been invested in any sort of infrastructure for jazz that might provide national touring support, as happens in, for example, Europe or Australia. In the United States, the approach to the arts stems from the belief that the efficient conduct of society's affairs is best managed by business. Accordingly, during the Reagan–Bush years government eroded public funding of the arts through agencies like the NEA, instead favoring a "supply side" philosophy that argued artists should be able to advance their careers solely on their own resources, with no call on the public purse because, government alleged, a conservative public has little interest in endeavors that satisfy a "liberal" elite. As Dr. Lewis Porter wrote in *Jazz: A Century of Change*, "Government support for the arts, jazz included, has decreased, even while respect for jazz is on the rise."

As work opportunities for jazz musicians continued to diminish in the face of an increasingly competitive, corporate-driven entertainment industry, Jazz at Lincoln Center, along with similar institutions around the country that have sprung up in its wake, began to absorb a lion's share of charitable, private and corporate funding on offer. This has helped to contribute to the demise of the middle range gig; as the highly respected drummer and composer Bobby Previte has pointed out, there is no "jazz middle class" any more. Musicians have become more than ever reliant on teaching, either privately or in colleges and universities, and on the Japanese and European jazz circuits for work. As *Music & Media*, the music

trade magazine, headlined in 2003, "Jazz Players Head East for Eden –
Europe has replaced America as the Land of Opportunity for Jazz Music
and Jazz Musicians," while in contrast, a feature in *Village Voice* in 2002
had pointed out how the jazz club circuit outside New York had shrunk
drastically and a 2004 *Downbeat* editorial noted that, "Touring opportunities for instrumentalists are bleak." Against this backdrop, it begs the
question of whether the vast sums of money (in jazz terms) spent on Jazz
at Lincoln Center and similar institutions might have been better spent in
subsidizing a national jazz infrastructure with subsidized venues, tour support and assistance with recording projects, as happens in several European countries to better secure jazz as part of cultural life in the United
States. "If we take a look at jazz in the USA now, at the beginning of the
21st century, it exists only as a historical niche culture," says Steen Meier,
chairman of the Nordic Music Council and Copenhagen's JazzHouse,
"musicians can hardly make a living in a society which offers no subsidies
to this musical genre." Indeed, the Jazz Center of the Universe—as the
Lincoln Center program has been touted – may turn out to be instead a
black hole, sucking the life out of a beleaguered jazz economy.

4

DÉJÀ VU TIME ALL OVER AGAIN: JAZZ SINGERS AND NU-CROONERS

Are vocalists saving the jazz industry?

Jazz Times, **December 2003**

Just a year after her debut album *Come Away with Me* was released on the Blue Note label, the twenty-three-year-old singer-pianist Norah Jones won five awards at the 2003 Grammy ceremony. After Bonnie Raitt and Aretha Franklin presented her with the Record of the Year Award, she said, "I never thought that the music I made would become popular music, so this is amazing." By then her album had sold over 6 million copies and topped the album charts around the world. Jones's ascent to megastardom had been built on the most traditional of virtues: wistful melodies, understated playing, and engaging vocals. *Come Away with Me*, whose sales had rocketed to over 17 million worldwide by 2004, included originals that "sounded" as if they might be standards and the real thing by the likes of Hoagy Carmichael and Hank Williams delivered in the breathy style of a 1950's cabaret chanteuse. According to the album's producer Arif Mardin, the album marked a changing point in musical consumerism. "People were ready for heartfelt music," he told *The Observer*. "Norah is in the vanguard of another kind of pop music listeners have been yearning for. We're now in a period where listeners are looking for real artists."

Jones was Blue Note's response to the success of Diana Krall, who had been shrewdly marketed by Universal/Verve. After her first album, *Stepping Out*, for the Canadian label Justin Time in 1993, Krall was snapped up by Universal. Her major label debut followed in 1995 with *Only Trust Your Heart*, followed by *All for You* in 1996, dedicated to the music of the Nat King Cole Trio, a disc that stayed in *Billboard*'s jazz top ten for 70 weeks and won her a Grammy nomination. In 1997 came *Love Scenes*, which took two Grammy awards and a Grammy nomination. Encouraged by this success, Universal marketing became increasingly aggressive; in 1999, *When I Look in Your Eyes* went platinum, winning a Grammy for Best Jazz Vocal Performance. In 2001 Universal pulled out the marketing stops with *The Look of Love*; across London, for example, Diana Krall posters could be found in bus shelters and in the underground, and the album was advertised on U.K. television. The success of the album, over 2 million copies, made the record business sit up and take notice. It went three times platinum in Canada and gained platinum status in New Zealand, Poland, the United Kingdom, and Portugal, and gold album status in the United States, Australia, France, and Singapore.

"There is no doubt that there's copy-catting in the record business," observed Nathan Grave of Add Music and former head of jazz at Universal UK, referring to Blue Note's signing of Norah Jones. "Companies see something working and say 'Let's take this direction.' A turning point in the popularity of the 'jazzy' singers was the crossover success of Diana Krall. Usually no-one in the media particularly likes jazz. But she had media exposure, people read about her in the press, heard the album on the radio, saw it advertised on TV and bought into her style."

Krall's success was dwarfed by Norah Jones's enormous sales of *Come Away with Me*. It inspired a search for more young, "jazzy" singing talent by the major record labels and many independents. Among the post-Norah signings were Britain's Jamie Cullum (signed in 2003 for just under $2 million by Universal), Clare Teal (signed in 2004 by Sony in a deal reported to be larger than Cullum's), Gwyneth Herbert (signed in 2004 by Universal), and Katie Melua (signed in 2003 by Dramatico), and America's Lizz Wright (signed by Universal in 2003), Jane Monheit (signed in 2004 by Sony Classical), and popular Sinatra throwbacks such as Michael Bublé (signed in 2003 by Warner Bros), and Peter Cincotti (signed in 2002 by Concord, before moving to Universal in 2004). "It might have started off as something novel and new, the lounge scene, but all of sudden there were these really talented artists making some great records, artists audiences could go and see, and it kind of moved from there," says Adam Seiff, Sony's director of jazz for the United Kingdom and Europe. "Suddenly there's an audience who listens and appreciates these singers. What started off as a small area of the business is now the mainstream."

Unlike their counterparts in pop music, these young artists sang in a style that was popular decades before they were born, evoking jazz's relationship to time as nostalgia. To be nostalgic, the music these singers sang need not be "old," but it did have to have associations with the great singers of the American popular song and articulate those associations in the right way, gestures at past glories that were marketed as a promise of new ones to come. When Jamie Cullum's major label debut *Twentysomething* was released in the United Kingdom in 2003, it promptly went double platinum and shot to the top of the album charts behind Norah Jones and Katie Melua to give jazz albums the entire top three for the first time in forty-eight years of U.K. album chart history. The way public taste had shifted ingrained industry attitudes was remarkable, enabling the jazzy singers to notch up six-figure sales and cross over into the pop marketplace.

Their rise took the record business by surprise. A whole industry geared to the youth market, with their ear to the ground waiting for the next teenage rapper with an misogynist bent or a breaking indie rock band who had perfected the psychotic stare, were left scratching their collective heads at this clean-living bunch singing songs twice and three times as old as they were. Yet the major recording companies' sudden interest in capitalizing on the sales potential of jazzy singers was not simply an attempt to piggyback the success of Norah Jones and Diana Krall, but to appeal to an audience that was fast becoming the most important market left for popular music. But what had led to this and what did it mean for jazz?

The new millennium ushered in challenging times for the record business. According to figures from Nielsen SoundScan, 2001 saw a drop in sales of 2.8 percent, which was followed in 2002 with a decline of over 10 percent. "The ten top selling albums [in 2000] sold a combined 60.5 million units. In 2002 that number dove to 33.6 million," said *Billboard*. The music industry was in crisis, which, like all crises in the music industry, meant that nobody knew where the market was going or what its audiences wanted.

But this crisis was like no other. The global downturn of CD sales during the late 1990s and early millennium years was exacerbated by the threat posed to the music industry by file sharing on the web. Increasingly, music files were being freely swapped by enthusiastic listeners through computer programs like Napster (the leader through the mid-1990s when the music business successfully killed it), Kazaa, iMesh, Gorkster, and Morpheus. The industry bitterly complained this was causing them to lose sales as companies like EMI, BMG, and Universal spent millions battling what they called "Internet piracy." In September 2003, the Recording Industry Association of America (RIAA) took 261 defendants to court in an attempt to stamp out the practice of illegal file sharing on the net in a test case that seemed set to run for years. "We're doing it to get our message out," the RIAA chairman told *Newsweek*. The people they chose to sue were ordinary, working-class families; "I'm furious because I can't afford this," a mother of two told the magazine. Subsequently, the industry considered settlements, supposedly in the $3,000 to $5,000 range, from families who had been forced to scrape up the cash or risk financial ruin defending themselves in court with a possible liability in the millions. At the 2003 Midem music convention, Jay Berman, head of the International Federation of the Phonographic Industry, warned that 600,000 European jobs were at risk because of illegal downloading of music files. But even with high profile lawsuits, including an action instituted in the United Kingdom in 2004 against downloaders, many of today's young pop fans consider their favorite new release as something they can download from the Internet rather than an item that you might buy in a record shop.

The trend of declining CD sales was also exacerbated by the increased competition for media-entertainment dollars from DVDs, increasingly sophisticated cell phones, and the practice of "burning" CDR copies of new CD releases at minimum cost for friends and family. But perhaps the most important player in the youth market was the rise of video games among the eight to eighteen year olds. Playing games replaced listening to the transistor radio — or watching videos on MTV — for the latest pop hits. No longer did teenagers sit in their rooms wistfully listening to their favorite pop star as they had in the past, when, as Lawrence W. Levine pointed out in *Black Culture and Black Consciousness*: "Popular music constructed a universe in which adolescent innocence and naivete became a permanent state. Men and women (often referred to as boys and girls) dreamed pure dreams, hopefully waited for an ideal love to appear and built not castles but bungalows in the air."

Now adolescents were confronted with a wide range of choices to fill their leisure hours, choices that were collectively severely affecting CD sales. By 2004 pop artists could figure in the top ten in the United Kingdom with sales of less than 15,000. It was a new world for the music industry, a world where polyphonic ring tones had begun to outstrip sales of CD singles. When Universal released the Sugar Babes "Round Round" as a CD single in 2003, they also put out a ring tone of the song; the ring tone had the best sales. In 2004, with the sale of ring tones now exceeding CD singles, a Ringtone Top Twenty Chart was inaugurated by Mobile Entertainment Forum for the growing billion-dollar ring tone business. By 2005, the record industry was contemplating the total demise of the CD single, as consumers deserted record shops for their home PCs, where tracks could be downloaded legally from virtual record shops like iTunes at minimum cost. The popularity of downloading was further fueled by the introduction of the iPod, which could store thousands and thousands of album tracks in a small unit the size of the once ubiquitous Walkman. The music marketplace was undergoing a seismic shift, the long-term consequences of which were impossible to predict.

In the world of mass produced, glitzy pop music there were hard truths to be faced, including a perception that the industry had lost touch with its roots. In his history of the Warner Music Group, former Warner Bros. executive Stan Cornyn wrote, "What we had accomplished in '69 we had forgotten in '99. . . . When money changed from being a wondrous shower and became a ruler over all, everything suffered. Swarms of suits had, in the end, endorsed greed over boogie." Marketing decisions had replaced musical judgments and had diluted the product, as Andy Taylor, chief executive of the independent Sanctuary Music Group, told *The Guardian*: "The fall in CD sales is more due to a lack of decent music than piracy. People are not buying CDs because a lot of the new stuff is not very good."

As the major recording companies gazed at a huge hole in their balance sheets in 2002, they saw that, over the past decade, consumers aged forty-five and above had nearly doubled, to 23.7 percent. Buyers over thirty now made up 54.5 percent of the market as compared with 36.1 percent for those between fifteen and thirty, according to figures from the RIAA. The over-thirties age group were now the fastest growing segment of the music-buying public, and the major recording companies, after much procrastination, identified them as an audience that did not usually download or were not much engaged in video games and set out to woo them. "As the youth market hemorrhaged, recording companies were forced to realign their marketing plans," said Nathan Grave of Add Music, formerly Universal's head of jazz for the United Kingdom.

Equally importantly, the thirty- to sixty-year-old demographic has the highest net disposable income; the [London] *Sunday Times* reported that the over fifties held 80 percent of private wealth, estimated at $390 billion in the United Kingdom alone, and were not adverse to spending it. When they shopped for music, it was not unusual for them to purchase five or ten CDs at a time. It explains why, from around 2000, the singles and the album charts increasingly bore little relationship to one another; the singles chart became the province of teen hits, dance music, and the occasional novelty song while the album charts began to take on a distinctly more adult-orientated feel, with artists such as Norah Jones, Diana Krall, Michael Bublé, Peter Cincotti, and Jamie Cullum vying for position with albums by legacy artists (rock stars from the 1960s and 1970s), chill-out music, and compilation albums. For the first time since the pop explosion of the 1960s, people in their forties were buying more albums than teenagers, with the fifty somethings not far behind.

Targeting the thirty to sixty year olds represented a striking departure from the recording companies' once inviolate principle of going after the youth audience. In the past, older audiences had seldom been exploited by record companies because they were never really sure how to sell to the more independent-minded listeners with established musical tastes. But the feeling was that if you *could* appeal to them, you'd have a smash hit; in the 1980s Linda Ronstadt did just that with an album of standards arranged by Sinatra's long-time arranger Nelson Riddle and in the 1990s Natalie Cole swept the Grammys and dominated the charts with an overdubbed "duet" with her late father, Nat King Cole. Back then younger audiences, more prone to buying in packs, were easier to target, and, as long as that sector was buoyant, why waste time bothering with older audiences? But as the market demographics began to change, recording companies *had* to make a play for the thirty to sixty year olds. As David Foster, Michael Bublé's producer, told the *New York Daily News*, "This is the last vestige of the music buying public. If the [record companies] don't go after them, they'll have no business at all."

One response to targeting this prime demographic was the repackaging of rock stars from the 1960s and 1970s. For years these "legacy artists," as they were known, had been selling out live shows. In 2002, for example, Sir Paul McCartney dominated the list of top grossing tours with a record $126.2 million in ticket sales according to *Billboard*. In fact, fourteen of the top twenty-five grossing tours that year had been active in 1972, a list that included the Rolling Stones, Billy Joel, The Who, and Bruce Spring-steen. "You didn't see this 20 years ago, 55 year olds going to arenas," Dennis Arfa, president of Artists Group International, told *Billboard*. Clearly, the millions that flocked to see these artists at around $50 (or more) a concert ticket were in the market to buy their albums as well, and artists who hadn't been on the album charts for years, like McCartney, Elton John, and James Taylor, were now fighting for the top chart spots with performers young enough to be their grandchildren, courtesy of the older record-buying public.

Back catalog provided another avenue of plugging into the older demo-graphic. "In the late '90s, labels began to wake up and say, 'These artists still sell out arenas,'" Bruce Resnikoff, president of Universal Music Enterprises told the *Washington Post* in 2002. "They were once a market-ing afterthought. Then we all set up separate departments to sell back cat-alogue." Successes that year included sales of *Chicago's Greatest Hits*, which exceeded 400,000 units.

But it was the huge success of Norah Jones's *Come Away with Me* in 2002 to 2003, that concentrated record companies' minds in a way that only the sale of 17 million units worldwide can. Here was another route of tapping into the over thirties market. According to Jones's record label Blue Note, the buzz about her multiple Grammy-winning album started with consumers in their forties and fifties and took off from there. It was NPR, not MTV that introduced her to her audience. In their end-of-year survey for 2002, *Billboard* concluded, "This time last year, it was looking like a challenge to sell jazz records at all, whether contemporary or tradi-tional. That was before releases by Norah Jones, Diana Krall, Jane Mon-heit, Natalie Cole and Karrin Allyson exploded into the top 10 of the jazz charts, selling better than respectable numbers and infusing the jazz world with hope."

As the success of the nouveaux jazz singers began to take off, their potential was identified in the marketing plans of the then five major record corporations — Universal-Vivendi, EMI, Sony, Warner AOL, and BMG — as well as several independents. As the *Boston Globe* noted,

"Every jazz label is scouting and signing young, attractive talent." The Maxjazz label in St. Louis, an important player in the jazz independent market, even launched a specialist vocal imprint, the "Maxjazz Vocal Series." The jazzy vocal boom was — as Norah Jones told *Jazz Times* — "all about money." After Ron Goldstein was promoted to president and CEO of Verve in January 2003, singers became a significant presence on the label. "The emphasis has to be on things that can have some commercial success," he told *Jazz Times*. It was about creating a product that would sell to a specific audience demographic, an audience who helped Robbie Williams become $128 million richer through the success of his jazzy Frank Sinatra homage *Swing When You're Winning*, actually recorded in Sinatra's old stomping ground, Capitol Towers on the West Coast, and the millions who put singer Rod Stewart back on the map with *It Had to Be You . . . The Great American Songbook*, in other words, the audience beyond jazz. It was in this context Verve spent almost $2 million on signing singer Jamie Cullum in an attempt to plug directly into this older, crossover audience.

Far hipper than Robbie Williams's calculated, one-dimensional Sinatra "tribute," Cullum's youthful energy, optimism, and confidence had attracted star-in-the-making whispers following his 2002 debut album *Pointless Nostalgic* on the Candid label, a U.K. jazz indie. The album's title track, cowritten with his brother Ben, a session musician and early influence, was intended as a teenager's reflection on his nostalgia for an evaporating childhood and the beginning of a new life as much as it was questioning whether young artists performing the classic popular songbook was more about nostalgia than the music. Once the album was out, the step from playing the bar and jazz club circuit for union scale to Universal's seven figure deal took just over a year. "When we saw Jamie Cullum, we felt that there was no young, under 30 year old male jazz-related singer in the market that could crossover to adults and yet still appeal to a twenty-something audience," recalled Nathan Grave:

> Many gigs were attended and the courtship began. It was a long process of meetings with Candid records, the UK label that had signed Jamie first. Finally, on the eve of the final deal being agreed, over 12 Universal employees were invited to see our new addition to the label at a gig at the Pizza Express jazz club in London's Soho. To our horror, a veteran executive A&R director from Sony Music walked in. He didn't stay for the entire concert, but two days later we had notice that Sony had made a bid considerably higher than Universal's previous offers. This set the

boardroom agenda with the chairman, who asked "Is this kid really worth it?" I said, with my colleagues support, that we had something special here. The whole package was right: a musician and entertainer with good looks, humor, and youth on his side who could deliver a great song. He was a rare talent and a true find. We went about counteroffering and making it a last — take it or leave it. Alan Bates, owner of Candid, insisted Jamie was released in the US so we had the head of Verve Music Group — Ron Goldstein in New York — make a call to Candid assuring them a release for Jamie. It paid off and the deal was signed, much to my relief. Jamie was a key signing for Universal in the UK since the division of Universal Classics and Jazz had never spent so much on a deal.

On release in the fall of 2003, Cullum's much publicized debut on Universal, *Twentysomething*, took just five weeks to go platinum in the United Kingdom, going double platinum a few weeks later, enjoying crossover sales in the *youth* market after Universal cleverly promoted him in the teenage magazines. Consequently, Alexis Petridis in *The Guardian* noted that:

> Walking into a Jamie Cullum concert is a disconcerting experience. It is like being transported into a record company executive's fevered dream. The venue is packed, the audience incredibly diverse. There don't appear to be any Amish present, but every other section of society appears to be here: pensioners, teenyboppers and —this is where the dream gets really good — people laboring under the impression that a gig is something one must dress smartly for, like a fancy restaurant. This intimates they never normally go to gigs. Cullum has attained commercial nirvana, winning over those who usually ignore music.

Able to spin their web around both jazz and general audiences alike, the jazzy singers were often achieving sales and album chart positions higher than many established pop artists. Aware that their albums were now being bought by far more pop than jazz fans, the mainstream media resisted the industry trend to classify the nouveaux singers as "jazz." Thus: Cullum, who was featured on the cover of the U.K. magazine *Jazzwise* when *Twentysomething* was released in 2003; Diana Krall, who was cover feature on *Jazzwise* and *Jazz Times* with the release of *The Girl in the Other Room* in 2004; and Norah Jones, who was cover feature on *Downbeat* following her 2004 release *Feels Like Home* (which debuted at the No. 1 spot on *Billboard's* 200 chart and remained there for six weeks), were now being picked up in the *pop* columns of the broadsheets, tabloids, glossies, and lifestyle magazines. The nouveaux jazz singers had quietly become *über-pop* stars.

"Live, it's definitely a bit more rock 'n roll. It's about presenting the music in a different way without contradicting myself," said Jamie Cullum. "The general attitude is to make the show a bit more like the visceral shows I used to go to. To make it a bit more of a performance, more entertaining to the type of punter who doesn't know you have to clap solos." Peter Cincotti, on making his eponymous debut on Concord records in 2003 at the age of nineteen, became the youngest artist to play the Algonquin Oak Room in New York. He not only topped the jazz charts but, as *Jazz Times* observed, "appeared seemingly in every form of non-jazz media, from *Vanity Fair* to *Spider Man 2*." Perhaps the key in crossing over into nonjazz markets was that the jazz singers did not come with the stigma of manufactured pop attached to them, as Jason Koransky, editor of *Downbeat*, underscored: "It's easy to feel abandoned by the record industry at large today. It seems like everything is geared toward the teen audience, and there's been a backlash — and crooners are part of it."

Generally speaking, thirty-plus consumers were past the point of wanting to be moved or inspired by pop. The young nouveaux singers, purveyors of the intimate, confessional love song frequently addressed to the inamorato, often fulfilled the function of providing a background ambiance that could tastefully decorate a home for a dinner party or as an accompaniment to making love. Diana Krall's best-selling *The Look of Love*, for example, was an album that cleverly sustained an intimate mood by the choice of slow-medium tempos. Each tune picked up from where the previous one left off, avoiding the disjunctive effect a faster tempo might have. Together with a haunting use of strings arranged and conducted by Claus Ogerman and a series of carefully chosen love songs by the likes of Victor Young, Johnny Mercer, George Gershwin, Hoagy Carmichael, and Burt Bacharach, the album successfully fulfilled the function of "furniture music," Erik Satie's term for undemanding background music that filled social spaces. It was the perfect canvas on which a mature, over-thirty audience could hang their aesthetic aspirations, affluence, and metropolitan attitude. As Adrian Jackson, director of the Wangaratta Festival of Jazz in Australia pointed out, "The Diana Krall–Norah Jones phenomenon has whetted the audience's appetite for what I call 'jazzy' singers. If the music is easily digested and marketed well, the audience will go for it, and congratulate themselves for having the sophistication to enjoy 'jazz.'" In an increasingly affluent consumer society, people were becoming defined not so much by how much money they earned, but the lifestyle choices they made, and the jazz singers plugged into this. "Musical taste is intimately tied to personal identity," wrote popular culture commentator Simon Frith. "We express ourselves through our deployment of other people's music."

In many ways, the thirty-to sixty-year-old audience viewed jazz as a music that was cool and hip, a perception that had been helped by two discrete factors: (1) the way it had been projected in certain Hollywood movies and (2) the function it fulfilled in certain television advertisements. Hollywood, a major force in influencing social attitudes, style, and fashion, has long monitored the kind of audience demographic its films attract and what their expectations are. The vast corporate complexes like Time-Warner or Disney-ABC make use of subliminal advertising — generating revenue through the on-screen use of particular consumer goods from a brand of beer to a breakfast cereal — or linking profit-making formulaic genres to burger outlet giveaways, "news"-source PR, video, DVD sales, and games. From the 1990s Hollywood had begun discreetly "signifying" on jazz as sophisticated and chic, the ultimate urban attitude, in its "human interest" dramas aimed at the over thirties, which is to say non-blockbuster movies. In *The Talented Mr. Ripley*, the doomed hero, a closet jazz fan, rattles off a stunning jazz trumpet solo (played on the soundtrack by Britain's Guy Barker); suave loner-at-home Clint Eastwood relaxes to Miles Davis's trumpet in *In the Line of Fire*; the Sean Connery film *Finding Forester* makes extensive use of classic contemporary jazz recordings by the likes of Ornette Coleman and Miles Davis; a group of high school children are intellectually awakened to Miles Davis's music in *Pleasantville*; and in *Runaway Bride*, Julia Roberts gives Richard Gere an original vinyl copy of Miles Davis's *Kind of Blue* as a token of her undying love.

Equally, the portrayal of jazz as the hip music of choice for suave urban thirty somethings was exploited by advertising agencies as a means to plug into a specific demographic, the over–thirty-five-year-old consumers with high net disposable income. In 2003, for example, glossy lifestyle magazines featured Wynton Marsalis in an advertising campaign for Movado watches, and Diana Krall and Tony Bennett in similar campaigns for Rolex watches. Television advertisers, skilled communicators who appeal to our emotions and unconscious biases, are well aware that setting a text to music can improve recall of its message. Increasingly, jazz recordings have been used as a soundtrack for goods and services that "sold something extra": Billie Holiday's "God Bless the Child" was not used to sell an auto-mobile, it was a luxury German production car; Dinah Washington's "Mad About The Boy" did not advertise a brand of jeans, it was a designer brand of jeans, and Sarah Vaughan's "Make Yourself Comfortable" did not tempt you to buy ice cream, it was to indulge in an expensive brand of ice cream. One striking early success was the use of Nina Simone's "My Baby Just Cares for Me," used on the soundtrack of a perfume advertise-ment — not just any perfume but "Chanel No 5." Its remarkable success resulted in the successful rerelease of the record and something of a career renaissance for the singer in the later years of her life.

In the context of television advertising, where the perceptible, the imperceptible, and the symbolic are combined to create what is hoped will be a lasting impression on the potential purchaser, jazz was used in an exclusionary way. The people to whom the sales message was directed were the mature executive class who could afford the goods or services being promoted, and jazz, with its aura of chic sophistication, was intended to resonate with their tastes and aspirations. This subtle tuning of consumer taste, by both Hollywood and television advertising in position-ing jazz as a culturally situated lifestyle accessory, helped create an aware-ness among a specific demographic that jazz had a cachet that neither pop nor classical music had — highbrow appeal from a lowbrow art form.

A key tool employed by major recording companies to market the jazzy singers was TV talk shows, because they appealed to precisely the same demographic that bought their albums: the thirty to sixty year olds, an age group more likely to be in on a Saturday night watching television than out at a rave. Rod Stewart, for example, pointed the way by promoting *It Had to Be You . . . The Great American Songbook*, an album of standards by the likes of Gershwin and other classic composers of the American popu-lar song, on the chat shows and morning television slots such as the Char-lie Rose Show and Connie Chung's show; Larry King was particularly good to Stewart because he appeared on his show twice. In the United Kingdom, the popular television Saturday night talk show *Parkinson*, with a reach of 6.5 million and hosted by a genial sixty-something Yorkshire-man Michael Parkinson, played a key role in determining the careers of musicians who got to play a couple of tunes between the banter. Two jazzy singers who appeared as virtual unknowns during his 2003 series, Michael Bublé and Jamie Cullum, quickly found themselves moving up the Top Twenty album chart and generating the kind of six-figure sales that few pop debutantes achieve without a campaign of massive hit singles preparing the way.

Where general entertainment talk shows had once been viewed by the record companies as largely irrelevant to the business of persuading fans to purchase their products, they were now queuing up to get exposure for their artists. In the case of daytime TV, it was quickly discovered the cleanly defined images of the nouveux jazz singers were attractive to a large potential market of housewives. Adam Hollywood, director of marketing for Michael Bublé's label, WEA, told *The Guardian* that record companies were now taking note of the rise of what he dubbed "the young housewife" audience: "For years this was a disenfranchised audience, one that was never marketed to before," he said. "Daytime TV is very powerful . . . shows are aimed at women at home with disposable income, and they are full of record advertising. Plus there's supermarkets: five years ago, they weren't really in the game, but now as you're getting your weekly shop, you can get a bit of Bublé in your basket."

These new marketing strategies employed by the majors for the nouveaux singers was, as Nathan Grave points out, key to their success:

> I think the public bought into the new jazzy singers because they were presented in a new way — not at all in the "old school" jazz way.
>
> They were promoted as fresh and new by younger people deeply involved in the marketing process. Not that past experience isn't valued, but marketing in jazz departments had not evolved very much over the years. Pushing artists through the "jazz only" press and media had become self limiting exercise. Selling records in volume means exposure in the mainstream media. That means finding acts that can appeal to a wider demographic than the "jazz only" audience, even if that means "jazz related" artists who can open up the new audience for the more core instrumental acts to follow, like Acid Jazz did for me in the 1980s.

These various marketing strategies employed by the majors — whether in the United States, Australia, Japan, or Europe — quickly proved successful and assumed priority status for all the major recording companies. As Adam Hollywood said, "It's probably easier to market this kind of artist than it is an alternative rock band now."

Some jazz musicians positioned their music to take account of the jazzy singer's popularity, a strategic response by recording companies to preserve instrumental jazz's relationship with the record-buying public. Saxophonist David Sanchez, recorded a moody album of ballads accompanied by strings as did pianist Eliane Elias, who went a step further by taking a leaf out of Diana Krall's book by providing her own vocals on 2004's *Dreamer*. Others included an airplay friendly track with a guest vocalist, such as Dianne Reeves on Wynton Marsalis's *Magic Hour*; Tony Bennett and Shirley Horn on Bill Charlap's *Stardust*; James Taylor on Michael Brecker's *Nearness of You: The Ballad Book*; Joni Mitchell on Brian Blade's *Perceptual*; and a whole host of vocalists including Diana Krall, Jane Monheit, Dianne Reeves, and Cassandra Wilson on Terence Blanchard's *Let's Get Lost*.

As the market for the jazzy singers broadened, so did their repertoire and notion of what constituted a "jazz singer," a concept that was becoming more and more fluid as recording companies seized on a *simpatico* media ear and a well-defined marketing strategy to reach their target audiences. "Ella and Carmen as well as June Christy and Anita O'Day had to be able to step into a composer's world and have the music arranged around their singing," singer Rebecca Martin told *Downbeat*, "That was the tradition and it was a luxury situation. Today, for singers to get work they have to lead. And they also want to write." Diana Krall, who for seven albums remained true to the American popular song (other than a Joni Mitchell song on *Live in Paris*), broadened her palette on 2004's *The Girl in the Other Room* to include six original collaborations with her husband, rock and roll singer Elvis Costello, and numbers by the likes of Mose Allison, Tom Waits, Bonnie Raitt, and Costello himself. "It was good for Diana Krall to write all those songs on her new album," singer Anne Hampton Callaway told *Downbeat* in 2004. "And Norah Jones? She gave us all permission to be intimate."

New young signings were now less influenced by an Ella Fitzgerald, a Billie Holiday, or a Sarah Vaughan, and more influenced by singer-songwriters like a Nina Simone, a Carole King, a Joni Mitchell, or a Laura Nyro. As the jazzy singers increased their appeal to the collective consciousness of an audience beyond jazz, Ann Hampton Callaway observed that people seemed drawn to singers who told stories and had a point of view: "People are lonely. We have so many more means of communication like e-mail and cell phones. And couples are dating on the Internet without having met. We're hungering for personality."

It had taken since the 1960s and the rise of the singer-songwriters in pop, who almost overnight brought about the demise of Tin Pan Alley, for jazz singers to realize that to release themselves from eternal competition with the great interpreters of the American popular songbook such as

Ella Fitzgerald, Billie Holiday, Frank Sinatra, Peggy Lee, Nat King Cole, et al., they needed to either write their own original material or seek out songs not normally associated with jazz and personalize them in a unique way. A good illustration of this was when Blue Note signed singer Patricia Barber. An original song stylist whose own material was often more interesting than the quirky slant she could lend to the American popular songbook, she debuted on the label with *Nightclub*, an album of tried and tested standards. The album was something of a disappointment, however, because her idiosyncratic style was somewhat miscast searching for new meanings among standards whose old meanings had been almost exhausted, standards such as "Autumn Leaves," "Yesterdays," and "Bye Bye Blackbird." Her next album *Verse* (2001), composed entirely of her own material, was far more successful. With longtime accompanist Michael Arnpool on bass, Neil Alger guitar, and Joey Baron on drums plus guest Dave Douglas on trumpet (who first appeared with Barber on her album *Modern Cool*), the singer was far more sharply defined, delivering her lyrics, if not dispassionately, then on a take-it-or-leave-it basis. This hard-to-get ploy worked; far too many young jazzy singers threw themselves at their audiences with a cheerleader's zeal. In contrast, Barber is unsettling yet hypnotic — you could return to tracks like "If I Were Blue" (a new standard in the making?) or the seductive "I Could Eat Your Words" time and again and discover a new nuance or crafty innuendo with each listening.

Barber made her recording debut in 1989 with *Split* on the poorly distributed Floyd Records, although it was her next album, *A Distortion of Love* for the Antilles label in 1992, that brought her to the attention of the public. After three albums for the Premonition label, she was signed by the Blue Note label in 2000. A classically trained pianist, a fan of Morphine, The Cranberries, and R.E.M., a whole lot else has gone into the mix to produce an individual, edgy, yet class operator in a very crowded field. Gradually expanding her little niche in jazz from her hometown of Chicago, where she regularly played the Green Mill, *Live* (2004) was her eighth album, a mixture of five smart yet intense originals that seemed to totter on the brink of neurosis and five sophisticated popular songs. Neurosis? In her lyrics for "Gotcha," she sings about of thinking about a piano falling on people's heads and the wisdom of looking over your shoulder. Barber was far removed from the easily assimilated jazz singers that were coming into vogue, since most of her albums have depth and meaning that do not reveal themselves in one sitting. She has a knack of writing love songs that make being loved by Patricia Barber seem only marginally more enticing than a barium enema, yet there was a sophisticated wit at work as well, whether it revealed itself in cautiously adventurous instrumental "Crash," or in the dark art of sexy, midnight moods on "Dansons La Gigue!"

In many ways it had been Cassandra Wilson who was ahead of her time in forcing audiences to reconsider the role of the vocalist in contemporary jazz in terms of both musical context and repertoire. When she signed with Blue Note in 1993 her artistic vision came into sharp focus under the direction of producer Craig Street. Two albums, *Blue Light 'Til Dawn* (1993) and *New Moon Daughter* (1995) with minimalistic backings followed under his stewardship, exploring the expressive and emotional force of her voice that delivered on the enormous promise she had revealed since making her New York debut in 1982. Never one to make it easy for her audiences, either singing from within the prickly thickets of her own originals or through a thoughtful choice of blues from Robert Johnson or Son House through to songs by Hank Williams, U2, Joni Mitchell, Sting, Patsy Cline, or the Monkees, she succeeded in making the material a personal expression of self, claiming it as her own, the ultimate goal of any jazz singer.

Wilson's highly personal choice of repertoire underlines the fact that back in the 1980s, she could have had the jazz world at her feet singing the well known Broadway standards that Ella Fitzgerald and Sarah Vaughan used to inhabit, as she did on *Blue Skies* (1988). But she never showed any interest in taking this obvious route to success, saying, "We have to take what we can and learn from the masters, but by repeating what they do, we're not really doing justice to the tradition. I think the whole point in jazz is to establish some kind of identity and help propel the music forward, make it speak of our needs today."

Her Miles Davis tribute *Travelling Miles* (1999) drew together several compositions with a Davis connection and her own originals that matched the mood of the album. Stripping songs down to bare skeletons, the dark timbre of her voice vibrated personal meaning through the lyrics, a gift that could be scary, as Billie Holiday once showed. *Belly of the Sun* (2002) and *Glamoured* (2003) followed, which saw Wilson working with a basic configuration of two guitars, bass, drums, and a percussionist (a grouping that could be augmented or pared down depending on the material to hand). This musical context was intended to distance herself from Holiday, Fitzgerald, and Carter from whom she is descended musically (traces of the former and latter swim through her style), and whose memory she wants to move beyond. In so doing she seemed to move closer to the singer she always wanted to be, a singer of the past, the present, and the future.

But while Wilson succeeded in creating her own space in jazz, elsewhere jazz singing was becoming a very crowded field as albums by the likes of Erin Bode, Jillian Lebeck, Madeleine Peyroux, Renee Olstead, Claudia Villela, Judy Niemack, Claudia Acuna, Carla Cook, René Marie, Christine Hitt, Mary Stallings, and Laverne Butler vied for sales against the more established names and reissues of classic albums by Ella, Billie, Sarah, et al., in the music marketplace. But even before Norah Jones broke, the Norwegian jazz singer Silje Nergaard had seen her album *Port of Call* go to the top of the pop album chart in Norway above the likes of Madonna, Britney Spears, and Radiohead in 2001 — an unprecedented event for a jazz album not just in Norway but anywhere before the upturn of interest in the jazzy singers. She followed it with *At First Light* (2001), which went to the top of the Norwegian pop chart on release, the first ever jazz album to achieve this feat, and became Norway's best-selling jazz album of all time. It was followed by *Nightwatch* in 2003, a series of reflections on a world watched over by the moon. On these albums the majority of the material was written by Nergaard with lyrics by Mike McGurk that neatly avoided the jazz singer's stock-in-trade, the American popular song, so allowing her to define her own musical personality with, as she pointed out, "The kind of musical stories that mean something to me. I guess it is the Scandinavian way not to look to America and try and copy that way of doing jazz. Maybe we're influenced by mountains or long winters."

Nergaard's accompanists were Tord Gustavsen on piano, Harald Johnsen on bass, and Jarle Vespestad on drums, who, as the Tord Gustavsen Trio, made their best-selling debut on the ECM label in 2003 with *Changing Places*, which by 2004 had sold in excess of 60,000 copies. But despite the international success of the album, both singer and trio kept their diaries in synch, and continued to tour together extensively, appearing at Jazz at Lincoln Center in 2004, preserving the unique empathy that evolved between singer and accompanists.

Nergaard comes from Tromsø in the windy north of Norway where, she says, "You have to shout to be heard." Born to two teachers who also happened to be jazz fans, she was brought up on a healthy diet of Ella Fitzgerald, Stan Getz, and Oscar Peterson, and learned the lyrics to many American popular songs. She also learned piano from a young age and was soon playing and singing along with the records and trying her hand at songwriting. As a sixteen year old she hitchhiked to the Molde Jazz Festival and was encouraged to sit in with a band of visiting Americans at an after hours jam session where she scored a huge hit. "One night Jaco Pastorious played and after the concert there was a jam session but somehow I talked myself into it. I ran up there and Delmar Brown, the piano player with Jaco Pastorius, was playing and singing and I started to improvise something with him."

The following day the Norwegian press was full of news of a new jazz sensation. Yet instead of pursuing a career in jazz, she turned to pop music, convinced she did not yet have the experience and depth necessary to become a jazz singer. She moved to London, and her first album got onto the playlist on BBC Radio. Seemingly poised for success, she promptly took a four-year break from music and returned to Norway, convinced pop music was not for her. "I had a kind of war going on in my head saying, 'Who are you?' 'What is this?' 'Why do you actually want to sing jazz songs?' I realized I was much more playful and spontaneous as a person and also as a performer and I couldn't stay within these walls of pop music, they were too strict, the rules were too strict, so what happened was during those four years I made a decision to go back to my real background which was jazz."

The album *Port of Call* marked her return to jazz, entering the Norwegian album charts at seven, it remained in the top twenty for twelve weeks. Her decision not to rush into jazz singing but find her own voice in a competitive field was vindicated. "It was very surprising," she reflects. "I hoped for success, but it was still a jazz album, so it proved people are open to hearing melodies and something that is more meaningful than pop music or rhythm and dance." The album opened doors for her across Europe at jazz festivals and clubs, including an appearance with the sixty-piece NRK Radio Orchestra for a televised live concert.

Nergaard had no formal jazz education, but her experience in both jazz and various styles of pop music meant she approached jazz singing from a fresh direction. In particular, her decision not to embark upon jazz singing too early seems a wise one; so many songs in American popular songbook tradition deal with broken or unrequited love, and because many singers are simply too young to have had the kind of experiences about which they are singing, they appear inauthentic. Instead, Nergaard was able to be herself. "Maybe these young singers today learn too many rules," she says. "I wish sometimes I went to jazz college and learned a lot about theory, but the good thing about not learning all those rules is that I can make my own rules. I have no rules, it makes me more creative because the walls are torn down I am free to wander where I like!" The best known of a new breed of young Scandinavian jazz singers, she followed in the tradition of highly acclaimed Nordic jazz vocalists such as Alice Babs, who famously sang with Duke Ellington, Karin Krog, Ratka Tonef, and Sidsel Endressen, who began singing with the Jon Eberson Group in 1981. Endressen evolved a wholly personal approach to singing that developed on the Munich-based ECM label and the Jazzland record label that has grown into a "language" of nonvocalized sounds mixed with her own haunting lyrics and evocative poetry.

Endressen also teaches jazz singing at the Oslo Music Conservatory, where one of her pupils was Solvieg Slettahjell, who went on to earn her Masters in 2000. Slettahjell's style is both distinct and very personal. On her debut album *Solvieg Slettahjell* (2001) with her Slow Motion Orchestra (trumpet, piano, bass, and drums), she gave several pointers to how her style would subsequently evolve: a preference for slow tempos, total lack of vibrato, a love of long notes held agonizingly long to explore their timbral density and an understated expressivity that somehow went to the very kernel of a song's meaning in the way a thin stiletto can be more devastating than a meat cleaver. Slettahjell was less interested in original material, but sought out tunes on which she could impose her powerful musical personality and so claim ownership of them with her own distinctive interpretations. Her approach was both original and compelling; her accompanists seemed to inhabit a parallel musical universe, deconstructing a song and reassembling it in a completely unexpected form, yet their efforts somehow coalesced with the singer with great symmetry and musical logic. It had the effect of totally recasting songs in a new light, forcing listeners to reconsider the material afresh from a completely different perspective. With *Silver* (2004), all the aspects of her style were now in place; even familiar tunes such as "Second Time Around" or "You Won't Forget Me" were sung at the slowest tempos, making short notes long notes, and long notes even longer, which automatically revealed hitherto unimagined nuance, the melody somehow hanging in the air supported by her remarkable vocal technique. Her voice, pure, haunting, and with inch perfect intonation unwound with perfect control, created an approach and mood quite unique in jazz. "It's not about me," she asserted. "It's about the music, we all have our roles within the band to try and create something special."

Another product of the fast developing Nordic scene was the Danish singer Cecilie Nordby, wife of bassist Lars Danielsson and signed by the Blue Note label. Equally, the jazz scene in Sweden has had no shortage of gifted jazz singers. Monica Zetterlund was one of the first Scandinavian singers to hint at a "Nordic tone" by suggesting Swedish folklore elements in her music. In 1997 she celebrated forty years as a jazz artist with an extensive tour. In a career that included many highlights, including working and recording with the Arne Domnerus orchestra and Americans such as Zoot Sims, Thad Jones, and Jimmy Jones, she recorded the album *Waltz for Debby* (1964) with the Bill Evans Trio, which is now regarded as a classic. Her 1997 album *Det Finns Dagar* revealed her art had only grown deeper with the passing years.

Of the younger artists, Jeanette Lindstrom has excited praise from the former jazz musician and arranger and now record producer Quincy Jones. Her debut album *Another Country* included just one American standard; the rest were her own compositions, which she describes as, "Air and light with a bit of earth mixed in." Subsequently, *I Saw You* succeeded in focusing on the meaning of the lyrics while balancing her soft yet deft musicality. Lina Nyberg, who moved from lyrical moods to raw blues, worked with some of the best known young musicians in Sweden, including Esbjorn Svenssön (on the album *Close*) and Per "Texas" Johansson. Singing only songs with lyrics that had a personal meaning to her, albums such as *When a Smile Shines Through* and *So Many Stars* revealed a singer of great promise. Victoria Tolstoy (a descendent of the great Russian author), who has also worked with Esbjorn Svenssön followed a similar pattern. Her album *Russian White* saw her becoming the first Swedish artist to record with the Scandinavian Blue Note label imprint, which was followed up with *Blame It on My Youth*, which explored American standards.

In the United Kingdom, Clare Teal, after a decade of honing and refining her talent on the U.K. jazz circuits, was signed by Sony; *Don't Talk* (2004) revealed her ability to swing as few of her young competitors on either side of the Atlantic could. Entering the U.K. album chart in the first week of release with sales of 13,500, it was the first jazz album to make the top twenty since Jamie Cullum's *Twentysomething*. At the same time, Gwyneth Herbert made her debut for Universal with *Bittersweet and Blue*. Herbert's voice was like that of a mature, 1940's nightclub chanteuse transplanted into the body of the high school netball captain. Even so, she seemed like a star in the making. Clearly the jazzy singers' vogue was revealing some very talented singers, and by 2004 there seemed no shortage of great talent in the wings, such as the U.K.'s Jaqui Dankworth or Norway's Rebekka Bakken (resident in Austria).

The mood created by the success of Norah Jones and her contemporaries escapes easy definition, but the Norah effect was one of melting barriers between generations and genres, of pop, easy listening, and jazz conflating at their respective margins. Having taken the concept of the "jazzy" singers from the margins to the mainstream, the record business was setting itself up to squeeze as much nectar out of the trend it could. Alongside the out-and-out jazz singers, there were singers who affected the whimsy of a Norah Jones, there were soul singers singing jazz material, there were pop singers singing jazzy sounding material, and there were young singers who record companies thought were worth taking a chance on, with the hope of appealing to playlist compilers. Best-selling artists such as Katie Melua and Amy Winehouse, usually bracketed with the jazzy singers, were really jazz-inspired pop acts. Winehouse's Sinatra-inspired *Frank*, a boldly written collection of thirteen spiky songs, including "Fuck Me Pumps," a caustic commentary on the shallow celebrity culture, saw her dissect love in her "four bottles of red wine, thirty Gitanes" voice, despite the fact she was just nineteen when she recorded it. "Call it almost jazz, easy listening or just plain pop (and if [Norah Jones's] 17 million sales aren't pop, what is?)," said *The Observer*. "Part of the Norah effect has been to move the parameters of 'jazz' beyond the reach of its self-appointed guardians."

Blue Note records (whose proud boast is "The Best in Jazz Since 1939") signed Van Morrison and Al Green, and included Country and Western singer Dolly Parton as a guest artist on Norah Jones's 2004 follow-up album *Feels Like Home*. As label boss Bruce Lundvall explained to *Downbeat*: "Norah has changed our direction to a degree. Our story now is that we've dropped the boundaries and opened the borders." Blue Note was not alone; Verve signed Linda Ronstadt, Aaron Neville, Me'shell Ndegeocello, and Jonatha Brooke, while Concord Jazz signed Barry Manilow and issued Ray Charles's posthumous album *Genius Loves Company*, on which he duets with a range of pop and country singers. In 2004 Rebecca Martin was signed by the independent label Maxjazz for their Vocal Series imprint and debuted on the label with *People Behave Like Ballads*. "Without a doubt Norah's success made someone like [Maxjazz president] Richard McDonnell more open to what I was doing," she told *Downbeat*. "Categories are far less important because in this day and age things are changing and evolving so fast . . . I used to say no [I wasn't a jazz singer], but I was thinking in the traditional sense. But today I say absolutely, in the modern sense. At its simplest, jazz has swing and improvisation. That's there in my music, but not in the way we're accustomed to."

As the jazzy singers blossomed into a key area of record company activity, Glen Barros, president of Concord records told *Jazz Times* that, "Naturally the industry is going to devote more resources to that which is working." Ultimately, there is always going to be an audience for good songs sung well. Some songs, including those from the twentieth-century American songbook, are as much the property of popular culture as jazz. They are a marriage of words and music that the best singers could charge in a way that communicated with an audience in a way that an instrumental solo did not. This carries with it the implication that the vocal dispenses something of the common touch, which is probably quite true. Jazz vocalists have always been more likely to be understood by a broader audience than their instrumental counterparts because of their story-telling privilege. The success of the jazzy singers traded off this ability to cross over into other, nonjazz, markets, and as long as they did so, the trend seemed set to continue. "Meanwhile, some of the more adventurous jazz singers . . . continued to get results associated with music towards the 'adventurous' end of the spectrum: glowing reviews, the respect of their peers and modest sales," said Adrian Jackson. The success of the jazzy singers, it seemed, may have been good for the music industry, good for those jazz singers who were able to benefit from it, but sadly was doing instrumental jazz no favors, as an end of year survey in 2002 for *Billboard* noted, "It prompted many to ponder the fate of the unsung heroes behind the vocalists, namely the instrumentalists. Even as jazz vocalists were brought to the forefront of the public's consciousness, it seemed that instrumentalists were losing ground." They were indeed, and by 2004, Jason Koransky would point out in a *Downbeat* editorial that, "The major jazz record labels (what's left of them) aren't signing instrumentalists," forcing artists to examine new channels of sales and distribution for their product on the Internet, such as Artistshare. The business of recording instrumental jazz was entering a new and uncertain future.

5
TEACHERS TEACHING TEACHERS:JAZZ EDUCATION

There are a lot of Conservatoires that teach jazz — the techniques of jazz — but not the spirit and the spirit, you have to look for it. The point about jazz is not to imitate or play the techniques, but to try to understand the spirit. This is the hardest thing.

Julien Lorau, saxophonist

Today, practically all contemporary jazz musicians under the age of thirty-five are likely to have been exposed to some form of jazz education, the majority at college or university level. The institutionalization of jazz education in the final decades of the twentieth century has meant it is now playing an increasingly important role in helping shape jazz in a way it did not in the past. "Jazz education has taken the place of the jazz-apprenticeship system that has largely disappeared because of economics, changing times, and the deaths of the Miles Davises, Woody Hermans, and Art Blakeys of the jazz world who, with many others, gave valuable professional experience and seasoning to countless young musicians," points out saxophonist, educator, and jazz historian Bill Kirchner. "Given the current scarcity of working jazz groups, jazz education — with all its imperfections

99

and limitations — is the best way we now have of sustaining the mentoring process and enabling students to interact with their peers."

As more and more of jazz's great master musicians — often autodidacts — departed the scene, the last traces of a true oral tradition disappear with them, and in its place the age of the college-educated jazz musician has become a reality. Yet despite the crucial role jazz education now plays in the music, very little, if anything, has been written about it from outside "the academy." This seems odd, particularly as the great paradox of jazz education is that the goals of the academy do not always coincide with the expectations of the jazz consumer.

To put this in its most simplistic terms, universities and colleges are judged on the number and quality of degrees each academic year produces. Yet consumers do not judge jazz performers by their academic qualifications. In fact, for them it matters little that a performer might possess a B.A., an M.A., a Ph.D., or have no academic qualification at all. Audiences are more concerned with whether the music engages them, whether it moves them, or arouses their emotions and interest in some way. There are two different value systems in play here; they are not mutually exclusive, but there is, inevitably, a tension between them. As Simon Purcell, professor of Jazz Improvisation and Piano at the Guildhall School of Music and Drama in London, has written, "Conservatoire teachers now find themselves torn between the cultivation of high artistic ideals and the maintenance of a tradition, while preparing students for a rapidly changing range of professional practices. A utilitarian training for professional competence alongside a response to market values could never be at such odds with the authentic vision of artists and musicians."

The style of jazz taught in high schools, colleges, and universities is derived from the conventions of the bebop–hard bop style of the 1950s and 1960s. "In America there is certainly a common practice and assumed language for jazz," observes Paul Rinzler, director of Jazz Studies at Cal Poly State University. "This would be apparent at a jam session at which fundamentals are expected to be assumed so the jam session could function. That language is the core of the American jazz pedagogy. The argument for a narrow jazz pedagogy is that one should be able to speak this common language before moving on to variations of it and the wider aspects of jazz."

This common language, its foundations based on the conventions of the bebop style, is, as Mark Levine has pointed out in his excellent *Jazz Theory Book*, "explainable, analyzable, categorizable and do-able." The problem was that by the end of the 1990s, rather a lot of jazz on CD and at clubs and festivals played by many younger musicians was *sounding* as if it was "explainable, analyzable, categorizable and do-able." Many critics ascribe this to the homogenization effect of jazz education, because most students follow broadly similar pedagogic routes to graduation while at the same time following broadly similar sources of stylistic inspiration. "The lowest common denominator is what academicization is about," observes Dave Liebman, one of the great saxophonists of the post-Coltrane era and an internationally respected jazz educator in his own right. "With the proliferation of jazz education at all levels and people like myself explaining the nitty gritty, the obvious byproduct of streamlining is conformity."

Lack of individuality, or originality, in jazz is, of course, a very subjective issue. Every era of the music's development has had its share of players who have attracted this kind of criticism, but because all historical study involves making a selection and history is usually constructed around great men, the contribution of jazz's foot soldiers has been largely ignored at the expense of its high-flying generals. But in contemporary times, there appears to be rather more players lacking individuality than in the past, a belief that has grown rather than receded in recent years. "Everybody's bitching these days about how the new students and young players all sound the same," says pianist and educator Hal Galper, a former sideman with the likes of Cannonball Adderley, Stan Getz, Phil Woods, and Chet Baker. "What else can be expected of a jazz education system that is becoming increasingly codified and standardized? This tendency to over-organize jazz pedagogy has not been in the best interests of those who strive to develop their own voice. When you have a large classroom of students being told 'you play this scale over that chord,' they're all going to play that chord that way."

Critics point to the increasing numbers of young players coming off what they call a jazz-education production line every year, all of them sharing a broadly similar stylistic approach to jazz. "The standard of playing among so many young musicians today is remarkably high," acknowledges drummer and educator John Marshall, a veteran of Soft Machine and Ian Carr's Nucleus in the 1970s. "You raise the bar — the standard technical ability of everybody — through teaching bebop and big band, which are the easiest to teach in the sense there are rules — you teach them the rules and they negotiate the obstacle course, as it were — but the results, to me, seem a little bit passionless. What happens is idiosyncrasies get ironed out, or not valued, or get lost in a mish-mash of bland, but well played, stuff."

The debate about lack of originality among young musicians today warrants exploration and discussion because it is an issue increasingly laid at jazz education's door; but is jazz education to blame? "Surely jazz educators would have the greatest tendency to encourage individuality compared to other educators, given the natural affinity in jazz for individuality," argues Paul Rinzler. "However, there is a balance between learning the basics of the style and individuality. It would be just as wrong to not encourage individuality in jazz as it would be to not require students to grasp the basics of the style. Whether the opportunity to encourage individuality is grasped or not is an empirical question that hasn't been explored to my knowledge (one would have to define individuality)."

The challenge facing jazz education in the new millennium, it seemed, was the eternal dichotomy of skills building versus creativity. Today, these programs are capable of producing young players whose technical ability might have stunned the jazz world fifty years ago. However, the real challenge for musicians is the same as it has always been: developing a musical vision, a defining voice, and the imagination to create an original context in which to function as a jazz musician. As guitarist Pat Metheny emphasized in his keynote address to the International Association of Jazz Educators Convention in 2001, "It's simply not gonna cut it to just keep looking back, emulating what has already been done with just a slightly different spin on it. . . . We have to get our collective imagination working hard on a vision that is more concerned with what the music can *become* than what is has already *been*." But was American jazz education addressing this? Could it learn from other models?

By the end of the 1990s, jazz education in America had become big business in a way impossible to imagine a decade or two earlier. For example, the 31st Annual Conference of the International Association of Jazz Educators held in New York in 2004 attracted almost 8,000 educators, musicians, and music-industry types, who turned up for what was billed by the organizers as "The world's largest jazz gathering." Over a four-day period these delegates, all involved in some way with jazz education, attended seminars, conferences, master classes, workshops, concerts and events devoted to the educational process of teaching jazz. When they weren't attending workshops, they were milling around a record number

of trade stands displaying all kinds of musical instruments, music para-
phernalia, and, of course, a huge library of literature dedicated to jazz education: solo transcriptions, patterns for improvisation, "teach yourself"
books, theory books, instrumental "method" books by jazz stars, play-
along albums, "real" books of standards, and artist-by-artist compilations
of original jazz compositions.

Since the 1970s, the business of jazz education has flourished in
America in a way that the business of jazz has not. "Vested interests in
jazz academia are making a lot of money," Hal Galper points out:

> There are thousands of music departments in the U.S., and a lot of peo-
> ple are making their living from teaching the notes and theories behind
> the music. Most jazz education today is being destroyed by the profit
> motive and an overloaded curriculum and acceptance of music students
> that are loading down faculties. Just look at the figures! Berklee College
> of Music gets 30,000 applications a year, of which they accept only
> 3,000. Those turned away go to other schools with an average annual
> tuition of $10,000 per student as the jazz education industry grosses an
> estimated $300 million per year.

The commercial environment in which jazz education operates brings
with it issues that Dr. Elizabeth Peterson, a former linguistics lecturer at
Indiana University and sociolinguist at The center for Applied Linguistics
in Washington D.C., believes should be viewed in the broader context of
higher education as a whole in the United States. "It comes as no surprise
to me that jazz education, like all things American, has become big business," she says:

> Inevitably, the ability to pay becomes separated from academic ability
> and is a complaint that runs throughout higher education in the U.S.
> More and more, as fees skyrocket, higher education becomes less the
> province of the smart and talented and more the province of the wealthy,
> who in many cases take a lot for granted. In my experience — and I
> know this view is shared by many colleagues — students who have had
> everything in life handed to them on a plate in childhood believe this
> continues into academic life. Consequently many don't want to work for
> grades, they expect to be given them. The universities tend to respond
> by rewarding these expectations — the bottom line is that universities
> need the dollars, so they want to make the students and the student's
> families happy. This has led to gross grade inflation during the past cou-
> ple of decades and with it a general lowering of academic expectations

and a good-bye to the ideals that academia can offer — hallowed halls full of studious pupils with hushed respect for learning and intellectual pursuits. Professors complain nonstop about being torn between really wanting to teach good content and run a well-disciplined classroom and being forced by the administration to give away good grades. I can't even begin to count how many students have come to me saying, "But I have to get a A!" — as if that alone is sufficient reason for me to determine that they actually deserve an A. The dumbing down of universities is a well attested phenomenon.

Similar problems were experienced in the 1980s by pianist Jack Reilly, while chairman of Jazz Studies at the New England Conservatory of Music in Boston, Massachusetts. He calls his experience the "Image vs. Truth" of jazz education and cites the occasion when he wanted to raise the admission requirements. "Wow! Did I hit a funny bone," he recalls. "A roaring NO! came back. They said, 'We need the average talented student so we pay the rent and pay the salaries. We must not challenge the incoming freshmen.' Many students confided in me they just wanted their degree, period. They weren't interested in serious study or learning, let alone developing their own voice in jazz."

Balancing the tensions between business and education is clearly an issue that both jazz education and higher education as a whole has to grapple with. But it remains a fact of life that the business of education requires student fees to sustain an institution's academic life in America. The student numbers required for financial viability can, in some instances, mean large class sizes, which in turn can lead to a reliance on a rigid pedagogy that makes it difficult to cater to the special needs of the individual. However, not all jazz educators feel the pressure to meet financial goals; as Paul Rinzler points out: "For myself, I feel no business pressure to not vary my pedagogy [i.e., maintain a curriculum based on big band and bebop styles] because of student numbers. Jazz educators respond to business pressures by different means. Largely through recruiting via jazz festivals at colleges and universities that invite high school bands to participate, rather than not changing pedagogy. If pedagogy doesn't change, it is more probably due to musical reasons rather than business reasons." Today, the bebop-based jazz pedagogy has been an important musical experience for the majority of practicing jazz musicians. Formal, classroom-based instruction has enabled them to focus on key areas of their musical development, eliminating much of the trial-and-error approach used by earlier generations of self-taught musicians.

In the 1950s and 1960s, the first big American university jazz courses emerged, such as those at Berklee College of Music or the University of North Texas. As this occurred, Charles Beale in *The Oxford Companion to Jazz* notes, "The need to justify jazz education as worthy of institutional and cultural attention led to a clear, if in retrospect slightly limited, definition of a single jazz style and related skills." Effectively, the price exacted from jazz in exchange for entering academia was that for it to be taught, it had to be defined, otherwise the argument goes, what, precisely, are you teaching? "It seems inescapable to say, at some point, this is jazz and this is not," continues Rinzler. "If one never said 'This is not jazz,' then any music could be jazz, even Beethoven's Fifth Symphony, but that situation is clearly absurd. The line must be drawn somewhere. Where the line is drawn is another question."

Yet during the 1950s, 1960s, and 1970s, jazz was typically regarded as a work in progress, where change was regarded as both inevitable and necessary; as Gunther Schuller noted in *The Swing Era*: "True jazz by its very nature cannot be held to a formula or be based on some stationary perfection." However, by defining jazz for the purposes of education, a line is metaphorically drawn in the sand: cross this line and it ceases to be jazz. Pedagogic utility has actually helped reinforce a closed, static definition of jazz, and increasingly, students have become aware of a limit to their art. As pianist Ted Gioia, author of *The History of Jazz* points out, "Jazz educators and other members of the jazz superstructure often embrace . . . static models of jazz because doing so simplifies their job."

In part through the dominant bebop-hard bop-postbop pedagogy that has emerged as an alternative conservatory style for training young jazz musicians, the 1980s and 1990s saw a hardening of the American paradigm of jazz. As Charles Beale described it, "The first bebop flowering of jazz education established important and influential norms . . . for some, this has tended to codify jazz education and slant the players it produces toward the mainstream styles and tunes of the United States." On the one hand, the bebop tradition gives students an insight to jazz improvisation at the highest levels through a series of modules that move through compositions with relatively static harmony to complex chromatic reharmonization. On the other hand, young musicians are in danger of becoming custodians of a music with carefully proscribed parameters. The original bebop improvisers learned to fit the elements of their style together in a way that created something exceptional; they were imitated by other members of the musical community, and key elements of their playing were quickly assimilated into the broader syntax of the music. Certain key phrases or licks, exercised within the parameters of the bebop style, had, even by the mid-1960s, become widely disseminated and imitated.

Today, like an inverted triangle, hundreds of thousands of students and thousands of teachers study this narrow repository of stylistic inspiration (the pantheon of truly "great" bebop players in all of jazz is probably less than fifteen musicians), which for many students has resulted in both a similarity of concept and execution. Consequently, many have expressed the view that what jazz has gained in mass production it has lost in individuality and creativity. "I think one of the problems with many American programs is there is too much studying the masters and not enough time studying yourself," observes American saxophonist and educator Frank Griffith of Brunel University, London. "They've got classes in American universities just devoted to one style, the music of Horace Silver for one semester, for example! By the time they are ready to study themselves they've got their degree and they're off! The next stage of their development is to prove to their audiences and peers what they've learnt at college."

During the learning process, the apprentice jazz musician must learn many, many standard songs. For example, in *The Jazz Theory Book*, Mark Levine lists 965 tunes in his chapter called "The Repertoire." Some tunes are marked with an asterisk that denotes a "must learn tune," and comes with the following caution: "Do not move to New York without knowing most of them." The challenge for a young musician when building a repertoire, from blues tunes to the classics of the American popular song, from contemporary tunes to modal tunes, and from free form tunes to jazz standards, can be a daunting process, but one that every jazz musician must undergo, a process that never ends. To unlock the complexities of improvising through unfamiliar chord progressions, students are introduced to pattern running, or sequencing as it is sometimes known, be it melodic sequencing or rhythmic sequencing. But Ted Gioia is cautious about the prominence of pattern-based study in the pedagogy. "Young musicians are taught to memorize certain licks," he observes in *Future Jazz*. "I have seen them labor over warmed over phrases for ii–V progressions with the fervor of disciples memorizing Holy Scripture."

As Professor Simon Purcell points out, a deeper appreciation of improvisation and its range of educational potential can actually be hindered by the proliferation of study aids in jazz that offer various permutations of patterns that he believes preys upon the acquisitive nature of students.

These compendiums of "hot licks and cool grooves," he contends, pay "little attention to the whole range of processes that characterize musical or artistic development." Even among advanced students who can draw on rhythmic energy and technical facility in the application of these "licks," the results can often sound like exercises from study aids such as *Patterns for Jazz* that spell out how to negotiate a path through commonly encountered harmonic sequences such as II-V-I changes, turnbacks, the blues, "rhythm" changes, and so forth.

Reliance on the patterns and licks methodology, together with a rigid adherence to the bebop paradigm, suggests that a deeper understanding of the improviser's art is lacking, with some young musicians seizing the performing situation as an opportunity to showcase their technique, they are failing to adjust to the musical surroundings and context they find themselves in. This is something that concerns John Medeski, of the group Medeski Martin & Wood, himself a graduate of the New England Conservatory where he studied classical music: "I find a lot of times DJs are some of the best musicians to play with these days, because of the nature of what they do they tend to think more orchestrally and think about what *I* am trying to do — think about themselves in relation to the whole, as a composer would, whereas the new breed of, quote, 'schooled jazz musicians,' unquote, tend to play on top of you, play their STUFF on top of you."

In his book *Bebop and Nothingness*, Francis Davis wrote of the "deadening sameness" of what he was hearing on record and in clubs, pointing out that boredom was a reasonable response to "[a] lineup of soloists running down the chords to no apparent purpose." As drummer Dave King of the trio The Bad Plus observes:

> So often I'll hear a record and you have all these great players and they just sound like islands stuck together — like "I've got some stuff I'm going to put in here"; "I've got some stuff I'm going to put in *here*"; "I've *got* to get my two cents in!" It's the, "I've-got-all-this-vast-technique-and-I'm-going-to-throw-it-out-there, man, because-that's-what-it's-about!" syndrome. It's *not* about that. It's about being aware there's something esoteric underneath you've got to pay attention to.

The problem with basing the educational curriculum on a bebop-styled repertoire is that solos in this style — and it is a style that focuses almost entirely on solos — were becoming so circumscribed stylistically and technically it was increasingly difficult for musicians to say anything original in the idiom. This is not to say it was impossible (the work of Greg Osby, Brad Mehldau, or Jason Moran, for example), but in general the idiom has become so self-referential it may have lost its sense of linear and historical progression. It can be competitive (a tendency exacerbated by the status accorded to student competitions to find the "best young soloist" or "combo"); in the hands of some it can be emotionally narrow, and, as eventually happened in the first incarnation of the music in the 1950s and early 1960s, it can be taken to its logical extreme where it ends up communicating nothing other than virtuosity itself.

A parallel situation exists in popular culture. Simon Frith argued in his book *Sound Affects* that guitar-based rock music had become almost exclusively self-referential by the end of the 1970s: "There was no music a rock musician (however young) could not make that did not refer back, primarily, to previous rock recordings; the music was about itself now, whether it liked it or not." The similarities with the bebop idiom are all too plain: the music is about itself, with solos by many young jazz musicians seeming less art, more the product of assiduous assimilation of the bebop masters of the golden years of jazz in the 1950s and early 1960s. With the establishment of a broad, overriding jazz pedagogy (albeit subject to different emphases and priorities in certain institutions), a settled consensus about basic methodology has coalesced. But, as the Italian musicologist Marcello Piras notes: "The vast majority of jazz teachers push students toward copying a standard language, the results are endless repetition and boredom, no new genius ever surfaces, and audiences still purchase the classic jazz recordings, yet nobody steps back. No doubts, no ifs and no buts. And if you teach differently, you get isolated." Matthew Parris, who took up postgraduate studies at Harvard University after graduating at Cambridge University, notes in his book *Chance Witness*, "[In Academia] I learned an important truth: that academics, even very clever ones, fall into the grip of orthodoxies, become slaves to fashion, and are spectacularly craven about speaking out about ruling nostrums."

In his book *Self-Portrait of a Jazz Artist*, Dave Liebman called bebop the "calisthenics" of improvisation, a vocabulary that provides a coherent and harmonically sophisticated basis for exploring the art of improvisation. But instead of using it as a jumping off point to find an individual voice, it was increasingly seen as a form "in itself." This was something that was brought home to the Norwegian bassist Eivind Opsvik when he moved from Oslo to study in the United States in 1998:

When I came to New York I was surprised at how "traditional" much of the scene is. I think that's why nothing much has happened in jazz in the last thirty years because of the jazz schools [in America]. The program is so based on standards and learning the bebop language that people maybe forget about their own identity. If they had some personality the school can easily take it away if you're not a strong enough person.

Original voices were becoming increasingly hard to find, exacerbated by the fact that learning solos of the greats was seen as a pathway to acquiring familiarity within the syntax of bebop. "I tell my students, I know what the real world is like," says Bob Brookmeyer. "I try to gently tell them that there are probably 35–40,000 Coltrane tenor players and you ain't going to make much money or even a living if that's how you want to play, even if you play fantastically well. So being their 'Real World Representative,' I say it might be wise to broaden your spectrum, learn to become a musician rather than a focused imitator, which is what many of them become."

But during the late 1980s and 1990s, there was no need to go that extra mile in search of an original voice when the jazz marketplace — record companies, the media, club owners, and promoters — had bought into the prevailing *mode retro*, celebrating virtuosity for virtuosity's sake. As pianist and educator Geri Allen told author Gene Santoro in 1994:

It's really difficult to go for something that is not a traditional sound *per se*. . . . You can make a . . . choice and say, "People are gonna identify with John Coltrane because he pulled his weight . . . and it's still fresh." So you can think, "Why should I go through all this when I can really feel good about my playing and not have to go through the frustrations of doubting myself? Because if I'm gonna play like Trane, nobody's gonna put me down. How can you put something that great down?" So in a way I think that attitude is a safety valve. It's more the feeling of being a really good player and getting out there and dealing right away, because people understand that language. It's clear and it's been around long enough; it's not fumbling around trying to find a better way.

This impatience with the struggle that goes into musical growth and development reflected the tendency in the 1980s and 1990s for instant gratification, particularly among the young, encouraged by contemporary consumerism in general and advertising in particular. This desire for instant gratification has increasingly become ingrained into our culture, shaped by television and the media for a rampant consumer society, such as the thousands who rushed into dot-coms in the mid-1990s because they wanted to make an "instant" fortune before they were thirty.

It's hardly surprising that a search for quick results for time invested in the practice room should be reflected in jazz, where, traditionally, "fumbling around trying to find a better way" — trying to find an individual voice — has been so essential for artistic growth (jazz history abounds with stories of established greats struggling and eventually receiving recognition for their particular style played in their particular way). By copying the work of past masters, many students can acquire a superficial understanding of the art of improvisation, but they lack the deeper understanding of the processes involved that ultimately leads to originality of concept and execution. As jazz scholar and educator Dr. Lewis Porter, author of *John Coltrane*, observed, "a kind of 'unthinking adulation' of the past 'greats' has been accepted by the vast majority of today's students, coming out of the attitude promoted by Wynton Marsalis and others since the 1980s."

"As long as people are taught to emulate somebody else's ideas and style — hence emotions as well — the whole thing is doomed to failure," says the Italian musicologist Marcello Piras:

> In order to express emotions, people must primarily express *their own* inner life. And they need to find their own distinctive voices to that purpose. Current jazz pedagogy basically discourages originality, or (more accurately) encourages imitation of a narrow range of jazz heroes. . . . If you are taught that things must be done in one given way, and ONLY that way, and all you need is learning rules and tricks to get as close as possible to that given way, people will learn it but, to them, it will be exactly like learning chess. They won't express their emotions, which grew out of a life that is light years different from, say, Coltrane's own. Some gifted students, who have listened to Coltrane for years and assimilated his style, may come acceptably close to faking Coltrane's emotions. They will probably win some prize for young jazz talent, make their own CD, and disappear, for anybody would still prefer Coltrane. This is what I have witnessed in jazz teaching for some thirty years.

The result has often been a kind of predictable uniformity in the content of many jazz solos, which in many cases rather too faithfully echoed jazz's great master musicians. "Thirty years ago if somebody came up to you and said, 'Gee, I really enjoy your playing, you sound just like so-and-so,' that would *not* have been taken as a compliment!" said saxophonist Steve Marcus, a featured soloist for bandleaders Woody Herman, Stan Kenton, and Buddy Rich. "The idea was to play three notes and have everybody willing to bet their house on who it was. Individuality was much more important than it is today. Now, if you say, 'You sound just like so-and-so,' there is a tremendous sense of accomplishment."

"When you go to college to learn jazz you naturally stick with the things you are learning, and want to show people what you have learned," observes Odd Sneeggen of Svensk Musik in Stockholm:

> Art is something different, not "showing what you can do" but having something to say and having a unique way in which to say it. In America, jazz is so much more a business and musicians are sometimes unwilling to make a simple or even a naïve musical statement by peer pressure and business pressure. They are afraid colleagues or people in the music business or fellow musicians will think they haven't learned anything in college and unless they demonstrate their skill within the idiom of bebop they won't get work.

Jazz has increasingly become a shared language by which a technocratic elite advance their reputations among their peer group through prowess on the bandstand, an often competitive environment where others wait in the wings for their chance to claim the spotlight. As the internationally respected bassist and ECM artist Arild Andersen observed, "The mainstream of America is still playing fast and New York-ish and they're really burning, you have to play faster than the guy beside you otherwise you are driving a taxi. . . ."

This competitive tendency within bebop-orientated music has inevitably pushed it toward mechanical prolixity producing a materialistic approach to art, where musical productivity is increasingly valued above content or artistic statement. "When many young players play a ballad, it becomes a chance to play more notes," says pianist Kenny Werner in his book *Effortless Mastery*. "Often they can't focus on a melodic statement and convey emotion, but are driven by myopic concerns, such as 'burning.' Young singers are often so preoccupied with their scat singing they don't even check out the words to the song. They [all] have an opportunity to tell us a story and make us feel its meaning, but they miss the point."

The preoccupation with technique as a means of establishing a reputation in the jazz marketplace is in danger of creating a music that speaks only to itself: to other jazz musicians, jazz educators, music business types, and jazz critics. Saxophonist Branford Marsalis has spoken of how many young American musicians have increasingly come to regard virtuosity as the *sine qua non* of jazz. "Players are too insulated [from the public]," he told me. "It's the jazz dark ages, patterns, patterns; virtuosity is the enemy of creativity — 'I must get more fourths in my solo, I must get more tenths.' It's missing the point about what jazz is all about. Guys say, 'I'm working on my technique,' but what's that? Putting polish on polish!"

Evan Eisenberg, in his book *The Recording Angel,* observed that most jazz musicians "lived in a sort of musical Wild West where [they were] always subject to challenge by the new gun-slinger in town." This climate where musical firepower becomes a means of securing self-identity, of being able to "blow the opposition off the bandstand," is best illustrated by the centrality of the western myth in American consciousness, a universal code that underpins its national life. In the western myth, the frontier was tamed by violence, and the gunfight was a means of settling differences. Today, being fast on the draw has been replaced by a rush to litigation as a way to settle differences with the result that there are more lawyers in the United States than the rest of the world combined. Perhaps unsurprisingly, this combative approach is embedded in jazz folklore, such as saxophonists Lester Young and Coleman Hawkins "dueling" through the Kansas City night in the 1930s, for example. The bandstand was where reputations could be lost and gained, illustrated by Forrest Whittaker's portrayal of Charlie Parker's early travails to establish his career in the motion picture *Bird*, where instrumental prowess in the heat of the jam session "battle" finally wins through.

In the past, the adversarial legacy of the jam session helped raise standards. In the opening scenes of the film *Bird*, the young Charlie Parker fails to measure up to the shared values of his elders and has a cymbal thrown at his feet, forcing him to leave the bandstand and go and "woodshed" — put in a period of intense practicing — until he had acquired the requisite skills to hold his own among older, established professional musicians. This adversarial environment served jazz well, forcing standards up among musicians of all skill levels. But times have changed, and some educators feel the confrontational–adversarial environment of the jam session should be approached with caution as a means of advancing overall musicality, skills, and especially confidence building among young musicians.

Saxophonist and educator Frank Griffith was originally from Eugene, Oregon, and moved to New York to obtain his masters in Jazz Composition at the Manhattan School of Music, and subsequently studied with Bob Brookmeyer and Manny Albam under the auspices of the BMI

Workshop. He underscored the competitiveness of the jazz scene in the city:

> The New York City jazz scene has much to do with an American cultural microcosm of winning and being the best. When I started out on the New York scene I went to jam sessions, one was the Star Bar on 23rd Street, where they had a jam session every Monday night, and youngsters like me who weren't very well known would go there religiously in the hope of being noticed. We'd feel really nervous walking in — "I've got to prove myself," "Can I cut this tempo," "Can I cut the chords on the bridge," and so on. And you wouldn't get any support from your fellow players, they all wanted to be noticed too. So when you're nervous and agitated you're not going to be at your best. That's not a creative environment. It doesn't foster a "group" concept, for example. In New York there's all these jam sessions and they are not geared for the public at all, they're geared for the musos. So you have another problem, you are not addressing an audience, but musicians. It wasn't playing for an audience and it wasn't addressing the dynamics and the shape of music — leading a tune to a climax, ending a tune with polish, devising an intro and so on. It was just a jam session for the sake of "playing," and I'm not convinced that that type of playing is particularly good for creating a group concept that you can present to an audience or help you develop an original style.

On leaving music college, the young graduate who decides to pursue a career as a jazz musician is confronted with intense competition in the jazz marketplace to secure the kind of reputation and identity necessary for attracting the attention of potential employers, be they bandleaders, record company A&R managers, bookers, club owners, and all those engaged in the business of hiring jazz musicians. Many *animators* in the jazz business share a bebop-based value system, where technique and virtuosity are frequently marked high because it is believed paying customers value a high work ethic (plenty of notes) even at the expense of meaning. Musical productivity is perceived as representing "good value for money," particularly in a jazz club where the cost of admission and a cover charge entitles the paying customer to one set where the jazz musicians are expected to "deliver." Indeed, many jazz club stages are surrounded by iconography that reinforces such expectations, including photographs of perspiring saxophonists or trumpeters straining with bulging necks captured in the intensity of creation.

The "business" of jazz brings with it a form of conformity where peer pressure, business pressure, and an implied societal sympathy for uniformity make it more difficult to depart from the bebop paradigm in 2004 than it was in 1954. An enormous controversy erupted in the jazz press over the piano trio The Bad Plus, for example, whose covers of rock tunes by Nirvana, Abba, and Aphex Twin on their major label debut, *These Are the Vistas*, in 2003, and The Pixie and Iron Maiden on their follow-up *Give,* in 2004, prompted a *Jazz Times* cover feature titled: "The Bad Plus — Good, Bad or Even a Plus?" One critic inadvertently summarized the situation when he complained, "they didn't make *Give* for me or for Ira Gitler or Nat Hentoff or anyone who has spent too much time with stacks of Blue Note, Prestige, Riverside and Savoy recordings." This kind of pressure seeks to hold jazz in a kind of stationary perfection that is subservient to how the music was played almost half a century ago. But as bassist Reid Anderson of the group appositely comments, "What connection do I have to jazz of the 1950s, other than I like it? It's beautiful music but it has been done. Every time has its expression, every time has a personality to it."

"What we as teachers have to worry about is the codification of jazz," says Bob Brookmeyer. "Charlie Parker was the first one to codify the language. And I have a small voice that asks very timidly, 'Was Charlie Parker a good idea?' Because I watched Coleman Hawkins, who was a good friend of mine, Ben Webster and Roy Eldridge go out of business, literally, when Charlie Parker came in. You either did it like that or didn't. If you didn't, then you also didn't work."

Equally, the business of earning a living in jazz in today's big urban metropolises can contribute to the homogeneity of jazz. For musicians who move to New York City, for example, there is the expensive reality of simply living there. The musician's struggle to cover costs can have an impact on their music, as Frank Griffith discovered:

> Musicians come from all over America, all over the world, just to make it in New York. You know what they say, "if you can make it there, you can make it anywhere!" But when you get started it's very hard to make a living there, so you take whatever [work] is going. A bar mitzvah in Long Island, a wedding in the Bronx, so this means it's very hard to develop anything of your own. I was there in the '80s and '90s, and it hasn't changed much since then. You have to concentrate on a style — bebop — so that you can fit in, you don't get a second chance, so that when you get that call you're ready.

Most musicians earn their keep by freelancing in a number of bands because few leaders can offer the prospect of full-time work. "I read reviews of new players who can sit in with anybody or play with five different...bands in five nights—and everybody talks about this like its a positive thing," said pianist Keith Jarrett in *The New York Times Magazine*. Thus there is a necessity for a common language, which again imposes its own kind of conformity, because there is often little or no time to rehearse and explore alternative ways of approaching jazz. Norwegian bass player Eivind Opsvik, who earned his bachelor's degree in music in Oslo and moved to New York to study for his master's degree in 1998, faced this predicament:

> In New York you have to do five or six bands, most people teach a lot, or do wedding gigs, just to make a living. It's hard to concentrate and focus in on your own music. . . . In Europe you have more time to develop a group thing. At least in Norway you get support from the State, you get paid to do tours, you don't have to spread your things through so many different groups and projects to make a living, you can concentrate on one project, because you can get support from the government to do tours and also support to compose, so it's easier that way to concentrate on individuality than making a living.

Equally, regular working bands, in which musicians might refine and hone an individual style and collectively work out fresh approaches to the music were getting fewer and fewer. Pick-up bands, thrown together for a European tour, a series of festivals, or a club date were becoming the norm. "The effect on jazz could be disastrous," wrote Roxanne Orgill in the *New York Times*, "because without working bands the music can't develop." Once again the "business" of jazz was mitigating against evolution — "What are the consequences of jazz without working ensembles?" asked John Corbett in a *Downbeat* feature called "Fanfare for the Working Band" — "Are we cut adrift in a sea of jam sessions? Local rhythm sections supporting international stars in a never ending string of one night stands? Name based ad-hoc groupings brought together once in every five years? Superficial label-stable bands assembled by committee, custom cut to appeal to a certain demographic?" As trumpeter and educator Donald Byrd said in the same feature, "Now there's no place to nurture, to grow".

The struggle to make a living in what, for the majority of musicians, is not a well-paid business, was exacerbated when arts funding came under pressure during the 1980s and 1990s. The result has been an increasing number of professional jazz musicians turning their backs on the freelance life and entering academia as professors, lecturers, teachers, workshop leaders, artists-in-residence, or researchers rather than opting for the less secure life on the road. Many jazz teachers say they would prefer to make their living as jazz musicians, but it is too precarious a profession. As Charles Beale notes: "The financial and cultural health of jazz and of its mortgage paying and increasingly middle-class musicians is now sustained as much by educational activity as by performing."

However, experienced professional jazz musicians are far outnumbered by the countless graduates who have entered academia, sometimes with a minimal amount of professional experience. In practice, large numbers of graduates are taught by educators who themselves have come through the jazz-education system, many of whom have little or no experience as professional jazz musicians and for whom the "jazz life" of paying dues in the hope that modest success might eventually come their way is more abstract notion than lifestyle choice. Others, from families who have made sacrifices to put them through college and university, feel they have to take advantage of the degrees and diplomas they have accrued and become teachers and lecturers and acquire status in the community, rather than turn their back on family sacrifices and scuffle for their living as a freelance jazz musician. "Unfortunately we are currently bearing the fruits of the 'teachers teaching teachers, teaching teachers' syndrome," observed Hal Galper. The result is jazz graduates becoming jazz educators who reinforce a static paradigm of jazz by teaching jazz that is "explainable, analyzable, categorizable, and do-able" who often lack experience of other forms of nonbebop-oriented jazz.

Today, the way the business of jazz is structured in America, it is increasingly difficult to survive as a jazz musician without some involvement in jazz education, either privately or within the academy. Steen Meier, chairman of the Nordic Music Council and Copenhagen's famous JazzHouse, sees some form of government subsidy as being vital to enable musicians to sustain their careers within the cultural job market and ensure the music's vitality. "The almost blind belief in the forces of the market has produced thousands of well educated musicians and music teachers who are unable to ply their craft. You cannot have a unique cultural expression like jazz, which now increasingly lives in academia where teachers educate other teachers, who later educate other teachers, and expect it to survive in a society which has absolutely no intention to support a platform to express this unique musical language."

The expansion of jazz education, not only in the United States but around the world, reflects the interest and respect jazz has generated as an American twentieth-century art form. Many countries from Australia to Japan, South Africa to Brazil, and Scandinavia to Western Europe offer graduate degree courses in jazz or jazz modules in tandem with classical and popular music courses. "As a jazz musician I have witnessed the rapid growth of a global jazz education industry," says Professor Simon Purcell of the Guildhall School of Music and Drama in London. "Musicians and teachers have tended to identify either with the dominant technicist pedagogy (stylistically specific and content-based) or with a more liberal, group-composition based approach (student-centered, allegedly). . . . The key issue here and in all music education is to focus on issues of teaching and learning rather than stylistic or pedagogical adherences."

The value of the latter approach avoids limiting students to a fixed paradigm of the music, so spurring creativity outside the loop of tradition-based styles. "Much of the American educational approach revolves around bebop," says the British pianist and educator Tim Richards, author of *Improvising Blues Piano*. "The feeling is that if you can play bebop you can play anything. Perhaps it is time to remind ourselves that it is over fifty years since that style was new, and that it is now possible to build a successful career in jazz without having much knowledge or experience of bebop."

These views are certainly not unknown in American jazz education, with some institutions acknowledging the bebop-based paradigm works less well in contemporary music structures and offering courses in both jazz and popular music or jazz and contemporary music, and so on. The majority of educators, however, argue that the bebop tradition should remain the basis of the curriculum. "Clearly emphasis on bebop and repertoire studies had advantage for those who sought to legitimize jazz as a serious art form with its own set of objective standards and definable history," points out Dr. Tony Whyton of Leeds College of Music, "From an Afro-American perspective, the desire to construct and celebrate a rich definable cultural history is understandable in the broader context of American history. The downside of the American approach is that it encourages the presentation of history as a defined entity, rather than something in constant flux, constructed in the present. This can lead to the exclusion of approaches that do not conform to the defined benchmark."

In Europe, some institutions are less fixated with the dominant bebop-technicist pedagogy. As a jazz tradition was being shaped in America, a parallel tradition was being developed in Europe, shaped by its own aesthetic responses to the music. While this tradition hungrily absorbed the American vocabulary of jazz, some musicians sought to modify jazz from a European perspective. This legacy has a long history and is refracted in its jazz education today, which often follows American methodology, but can also reflect the needs and requirements of European jazz musicians and audiences.

The result has been the emergence of what can only be described as a European approach to jazz education that has grown out of, and often runs parallel to, the basic American model. "The 'American approach' to jazz education is not necessarily geographically located," says Dr. Tony Whyton. "It's an approach which seeks to unify and underline the jazz canon, celebrating the contributions of a handful of iconic individuals at the expense of a more pluralistic perspective. The European outlook on jazz is certainly more eclectic, reflecting both the multinational perspectives of its jazz communities and the fact that European jazz culture is less fixated with the idea of one 'authentic' canon."

"The European musicians are definitely not tied to bebop, 'the tradition.' It doesn't mean anything to them," says Dave Liebman. "They have respect for it. Some of them do it better than others, but it's not something that's part of their repertoire by necessity, which here [in America], of course, it is. So they have much more original music, much more combinations using classical, avant garde techniques, and of course, folk music because they have so much. So there's a lot more mixing going on and in my eyes much more risk taking and adventurous music than you would hear with the standard thing here in America. America you get pretty much up and down the line. It's wonderful jazz playing but not that creative to my mind."

Jazz in Europe was quickly located within the broader umbrella of the arts in general, and often absorbed into the cultural backdrop of its nation states. For the most part, it is seen as a living, growing art form that should continue to broaden its expressive resources. As Mikko Toivanen, principal lecturer in jazz at the Pohjois-Savo Polytechnic of Music and Dance in Finland observes, "I see jazz as an 'open system.' Bebop is one possible and a very fine way to speak jazz, but the concept of an open system is the *power* of jazz and a secret of its vitality. Only one 'legal jazz' means that you have to concentrate to keep it pure and free from real life.

Art means self-expression and self-expression implies individuality. If there is no risk, no mistakes, it kills the possibility of communication."

While this open construct of jazz is shared by many, but by no means all, European jazz educators, the practical application of this philosophy can vary. At Leeds College of Music, for example, jazz is viewed in the broader context of twentieth-century developments, not only as a linear construct (swing, bebop, cool, etc.), but also as a site for the cross-fertilization of ideas. Thus students become aware of jazz's changing identity and social function, and so are willing to question the boundaries of jazz.

European jazz programs are smaller than comparable U.S. programs, and therefore can emphasize more one-on-one teaching, with a greater flexibility in their curriculums. Finnish pianist Jarmo Savolainen, who studied at Berklee College of Music in the 1980s and teaches in the jazz department of Helsinki's prestigious Sibelius Academy, believes that this difference flows from funding issues:

> In America the schools are mainly funded by tuition fees, therefore the number of students has to be kept high in order to sustain the school's life. That leads to more industrialized or canonized teaching methods, and with large numbers there is not much room for individualism. In Europe, the schools are mostly government or municipally funded, therefore the number of students can be kept low and the cream of applicants accepted. In the Sibelius Academy, for example, 5 out of 100 applicants normally get in. This means a student's relationship with their tutor is quite different and even the courses can be shaped "on the hoof," according to individual needs.

Low student numbers allow teachers a greater degree of flexibility. Ola Bengtsson, the director of Jazz Studies at Royal College of Music in Stockholm, points out that in his institution: "The students can, after their first year, set up goals and design courses and we hire teachers who are experts in those areas to direct and grade them. This is possible because of the small amount of students we have in the jazz department — 100."

A similar ethos of low student numbers is shared by American institutions such as the Brubeck Institute, which accepts eight students every two years, or the T. S. Monk Institute, where tuition is one to one and free, but similar schools are not to be found on the scale of Europe's jazz departments. "In the USA jazz is treated primarily as a business," points out Wouter Turkenburg, head of Jazz Studies at the Royal Conservatory in The Hague, "In Europe, jazz schools are art schools while in the USA, jazz schools, with just a few exceptions, are trade schools."

"I have seen schools in New York, I've never seen Boston, but I noticed that the money is important. To pay the fees and so on," observed Gunnar Lindgren, assistant professor and former head of the Jazz Department at the University of Music in Gothenburg, Sweden. "The staff of one college complained they couldn't select the best students — they select the ones most reliable to pay the fees, you know? And they knew that in Europe most of the universities are free, and they noticed the European jazz education has an openness and were afraid in the future the American schools couldn't keep up in the same way."

One obvious result of this "openness" is that some European academies believe their jazz students should also pursue parallel studies in classical music as an aid to skills building (developing a foundation technique) and to acquire a broader musical perspective from which to view their art. "It is of the utmost importance to realize that historically, European culture has been developed over centuries within specific national, regional, local areas, and still, in spite of the European Union, is considered a unique culture with Europe our common frame, and variations within a common understanding of what European Culture is," says Steen Meier. "Therefore the Europeans historically have a common background, but many different cultural, social and economic inputs. Therefore there is no conflict in teaching jazz studies students the classical tradition, because even the so-called 'classical European music' has been influenced by other musical cultures through European history."

By placing jazz in the broader forum of art music, Wouter Turkenburg argues, a context is created in which to better understand their subject. "Most European jazz musicians have a thorough training in classical music," he says. "They know what art music is. They are drenched by it. It is their main point of reference. Almost every jazz school in Europe puts an important emphasis on learning how to play classical music. Not only to improve the technique but also to know and understand another realm of music better. All of my students have one hour with a jazz teacher and half an hour with a classical teacher per week. If they fail the classical exams it is hard for them to continue their study."

Classical music provides a huge reservoir of musical knowledge to draw upon. Pianist and educator Mike Nock of the Sydney Conservatorium Jazz Studies department, in Australia, performed and recorded with, among others, alto saxophonist John Handy and multi-instrumentalist

Yusef Lateef in the 1960s. He observed: "When I grew up as a musician, the stuff we used to listen to when I was on the road with Yusef Lateef included a lot of classical. I used to have my Stockhausen records, Pierre Boulez records. It wasn't that anyone told me, it was that we used to like to listen to all kinds of music, it was part of the thing. It *wasn't* about trying to play like so-and-so. It was all about acquiring the knowledge so you didn't *need* to."

While studying with Bob Brookmeyer, saxophonist and educator Frank Griffith recalls how he was pointed in the direction of classical studies. "Brookmeyer once recommended I copy out several score pages of one of Bartók's string quartets — by hand, so that I could see his creative process at close hand," he recalled. "I have also heard that aspiring writers copy out the prose of others to accomplish the same goal. This doesn't mean that you are going to sound or write like them, but maybe internalize something that may well inform your own process of creating an individual statement."

In the late 1940s, Charlie Parker was interviewed three times for features in the music press, and each time he revealed his love of classical music; indeed, the majority of interviews from this point to his death in 1955 reflect his interest in studying classical music. He expressed a wish to study musical composition with Nadia Boulanger in France and later, in an interview with Paul Desmond, to study with Marcel Mule at the Conservatoire Nationale de Musique de Paris. Immediately prior to his death, he had actually spoken to classical composer Edgard Varèse about studying with him. As Parker's biographer Carl Woideck points out in *Charlie Parker: His Music and Life*, "Parker held high hope that study of classical music would provide the knowledge required to advance his art to the next stage." Clearly it can only be a matter of speculation what Parker hoped to gain from classical studies, but it seems he felt the traditional phonologies and syntax of the bebop style needed to be expanded to enable him to reach new pragmatics.

One result of jazz's entrance into the academy in relatively recent times is that in matching the conventional notions of established culture with its own canon, history, tradition, and air of "permanence" and "respectability," it considers itself a "self-contained" art form, despite the fact the jazz makes use of the same harmonic elements as classical music, such as primary triads, melodic intervals, passing tones, diminished seventh chords, augmented chords, extended chords, chromaticism, parallelism, suspensions, concord and discord, whole tone scales, modes, and so on.

Certainly, interdepartmental rivalry might seek to establish jazz as a secondary and dependent art form based on certain commonalities with classical studies, which can cause jazz courses to resist the influence of other disciplines. Equally, some jazz educators argue that there is very little of the classical repertory that can be carried over into jazz in terms of "licks" that can be applied to the blues or standards. These views overlook how an understanding of the classical repertoire can acquaint students with the discipline of presenting melody and that its development and variation does not depend on "hot licks," as well as the importance of tone, articulation, expressivity, and dynamic control. This is particularly true because much jazz today is either transacted at a monochrome *mezzo forte* or falls into the fast-equals-loud or slow-equals-soft syndrome. As William Bauer, assistant professor of Music at The College of Staten Island/CUNY points out:

> When I hear student performances, I often wonder how much time and energy the teacher has devoted to guiding his or her students' development in the ability to establish and vary at will the music's tempo and dynamics — significantly, the two areas in classical performance where the performer exerts the most direct interpretive control (aside from phrasing and articulation). In my experience as a teacher, I've encountered many students who seem temperamentally averse to producing either a convincing *fortissimo* or a true *pianissimo*. Likewise, certain students seem to be ill suited to playing a sustained *legato* at a steady slow tempo or seem to hammer away at fast tempos with little sense of the sound they are producing. These students were not untalented and their technique grew to encompass a wide expressive range, from *niente* to *triple forte*, from *largo* to *molto allegro*. They just needed lessons in the handling of these musical elements. For further evidence of the neglect of dynamics and tempo in music education, take a look at any fundamentals textbook and see how much space is devoted to these areas which are so critical to the music's emotional impact.

Because jazz education is heavily reliant on teaching improvisation using the traditional cyclical chorus structure — the two most common being the 12-bar blues and the ternary AABA 32 bar song form — classical music introduces the potential of music making that does not rely on traditional song forms. Marcello Piras points out:

> Jazz teaching is overwhelmingly oriented toward giving a recipe — how to improvise in bebop or modal style on the chord changes of a chorus

format. I concede that arrangement and composition courses go beyond this, but the vast majority of students never step into those courses. They are taught that jazz can only be, and therefore must be, based on the chorus format, which is given as a dogma, not a product of historical circumstances. I have always explained that there are dozens of other possibilities, in tonal, modal, and atonal jazz, and illustrated the point by analyzing anything from [Jelly Roll] Morton to Weather Report. My students stared at me in disbelief when I showed them that the chorus format is not mandatory. Most of them ran away out of shock and went back to their bebop calisthenics. The happy few who stayed soon began to acquire a much higher level of understanding of jazz language. In fact, non-chorus, linear forms have to do with the perception of the arrow of time, and activate higher brain areas that may remain silent if you listen to blues and AABA forever.

Classical studies introduce students to nonstandard forms that go beyond the strophic, binary, and ternary song forms commonly used in jazz and extend to the sonata, four part, five part, and rondo forms to through-composed forms where material is not repeated during the course of the work. It opens a whole world of possibilities that have yet to be fully exploited in jazz.

Orjan Fahlstrom, the second principal of the Royal College of Music in Stockholm and a jazz composer and arranger in his own right, says:

> In our Conservatory we use the European composing tradition as a knowledge database. We then expand into jazz and post Stockhausen electro-acoustic music and we encourage our students to cross these three idiomatic disciplines as often as they want. For us, music is music, and absolutely the most important thing is the artistic expression. If you don't have anything to say from an artistic standpoint it's quite uninteresting what style you are using, that's why we think it is most important to include lectures on aesthetics. We think it most important that our composition students, no matter what direction, can develop contemporary techniques in order to create a futuristic soundscape.

Yet a so-called European approach to jazz education has by no means been formalized. Jazz education, after all, is an American construct, and although its basic principles are applied throughout Europe, there is now evidence of a different philosophy applied to its methodology, albeit varying in its application throughout the continent. As Steen Meier points out:

The "jazz education scene" in Europe is as variable as the "jazz scene" as such in Europe. The variety is enormous according to musical styles, tradition, connection to classical music, and many other aspects. If one dare to make a generalization, it is that the jazz is being used as an "open frame," close to the historic basis of the music when jazz as such was a collage music, meaning it took elements from any other adequate musical expressions, and made them a part of jazz expressionism. Jazz has always, within certain variable frames, been open to collect and use elements from other musical traditions. Thus the jazz in Europe is viewed as an "open" construct. The European scene of jazz education is younger than the American jazz education Scene, and for this reason, and for a lot of other reasons, the European scene is more open.

In a feature in *Music Teacher* magazine in 2004, educator John Robert Brown pointed out that there has been a move away from America as the source of jazz innovation. "Jazz is developing in interesting and exciting fashions beyond the cultural jet stream from the USA," he wrote. Quoting Peter Sklaroff, the admissions tutor at Leeds College of Music, Brown said some students want to sound more "contemporary" and European, focusing less on bebop or standard songs and emphasizing modal harmony and inner lines. "They often associate this style with artists associated with the ECM label," said Sklaroff, adding that the learning and use of traditional methodologies within jazz education seems less popular with some students than it once was. "This has been put to me as a way of avoiding sounding old fashioned," he said.

As the Finnish pianist and educator Jarmo Savolainen notes:

In the last 20 years there has emerged new generations of musicians in Europe who can swing convincingly, as well as connect with their own background, from wherever in Europe that may be, and create something different from that standpoint. Derived from the jazz tradition, it might have elements of 20th century classical music or folkloric elements and often has an elasticity and looseness of its own. This kind of thinking can be passed on in education and is an on-going process at the moment.

To borrow Stephen Feal's phrase, it is through the "encoding of multiple significances" that include local and national identity, culture, and aspiration that produces a hybridized local representation of jazz that can project its own distinctive features and assert its own local "identity" within the broader hegemonic jazz styles, a process known as "transculturation" in popular culture studies.

Even so, there are many academies in Europe whose approach to jazz education would be recognized by most American students, focusing on repertoire studies and using bebop and the ABC methodology (study aid literature written by jazz educators Jamey Abersold, David Baker, or Jerry Coker) to deal with scale–chord theory. However, as Jarmo Savolainen, points out, it is now possible to see both the American and European approaches at work in many colleges across Europe, "or even one department's faculty."

The Norwegian University of Science and Technology in Trondheim has a reputation for producing some of Norway's most experimental and adventurous young musicians, prompting *Time Out London* to note that, "Norway is home to some of the most adventurous music being made in the world." Department head Erling Aksdal, a pianist who studied at Berklee (1977 to 1980) and performed with, among others, Warne Marsh and Chet Baker and earned his master's degree at the New England Conservatory in 1984, says:

> Teaching may often follow the "American methodology," and we teach some of the American bebop codes, but not as a goal in itself. To develop skills — and I am talking about musical skills, not athletic — you have to indulge in a tradition, and you cannot be superficial. We develop strong aural control over the musical material based on in-depth work with a given musical style. It is therefore important not to confuse stylistic imitation as a goal in itself. We do not expect any Coltrane clones, but we do demand that all students be able to navigate through "Giant Steps" in a way that displays aural control, and we do expect and encourage individual signature subordinate to the group's total expression. We do not put an "equals" sign between bebop and improvisation, but we do use bebop (and related styles, after all we are talking about jazz education) to develop skills. The college acknowledges the musicians' own peer culture is often more likely to influence them than the curriculum. But always there is an emphasis on instrumental and aural training, so they can take their music where they like. This I think makes us different from many schools both in Europe and USA who tend to canonize bebop. Another important emphasis is upon group playing, and interaction in groups is experimented with both in traditional (many popular styles) and free settings often related to classical musical compositional thinking, especially contemporary classical music.

The practical implications of this approach are discussed by Per Zanussi, a Trondheim graduate who quickly established himself as one of Norway's leading young bassists:

> I think the diverse results of the college have something to do with the fact that although we have the same courses as the American students, most American musicians are more conservative and jazz history oriented than the Europeans. In the States you are taught a lot of respect for what came before. This is maybe the reason for the lack of individuality. In Norway 'the jazz tradition' is not as important as it is in the US. You can choose not to be too preoccupied with this. In Norway we also have a tradition of 'being different' on the jazz scene. The musicians imitating the bebop players in the 1950s and 1960s were never very successful internationally. Garbarek and the other Norwegian ECM artists have been successful mainly because they are original. Maybe the awareness of a "European" tradition also gives us some confidence.

Aksdal takes up this point of individuality, saying that while the basic jazz education tools are available to all, it is a question of how they are applied, and believes that the context of the culture that surrounds students can have a bearing on their musical outlook:

> Here in Norway, a very egalitarian society, there is not much respect for authorities — traditions included — and a strong belief in individual uniqueness and self-contained-ness, which we call the "Peer Gynt syndrome." The strong self-confidence this implies may sometimes result in something new. It does so as a paradoxical implication since it encourages people to pursue their inclinations believing that they are unique — although they most often aren't! It's a kind of innovation by accident. We also have an expression, "inventing the gun powder again" — making fun of launching old ideas as new. I think this mentality has made much of what Norwegian jazz has become renowned for.

Thus national, cultural, social, and local identity can play a role in how the jazz tradition is interpreted outside America and subsequently on how jazz is imagined in its host nations. While many musicians and academies outside of America make the conscious artistic choice to play in the "American tradition," others see the process of transculturation — a byproduct of globalization — as both natural and inevitable. While the importance of the American pedagogy is readily acknowledged as a means of securing foundation skills, many musicians and institutions see transculturation as a means of both asserting individuality and broadening the expressive resources of the music.

In America, the social forces that helped shape jazz, as in the past, have largely been replaced by jazz education. Within the context of American social and cultural history, the debate over the "ownership" of jazz and the preservation of jazz styles from its golden years has become an important social, cultural, and political issue, with repertory-based studies seeming set to grow in importance. "Often discussion is about who 'owns' the term jazz rather developing the *concept* of jazz," says Orjan Fahlstrom. "Jazz needs to be open minded in that it has to affirm development even though it might not go in the direction the traditional jazz musicians might like."

Whether the future of jazz education lies in the known stars and fixed horizons of the bebop-based technicist pedagogy or a more inclusive, pluralist approach, seems set to become a major area of discourse in jazz education. Yet Dr. Tony Whyton points out that neither approach need be mutually exclusive, "To overplay the essentialism of the European/ American divide, is unhelpful," he says. "An altogether healthier approach, I would argue, attempts not to force a choice between the two schools of thought but seeks to create a discourse between them."

6

ALTERED REALITIES AND FRESH POSSIBILITIES: FUTURE JAZZ

Jazz is changing . . . a variety of sounds and rhythms, many of which are alien to what audiences are used to, will find their way into jazz . . . progress is inevitable. Today's musical palette is just not adequate. All feelings relative to life and beauty cannot be validly expressed with techniques now in vogue. What is more, jazz is an evolving art; it is not meant to be restricted. The very nature of the music and its history indicate this.

— **George Russell, jazz composer, arranger, bandleader, and author of** *The Lydian Concept of Tonal Organizationin* **(1960).**

By the end of the 1990s, almost unnoticed and largely unreported, the sound of jazz at the margins of the mainstream had begun to change. Initially, what began as a trickle had become, if not a flood, then a small but noticeable flow of ensembles that included a musician handling "electronics" in their lineup. Albums began appearing with credits for mysterious tasks such as "sequencing," "programming," "sampling," "DJ," or "electronics." In 2002, pianist Brad Mehldau had a conversation with a promoter in London: "I commented on the large amount of DJs on the jazz festival rosters these days. He said that it reflects the fact that turntable technology, sampling and the like has now become part of the 'jazz vocabulary' — for better or worse!"

These changes had been influenced by two key developments that were taking place outside the world of jazz. The first was in the parallel universe of popular culture, where the art of the DJ-ing had developed in leaps and bounds since the 1980s, albeit out of sight and out of mind of most jazz musicians. The second development was the huge advances that had been made in computer science, which had evolved so quickly that by 2004 the average cell phone utilized more digital technology than the spacecraft that had put the first man on the moon. During the early millennium years, a new generation of computer software had become available that allowed far more sophisticated sound manipulation than in the old acid jazz days of the early 1990s when jazz musicians improvised over the old "wickka-wickka" of turntable scratching or the sound of a sample loop on a tape machine. With software costs tumbling, a wide variety of applications came within the price range of most musicians. "Since limitations of memory and processing power are continuously eroded by Moore's law, you can now get pretty much all the tools you need on a decent computer for $1700," says producer Leo @ Blu Mar Ten. "*Protools* was an early step in this direction. Now entire 'studios in a box' programs are available that sound excellent and are almost infinitely flexible." The result was that the bedroom could now function as a recording studio. As if to emphasize this, the Norwegian band Wibutee called their second album *Eight Domestic Challenges* (2001) because the recording, mixing, and processing of the album's eight tracks had all been done at home.

Now the improviser's art could be played out against new sonic backdrops colored by fragments of electronic sounds, rhythms, and samples swimming through the music, while digital computer editing — also known as "hard disc editing," where sounds are chopped up and rearranged inside the computer's virtual space — allowed for juxtapositions never dreamed of in Charlie Parker's day. As long ago as 1966, composer Milton Babbitt said: "As for the future of electronic music, it seems quite obvious to me that its unique resources guarantee its use, because it has shifted the boundaries of music." Yet jazz, widely admired for its invention and innovatory zeal in the twentieth century, had by the twenty-first century fallen behind the adjacent worlds of classical music and popular culture in terms of electronic experimentation.

But, as a technologically adept generation of jazz musicians, raised on home computers and video games, began to explore the new music software programs and the latest DJ equipment, they realized these tools had the potential to mold and shape sound, and recontextualize jazz within the jumpy, nervous, scary twenty-first century. "It should come as little surprise that all this is happening, considering jazz's history as a melting pot of music," said the *Boston Globe*. "Jazz artists who have until now eschewed electronic sounds . . . could look away no longer." But how were jazz musicians responding to these new challenges?

The impact of science and technology on our existence is no longer a whimsical excursion into science fiction. In the information-technology age of the new millennium years, life is now much more complex than it was a matter of ten or fifteen years earlier and seemed to demand a response from culture. The science and technology that is now at the heart of our lives is transforming not only the way we live but also the way we think and feel. It is perhaps unsurprising then that jazz should begin to reflect these changes. However, the use of electronics has always been a contentious issue in jazz, whether it be the simple matter of hooking up an acoustic double bass to a pickup, amplifier, and speaker, or the importation of electronic instruments into the music. But as early as 1961, music historian Jacques Barzun was urging audiences to overcome their prejudices toward electronic music:

> Most people of artistic tastes share the widespread distrust and dislike of machinery and argue that anything pretending to be art cannot come out of a machine: art is the human product *par excellence*, and electronic music, born of intricate circuits and oscillations and particles generated by Con Edison, is a contradiction in terms. Here . . . the answer is simple: the moment man ceased to make music with his voice alone the art became machine ridden. Orpheus's lyre was a machine, a symphony orchestra is a regular factory for making artificial sounds and a piano is the most appalling contrivance of levers and wires this side of the steam engine. Similarly, the new electronic devices are but a means for producing materials to play with.

The important thing about art is not the *means* used to achieve an end but the *end* it achieves. The question is surely whether the result commands our attention, whether it moves or fulfills us in some way. "Do we, after a while, recognize patterns to which we can respond, with our sense of balance, our sense of suspense and fulfillment, our sense of emotional and intellectual congruity?" asked Barzun. Electronics is simply another medium through which a jazz musician can express himself or herself, as trumpeter Dave Douglas points out:

> I feel the artistic, personal statement is the more important goal in creating new music. That this music is an inseparable part of our technological environment seems inevitable. Sonic issues [are] exciting, but that makes the eternal values in art seem much more important. All music has to be organic — has to come from the earth and the soul to be meaningful. Electro-acoustic music is no different.

Jazz did not evolve in a vacuum and has always adapted to and been shaped by technological as much as cultural and social forces. Brad Mehldau, who included subtle real-time electronics and original overdubs working with rock producer Jon Brion on 2002's *Largo*, says, "I can't deny that the musical decisions [in *Largo*], were informed by the technology: recording techniques, treatment of piano, et cetera. The actual sonic environment influenced how we played." Equally, Billie Holiday's art would have been impossible without a major technological advance of the early 1930s, the electric microphone. Sidney Bechet famously recorded clarinet, soprano, tenor sax, piano, bass, and drums on his "one man band" recording of "The Shiek of Araby" in April 1941, courtesy of the latest available technology.

When the LP broke through the three-minute barrier of old 78-rpm disc, a new world opened up for the improviser and composer. Magnetic recording tape replaced wax discs, offering further possibilities for manipulation of the original "takes." In the 1950s Miles Davis was using a large number of spliced takes, after-the-fact editings, drop-ins, overdubs, and postproduction work to produce classics such as *Miles Ahead*, *Porgy and Bess*, and *Sketches of Spain*. These studio creations demand to be heard on their own terms, for what they are, rather than what they were not, a "captured" live performance.

By the mid-1960s, the development of multitrack recording had made it possible to store different instruments, sometimes recorded on different dates, on different tracks, and in the final mix-down to add, rerecord, and alter the relationship one to another of these tracks. Thus the notion of jazz interacting and being shaped by technological advances is hardly new. Some classics of the genre have even depended on it, from Lennie

Tristano's "Requim" to Bill Evans's "conversations" with himself. Indeed, Miles Davis's jazz-rock work between 1969 and 1975 made extensive use of Teo Macero's tape editing and *musique concrète* (music constructed from recorded sounds) techniques to produce music that could never exist in real time: "[On a lot of Miles Davis's records] we would use bits and pieces of cassettes that he would send me and say, 'Put this in that new album we're working on,'" recalled Macero. "I would really shudder. I'd say, 'Look, where the hell is it going to go? I don't know.' He says, 'Oh, you know.' So he sends me the tape. I listen to it and say, 'Oh yeah, maybe we can stick that in here.'"

On Mike Westbrook's epic antiwar protest, *Marching Song Vols. 1 & 2* from 1969, the opening track "Hooray!" has crowd sounds — manipulated by Bill Price and worked into the big band mix — that capture the spirit of troops marching off to the carnage of the 1914 to 1918 war. On the title track of *Black Market* by Weather Report, made in 1975 to 1976, Joe Zawinul uses a tape evoking the hubbub of an African marketplace to open the title track. Both these examples situated the music in time and place, something that was repeated in live performance. Yet the music's "authenticity" was not derived from "effects" — how the music was actually made — but from the story the music has to tell in terms of its interaction with listeners. Later, Zawinul made use of the studio-as-an-instrument to broaden the range of his compositions, enabling him to create a seemingly limitless range of musical colors and textures on albums such as *Tale Spinnin'*, *8.30*, and *Mr. Gone*. "The availability of great electronic sounds has been here for a long time," says Dave Douglas. "Even more importantly, the availability of great electronic *players*. That's the key to me — people who can personalize the technology and sonic palette."

The speed with which audio culture has moved forward in the late 1990s and early millennium years presented jazz musicians with an almost unlimited range of sonic possibilities. One route to harnessing this potential was by adding a DJ-producer to the jazz ensemble to manipulate sound. At the end of Herbie Hancock's set at the North Sea Jazz Festival in July 2001, Hancock introduced his Future2Future band to the audience. Calling on each member to take a bow to the customary whoops of delight and wild applause, he finally turned to a lone figure tucked behind a small podium whose head was covered by huge earphones. "Well, I guess we have to call them 'musicians' now!" said Hancock. "DJ Disk on turntables!" The ironic tone was deliberate.

Hancock was signifying on an old musician's joke from decades ago: Question: "How many of you are there in the band?" Answer: "Five musicians (or whatever) and a drummer!" The DJ may have replaced the much maligned drummer as the butt of jokes, but just as the drummer finally became recognized as a musician in his own right, Hancock was conferring similar status upon the DJ.

The rapid rise in jazz of the DJ in recent times has not been entirely unexpected. According to retailers, sales of turntables among the young were already inching ahead of the once ubiquitous guitar by 2002. Part of the attraction of turntables for the neophyte musician is that they can produce "instant" music. "You literally don't have to know anything about music to put together your own compositions from samples and sound bytes," says Adrian Gibson, DJ at London's Jazz Café:

> One guy at the turntables can be a whole band. It opens up a whole new way of approaching music. There's the whole thing with "scratching" rhythms, then there's mixing one record into another and coming up with something new, then there's the use of sampling, tape loops — it's another world. These are the tools of the modern DJ and he's becoming just as integrated into jazz groups now as the pianist or saxophonist.

The unique musical domain of the DJ is made possible by the culture of recording, which Christoph Cox and Daniel Warner in *Audio Culture: Readings in Modern Music* describe as, "a culture in which music and sound circulate as a network of recorded entities detached from the specificity of time, place and authorship and all available to become the raw material of the DJ's art." Contemporary DJs don't simply "play records" or beat match two or three albums and layer them over each other, but see themselves as creative artists capable of making new compositions out of prerecorded media, such as DJ Spooky's *Dubtometry* (2003). These creative processes, says DJ Spooky — aka Paul D. Miller, who is also a musician, conceptual artist and writer — in his essay *Algorithms: Erasures and the Art of Memory*, is all about recombinant potential:

> Each and every source sample is fragmented and bereft of prior meaning — a kind of future without a past. The samples are given meaning only when re-presented in the assemblage of the mix. In this way, the DJ acts as the cybernetic inheritor of the improvisational tradition of jazz, where various motifs would be used and recycled by the various musicians of the genre.

The basic techniques employed by DJs in manipulating and sequencing samples of prerecorded sound, which can be "found sounds" or snippets from the vast libraries of pop, rock, jazz, soundtrack music, and so on, have become increasingly more sophisticated with the latest generation of sampling machines and hardware, as producer Leo @ Blu Mar Ten explains:

> The ways audio is manipulated began in the simple days of hardware samplers and included reverse playback; loops; cropping samples; playing at different pitches; panning left and right and playing louder and quieter. The newer functions that came in the later generations of hardware sampler and are also present in all current software samplers include time-stretch (made very popular by early jungle and drum n' bass in the early-mid 1990s); filtering (hi-pass, lo-pass, band-pass, which is effectively a very resonant moveable EQ); morphing (merging one sound into another); LFO assignment (assigning oscillators to any number of these parameters), and these values can then be quantized to move in time with the music giving a rhythmic dimension to any of these effects. When you stack this lot up it becomes very hard to work out what the original sound was, so you're creating a new sound from audio "matter" — Oh, what fun! And also these effects, which used to be only available in separate hardware units, are now available in software samplers along with everything else, so you can stack a ridiculous amount of things on top of each other like reverb (making a sound have an ambient "room/hall" type space); delay (simple diminishing repeats, think echoes across a canyon); compression (the black art of production, effectively squashing the dynamic range out of a sound so it bursts at you — a critical part of most drum production since the 1960s and 1970s). And so on . . .

The process of sampling analogous to the literary "cut-up technique," or "collage" in the visual arts. As Brad Mehldau points out:

> Collage was a comment *on* art from *within* art. The analogy to sampling is a pretty direct path: the artist would use bits of media — newspaper clippings, what have you — in the work itself. The painting was a comment, among other things, on the fractured world of modernity, full of reproduced images that are rendered meaningless. Framed in an artwork, though, they might recapture the very authenticity that they seemed to have destroyed, and glow in a sublime light. These bits of media, like a sample, have the distinction that they've already been produced, and now they are being *placed into* the artwork, rather than

created organically from scratch. So as an actual formal device, there is nothing particularly innovative about sampling. Like so many other devices that fall under the umbrella of postmodernism, it is actually just dressed up modernism.

In the early 1920s, the Hungarian born artist and theorist Lázló Moholy-Nagy, having earlier advocated the use of photography to produce abstract light compositions, suggested that the phonograph might be deployed as a means of musical production instead of reproduction. Moholy-Nagy's ideas forecast John Cage's experiments with phonographs, including his first phonograph study *Imaginary Landscape, No. 1* (1939) that manipulated variable-speed turntables. In the 1940s, Paul Schaeffer created compositions made entirely out of edited slices of found sound, and his first *musique concrète* composition, *Étude aux Chemins de Fer (Railroad Study)*, anticipated hip-hop and electronic dance music by decades. Cox and Warner suggest that "from Schaffer onwards, DJ Culture has worked with two essential concepts":

> *The cut* and *the mix*. To record is to cut, to separate the sonic signifier ("the sample") from any original context or meaning so that it might be free to function otherwise. To mix is to reinscribe, to place the floating sample into a new chain of signification. . . . DJ Culture also describes a new modality of audio history and memory. No longer a figure of linear continuity that, ideally, could be recalled in totality, musical history becomes a network of mobile segments available at any moment for inscription and reinscription into new lines, texts and mixes. In short, musical history is no longer an analog scroll but digital and random access. . . . Whatever one's position, DJ Culture marks out a fundamentally new cultural space. It has altered the very nature of musical production, opened up new channels for the dissemination of music and activated new modes of listening.

DJs were seized upon by jazz players to create a new sonic environment in which to function as a musician and recontextualize their music. "The language of the DJ has really expanded," says keyboard player John Medeski of the group Medeski Martin & Wood. "It's really developed from rhythmic scratching into a lot of things that produce a wide range of textures and colors the jazz ensemble never had before. Boundaries are being broken, the music's going this way and that, I think we're about to hear some amazing stuff." DJs brought a whole panoply of techniques to the jazz ensemble that might include using samples taken in real time, or prerecorded samples processed through a range of techniques integrated into the jazz ensemble as they perform. They might provide compositions constructed entirely of samples against which jazz musicians play in real time; they use these compositions as a backdrop for improvisation, a technique dubbed "Bluescreen" jazz after Jon Hassell called his group Bluescreen (the idea of "bluescreen" being to take something out of its natural element and integrate it into a new environment — a technique used in filming). It is a technique used, for example, by the French group St. Germain led by DJ-conceptualist Ludovic Navarre, where prerecorded material is used in conjunction with live musicians. DJs working in a jazz combo might also freely improvise within the ensemble, using a range of techniques from scratching to sampling to provide new colors within the jazz ensemble, or they might provide sampled or electronic beats as a basis for jazz improvisation.

Beat technology has developed into a sophisticated art in its own right, as composer and performer Ben Neill notes in his essay "Breakthrough Beats: Rhythm and the Aesthetics of Contemporary Electronic Music"

> The development and evolution of beat construction in current electronic music is a highly sophisticated art form in itself, which changes rapidly in its transmission through global networks. Just as composers in earlier historical periods often worked with a given set of large scale formal parameters (sonata form, dance forms, tone poems etc.), innovative pop electronic composers use steady pulse, loop-based structures and 4/4 time as a vehicle for a wide range of compositional ideas and innovations. Shifts of tempo, subdivision, sonic manipulation and complex quantization structures are making beat science the new jazz of the 21st century. Much in the same way that jazz soloists listened to each other and incorporated each other's licks into their own solos, beat makers around the world listen and learn from each other.

Saxophonist-composer-arranger-producer Bob Belden is one of many musicians who have embraced the potential that sampling technology offers. His collaboration with trumpeter Tim Hagans, on *Animation* and the Grammy nominated *Re-Animation: Live in Montreal*, a blistering, intense, freely improvised session, illustrates how jazz improvisation can be revitalized and recontextualized by the new medium. Belden sees the new technology as a potentially enormous resource for jazz — if used creatively:

As a composer, sampling offers an unexplored universe of sound and texture. In my group we view the turntable as a synthesizer of sorts, not confined to grooves and samples, but being free to do anything, which sampling machines can do. There are no rules anymore. There is a sense of freedom one gets from dealing in the new world of artificial reality.

The new modes of listening that have emerged as a result of DJ culture are not only having an impact on the sound of contemporary jazz, both live and on record, but also on the sound of the jazz classics from the past. In 2002, Verve Records released *Verve/Remixed*, an album of remixes of classic tracks from its jazz vaults by the likes of DJ-producers Masters at Work, Mark de Clive-Lowe, and Joe Claussell, that earned sales of over 100,000 units in the United States alone. The likes of Nina Simone, Sarah Vaughan, and Shirley Horn were recontexulized for dance club audiences with new rhythms, samples, and computer-generated sounds rising out of the mix. "A new hybrid of the jazz sound can be created by sampling it," says "Little Louie" Vega and Kenny "Dope" Gonzalez, who as Masters at Work are one of the most successful of all the remix teams. "Just one riff in a song that a musician played can become a new groove. And one tone of a bass, snare, etc. can create a new sound when you put it through a sampler. By truncating the sound and putting an effect on it you can give it its own sound. Scratching a part in a jazz record can give it a whole new groove. I see it as a way of introducing the jazz sound to all the young. It will hopefully make them want to go out and get the original. Then the job is done."

Blue Note — which had already let Geoff Wilkinson of the British band Us3 loose on their back catalog to produce the hit *Hand on the Torch* in 1993 and commissioned remixes of both contemporary and back catalog by a variety of DJs — sees the development of DJ technology as a growing trend. "I almost equate the DJs and remixers, who are truly gifted and innovative things, with the renegade jazz musicians — from bebop to hard bop to free jazz and fusion," Eli Wolf, their A&R Director told *Downbeat*. As musician and writer David Toop points out in his book *Oceans of Sound*, if the music is stored on a multitrack tape, floppy, or hard disc, there can be no such thing as a final mix, just an infinite number of possibilities: "The composition has been decomposed, already, by the technology," he says. The DJ is not just an entertainer but an information handler who selects and reorders the flow of audio data. "I consider the mixes created by a DJ to be mood sculptures," says Paul D. Miller. "Based on the notion that all sonic material can be manipulated with the same ease that computers now generate composite images, the DJ combines the musical expression of other musicians with their own."

If any point in history marked the rise of the DJ in contemporary popular culture, it was that moment back in the 1980s when Grandmaster Flash sealed his place in pop history with *The Adventures of Grandmaster Flash on the Wheels of Steel*, a never-to-be-forgotten seven minutes of existing recordings spliced together using three turntables and two mixers. A record made from nothing but other records? A record made by a DJ? At first Flash concedes he didn't think anybody was going to get it. The turntable collaging technique that he used utilized two copies of the same album to isolate and extend the key riffs and percussion "breaks" that gave hip-hop its original name, "break music." Not only was the record a huge underground hit, it's now regarded as the granddaddy of sample records, a record that changed music making forever.

In the wake of Flash, rap and hip-hop mutated from urban folk art to global phenomenon with surprising speed. The first major jazz musician to pick up on the trend was Herbie Hancock, whose 1983 album *Future Shock* was produced by guerilla bassist Bill Laswell. The opening track, the Grammy winning "Rockit," fused industrial sounds and turntable scratching from Grand Mixer on turntables. "When we put the record together, we used to go a lot at the time to the Roxy," recalls Laswell. "It was on 18th or 19th Street on the West Side [of New York]. The head DJ was Africa Bambaataa and inside of that crew was DST and Grandmaster Flash, everybody would work there, do their thing. I remember even before we did the track, the initial two tracks with Herbie, we took him to the Roxy and Bambaataa was DJ-ing."

"Rockit" became one of the biggest instrumental dance hits and videos of the 1980s, but perhaps surprisingly there were initially few takers from within jazz willing to follow Hancock's path, although Laswell would pursue the creative use of turntables, samples, and sound-on-sound technology with his group Material on albums like *Hear No Evil*, *Third Power*, and *Hallucination Engine,* and on a range of other projects, often for the Axiom label. Meanwhile, in popular culture, while most hip-hop DJs were now combing the vast libraries of pop and funk for that elusive new "break" that nobody else was using, some were turning to jazz samples to flavor their music, such as A Tribe Called Quest — which used samples from the likes of Freddie Hubbard, Lee Morgan, and Cal Tjader, and had Ron Carter add the bass lines to "Verses from the Abstract" for their 1991 album *The Low End Theory* — Delasoul, Eric B and Rakim, and DJ Premier and Guru's Gangstarr.

DJ Premier had good reason to include jazz samples in his music: his grandfather had been a jazz musician. When he got together with Guru, their debut creation, "Words I Manifest" — initially released as a single and incorporated on their 1989 debut album, *No More Mr. Nice Guy* — stood out among the late-1980s obsession with James Brown samples because of Premier's use of a sample from Dizzy Gillespie's "Night in Tunisia" on the chorus. His approach complemented Guru's taste for jazz (later explored further on his collaborations with Donald Byrd and Jazzmatazz) and a successful team was born. "I was taught well on what's jazz and what's not, the commercial and the authentic stuff," explained Premier. "During the time I started making beats, a lot of people were using James Brown, which I was too. But I wanted something different that would work with Guru's vocal style, so I started using jazz samples."

For a while, a fusion between jazz, hip-hop, and rap seemed like it was going to become a neat media phenomena. There were some notable success, including "Jazz Thing" (1990), Gangstarr's smart history of jazz from Spike Lee's *Mo' Better Blues,* which succeeded in saying more in three minutes about the music's history than Ken Burns did in fifteen hours; Miles Davis on *Doo-Bop* (1992); Donald Byrd and Gangstarr's Guru on *Jazzmatazz* (1992); Greg Osby's *3-D Lifestyles* (1992); Gary Thomas's *Overkill* (1995); Don Byron's *Nu-Blaxploitation* (1998); Charlie Hunter's *Songs from the Analog Underground* (2001); and Branford Marsalis's albums with his group Buckshot La Fonque. In 1994, the *Red Hot + Cool* project brought together rappers, funksters, and hip jazz musicians in various combinations to considerable commercial success. And since the late 1980s, Steve Coleman's experiments with arty, rococo funk with his band Five Elements have been a constant presence as he got deeper into grooves influenced as much by contemporary sources as ethnic music. In 2003, pianist Matthew Shipp produced *AntiPop Consortium vs. Matthew Shipp*, a collaboration with the rap group in the title, a reexamination of whether two strong musical blood lines could coexist. "I have always been a big hip-hop fan," said Shipp. "I've always wanted to do something with beats. I've always been a fan of a lot of contemporary music — one of my favorite albums is *Low* by David Bowie. I always wanted to do something that dealt with the modern landscape, but my own take on it, being a jazz musician."

Ultimately, however, the marriage of jazz and rap produced two uneasy bedfellows. Rap privileges the vocalist in terms of verbal invention and the ability to follow the rules of rhyme and meter. As it evolved into a mass mediated form of entertainment, it released the forces of contemporary communications technology onto language, objectifying the vitality of slang and the fragmented and reactive "utopian" language of the streets. A form of rhythmic "conversation" between performer and audience, an instrumental obbligato detracted from the text, while an instrumental solo between the rap choruses appeared secondary to the main attraction: the words. Indeed, at this point in hip-hop history, it seems to be stuck in one of its own loops, endlessly repeating itself, mercilessly cannibalizing its own corpse.

However, in the late 1980's, a London group of DJs began featuring complete jazz album tracks for the dance crowds in club culture. Jazz-orientated DJs like Paul Murphy, Gilles Peterson, and Patrick Forge featured jazz and jazz-influenced music in places like the Electric Ballroom, The Wag, and Dingwalls. "People developed their own style of dancing to it," says Gilles Peterson, "fast foot movements and that sort of thing. It was big in London. In '88 or '89 I was DJ-ing in clubs with acid house DJs. I was playing instrumental funk jazz and for a joke I called it 'Acid Jazz.'" The name stuck.

"The whole Acid Jazz scene came out of jazz musicians being inspired by DJs, not the other way around," Adrian Gibson is quick to point out. British DJ Geoff Wilkinson was very much a part of this scene, organizing events at London's Jazz Café and Orange Club, and bringing jazz musicians on stage with him to interact with rappers and the collages of sound and rhythm he created at his turntables. Instead of sampling funk tracks to hip-hop beats, Wilkinson sampled classic Blue Note grooves. When Wilkinson's Us3 project was signed by the Blue Note label in 1993, his album *Hand on the Torch* became the label's best-selling record up to that point, while a track from it, "Cantaloop (Flip Fantasia)," became the dance track *du jour* in club culture for almost two years. The artful deconstruction of Herbie Hancock's 1964 "Cantaloupe Island" with its repeated funky piano sample and a delightfully sinuous trumpet solo by Britain's Gerard Prescencer in real time went down a storm with dancers.

In 1990, Briton Maurice Bernstein and South African Jonathan Rudnick brought the acid jazz phenomenon to the United States, opening the jazz-meets-hip-hop club the Giant Step in the small, marble-pillared basement of New York's Metropolis Café at 31 Union Square. "We wanted to allow a new generation to create its own spin on jazz," said Bernstein, "rather than have it defined to them by their elders." As DJs Smash and Jazzy Nice took turns spinning an eclectic mix of hip-hop, jazz, and funk music, jazz musicians and rappers vied alongside each other to take turns improvising.

"I started hanging out in clubs in NYC during the early 1990s, including the Metropolis," says composer, arranger, and saxophonist Bob Belden:

> I met DJ Smash at Metropolis in 1993. He was spinning, as an uninter-
> rupted medley, "Sidewinder," "Song For My Father," "Maiden Voyage,"
> and "Adam's Apple." He set up a loop from "Speak Like a Child" and
> then Jay Rodriguez started to play a tenor solo. This was NY Acid Jazz.
> My first exposure to what we call "sampling" had been in 1973 when in
> college, which had an Electronic Music Department. I studied contem-
> porary classical music — Stockhausen, Boulez, Varèse, Crumb, Earl
> Brown, Cage, Carter — everything was examined. We would have
> called sampling "collage," a descendant of the French *musique concrète*
> school. Miles [Davis] reflected the "Darmstadt School" with *On The
> Corner,* while Steve Reich's experiments with looping on *Come Out* we
> would call "trance" today. So I never knew the difference between the
> idea of sound and the practice of sound.

Jay Rodriguez, together with percussionist Nappy G, trombonist Josh Roseman, vibist Bill Ware, and trumpeter Fabio Morgera, formed the nucleus of a ten-piece band called Groove Collective, and their albums such as *Groove Collective* and *We the People* reaffirmed the lost link between jazz and the dance floor, albeit using a drummer rather than turntables to supply the beat (although turntables and rap were a presence on their debut album, with guests DJs Nice and Smash). "All those guys who are recreating older styles and sounds . . . haven't come out with their own thing," said Nappy G, "We're trying to create something totally original."

However, despite successes of Us3, Digable Plants's *Reachin'*, or Ronny Jordan's *The Antidote*, the acid jazz craze flared briefly, but in the end commercial and market forces commandeered it. Any type of music, it seemed, from 1970s disco music to 1960s film soundtrack music, was dubbed "acid jazz." The phenomenon came and went, weighed down by too many interests trying to cash in on it. But the genie was out of the bottle. Several jazz musicians were now curious about the potential turn-table, and sampling technology had to reimagine their music.

"It was like the birth of bebop," says the French trumpet player Erik Truffaz. "It didn't come from just Charlie Parker or Dizzy Gillespie, it came from a lot of people, but afterwards we only speak of the well known. But maybe we all contribute by adding one small stone to build this castle." These musicians, working along similar lines and guided by their instincts, taste, and musical curiosity gradually began finding ways to integrate electronics — initially turntable and sampling technology, later adding computer programming — lurking around the periphery of jazz for so long, as new ingredients in their music.

By the late 1990s and early millennium, guitarist John Scofield observed in *Downbeat* magazine that the new technology had now become so pervasive it could no longer be ignored. Many artists began embracing technology, using it to enhance their personal visions. Trumpeter Dave Douglas's path into using electronics was one of gradual experimentation, to see what role it might play in his music. These experiments culminated in his 2003 CD, *Freak In*, which provides an excellent example of the thoughtful integration of the new electronic technology into the jazz ensemble. He explained:

> On previous records like *Sanctuary* and *Witness* I always wrote so that the [electronic] players would interact with the pieces and the band in real time. The idea was to document an actual performance in which the electronics participated in the flow of the music like in any other standard "jazz" performance. That's an approach that I revere and truly believe in as a player and composer. What I am about to say does not mean that I want to abandon that kind of playing, [but] I came to feel that that expectation for electronic music was unrealistic, that it was a handicap for the electronic players. Those sounds work much better under the microscope of the studio. The idea of *Freak In* was to create a sense of flow, of fluency that live bands get but with additional freedom of being able to really work the electronics in ways that their technology was created for. I think there is a big future for the use of this process in the music that's coming out of jazz.

Pianist Matthew Shipp began experimenting with the new technology as a sonic palette to color and broaden the expressive range of his music on *Nu-Bop* and *Equilibrium* for the Blue Series label in 2002 and 2003, respectively. Shipp has been a vocal critic of the jazz industry, which he calls the "death industry," pointing out how musicians only become "marketable" after they die, when their work can be easily and tidily "summarized." For Shipp, musicians who are reluctant to part company with the past are missing out on an opportunity to redefine their art in the present. "What a huge, huge waste," he says. "I've seen musicians sitting around drinking whiskey trying to pretend they're Lester Young or something — I guess I don't need to say how tired that is. It has nothing to do with how or why music is made today."

As a creative artist, Shipp incorporated electronic technology into his music as a means of reflecting the contemporary environment in which we live. "The music has to take into account that people's psyches are shaped by what is going around them," he explains:

> I live in an urban setting. There's lots of things I take in — sounds and the ambience of the street — that I soak into my subconscious just from walking around the city and feeling the rhythm of city and just knowing how our lives are changed now just because of the Internet, how our lives changed because of many machines we have to deal with. There's things in the environment, things in my consciousness, just living in the world today that I'm trying to connect to, and I've been feeling that making jazz albums as we've known has not been adequate for me personally to connect to those things.

For Shipp, samples provide the obstacles that inspire creativity. "What I find very interesting is dealing with the machine in my music, especially coming from a 'classical free jazz tradition,'" he says. "The machine is something that takes you outside yourself, but I'm actually finding the machine is allowing [me] to connect more inwardly with myself, it's a kind of a paradox but it's really fascinating how it's working out."

Shipp talks of creating a new emotional language for jazz in the twenty-first century, one that comes in bursts of information from a variety of sources:

> I'm interested in the idea of syntax feeding the nervous system, and discreet little musical phrases forming its own nervous system, and how acoustic instruments relate to the computer, and how all these things

form their own nexus, urban jungle, nervous system, information machine — whatever you want to call it. I'm interested in making my albums syntax generators, where you can soak your brain in the language.

When he became musical director of the Blue Series imprint of the New York–based Thirsty Ear label, Shipp had the opportunity to create a label with its own unique musical identity, something that he likens to early ECM, the Munich-based jazz label formed in 1969 that embraced musicians from the avant-garde who could also move freely between "inside" and "outside" playing. Under Shipp's musical direction, the Blue Series has become something of a standard bearer of this new direction in jazz in America, beating a pathway to a new jazz frontier through a diversity of approaches.

On *Masses* and *Amassed*, Shipp brings together Spring Heel Jack, the British electronica duo of John Coxon and Ashley Wales, whose roots are in drum 'n' bass, and a pool of improvisers that include himself, trumpeters Roy Campbell and Kenny Wheeler, reedists Evan Parker, Tim Berne, and Daniel Carter, bassist William Parker, and drummers Guillermo E. Brown and Han Bennink. The tracks were worked up in real time and then recombined, piece by piece, into a new jazz tongue. Shipp says that, as a jazz musician, he "had never conceived of putting an album together that way, and I know most of the albums we do I don't put together that way even though some parts are. But the idea of doing an album completely by samples, or completely by pasting together painstakingly measure by measure, that whole idea intrigued me — as far as being an improviser and a free jazz player I don't mind giving up the control to the production aspect to try and create a new sound."

John Coxon of Spring Heel Jack explains the techniques he and his partner Ashley Wales brought to the Blue Series projects:

> The thing about the records we've been making for Thirsty Ear is that each track is a different sound world. In traditional bands — whether jazz or any kind of band — you can't control the environment as much as you can now, the sonic environment. Basically you have the sound of the band doing their set live or in the studio, whereas now with the technology it is very, very easy to create a completely different sound world for those instruments to fit in.

In 2003, the Spring Heel Jack project took to the road with an eight-day tour through the United Kingdom with Coxon, Wales, and

"J Spaceman," the guitarist from Spiritualized, plus Evan Parker, Shipp, William Parker, and Han Bennink. The concerts at Brighton and Bath were released as *Spring Heel Jack Live* and offer two sets of fascinating, freely improvised dialogues, primarily featuring Shipp and Evan Parker, against a backdrop of samples and electronic sounds. "This wasn't like free jazz, or Spring Heel Jack. But it was an amazing, heartbreaking sound," said *The Guardian*.

The problem faced by many artists was that while they wanted to retain the legitimacy conferred on them by the jazz tradition, they also wanted to break free from its constraints. In March 2001, Eli Wolf, head of Blue Note Records A&R department, told the *New York Daily News* that he now felt there were young musicians out there "who possess a high caliber of musicianship but don't want to get caught in that historical quagmire. They're in tune with what is going on today in music and not just the past. Traditional artists sometimes get stuck back there."

By the early 2000s, however, a more inclusive view of jazz was being reflected by an increasing number of musicians, even those formerly associated with the more intractable line associated with the post–Wynton Marsalis neoconservatives. Bassist Christian McBride's 2003 album *Vertical Vision* paid homage to the electric jazz of 1970's Weather Report and incorporated electronica influences; trumpeter Roy Hargrove came up with a eccentric bag of influences from D'Angelo to rappers Common and Q-Tip and a whole lot more on 2003's *RH Factor*; while trumpeter Nicholas Payton, whose previous album *Dear Louis* was an amiable tribute to Louis Armstrong, released *Sonic Trance* in 2003 inspired by 1970's electric Miles Davis. "I knew after I recorded *Dear Louis* that I was closing a chapter on the kind of records I wanted to make," he said:

> I'm still playing jazz but from the perspective of a man of my age and experiences. All the musicians I love and respect, like Ornette Coleman, John Coltrane and Bill Evans made statements that had not only personal relevance to their lives, but cultural relevancy to the times in which they lived. It was significant for me to do a project that embodied that.

Although saxophonist Jan Garbarek built his reputation on acoustic playing, to the extent the album *Dis* was recorded with a wind harp, he began making sparing use of electronics on albums such as *All Those Born with Wings* and *Visible World*. However, on his 2004 album *In Praise of Dreams*, electronics became central to the album's construction. Garbarek composed directly onto a laptop and added the solos later in real time. "It is very exciting for me also to work with new sound possibilities — I just consider them another source of sound," he says:

> Some people are against using sampling or synthesizers or whatever. I don't have this distinction, they can be used for better or for worse. While on tour I had my computer and all the software I needed. I ended up doing more in the computer with all the sampling and synths, all those things available to me there. And then I realised I was well on my way to an album. I played the "sketches" [on computer] for Manfred Eicher [of ECM], and I had used some mock-ups, some samples of a viola, and he suggested right away that we try and get Kim Kashkashian. I also wanted to have Manu Katché because I wanted a drummer who could find his way in between all the other pre-composed drum patterns I had used, I didn't want to lose those, and Manu is very used to that sort of work.

In one step, Garbarek had recontextualized his music within the twenty-first century by deftly changing the musical backdrop. "That's the only thing I can change," he says. "I am only me, that's a constant, sometimes you look in the mirror and you want to see something else, but you have to face up to your face! One way of creating a difference is to change the surroundings, and Miles [Davis], he was the master of reinventing the context, he seems to me to be playing quite similarly, to my ears, throughout most of his career, as a trumpet player, but always found a different backdrop."

The Chicago jazz underground has over the years acquired a reputation as a hothouse of experimentation, in which electronics frequently play a part. Bands like Isotope 217, Brokeback, and Tortoise may be closer to the world of rock than jazz, but are refreshingly open minded and have acquired a dedicated following among progressive jazz audiences as a result. Tortoise, for example, was the subject of a major feature in *Downbeat* magazine in 2004. "We're not interested in being dogmatic about anything," percussionist John McEntire said:

One of the main concepts when we started the group is that we're not interested in formula or trying to do anything in a particular way. We're creating our own set of rules and expectations for everything that we do and that has more to do with the spirit of jazz than the spirit of pop, rock or doing things by rote.

It is this openness to musical ideas that has come to define the Windy City's jazz scene. "The most characteristic elements about Chicago's underground scene are its scrappy do-it-yourself attitude and a nonchalant openness to working with other forms and players from those other scenes," points out Peter Margasak, jazz critic of the *Chicago Reader*:

In terms of musical flexibility, Ken Vandermark's Spaceways project touches on hard funk and dub reggae, while his large-scale Territory Band project mixes extended composition with abstract electronic noise, first contributed by Chicago's Kevin Drumm and now by Norway's Lasse Marhaug. The Chicago Underground groups freely mix in electronic rhythms and textures, and it's wonderful guitarist Jeff Parker not only keeps busy playing in a wide variety of jazz contexts, but he's also a member of the adventurous rock band Tortoise. A younger, post-Vandermark crew has also emerged, dialing down from the free jazz bluster of the '90s in favor of a more contemplative approach that draws on everything from Morton Feldman to live electronic manipulations. Again, it's now the norm for these players to be involved in all sorts of disparate projects, regardless of genre. Various incarnations of the Chicago Underground Duo/Trio/Quartet are still intermittently active but Rob Mazurek now lives in Brazil, although he still spends a good chunk of time touring in Europe and the US. None of the most active venues today — the Hungry Brain, 3030, Candlestick Maker, and the Empty Bottle — are traditional or perfect, but they allow for cheap admissions and total creative control. Most of them are artist-booked. I think this modus operandi has influenced musicians from all over the US, applying a kind of punk rock ethos to creative music.

Across Europe, the rise of digital technology was quickly embraced by many young jazz musicians from the mid-1990s. Among the most innovative are Norwegian pianist–sound producer Bugge Wesseltoft and vocalist Sidsel Endressen. Their collaborative albums, including *Out Here*, *In There*, and *Undertow*, combine Endressen's haunting vocal style, which often dispenses with lyrics and imitates the ambient sounds of nature in the frozen north, with Wesseltoft's vast array of acoustic and electrically generated sounds to create memorable, improvised etudes.

An accomplished pianist who has appeared as a sideman on several albums by the likes of Arlid Andersen and Jan Garbarek, Wesseltoft had a fairly orthodox introduction to jazz from his father, a jazz guitarist. Taking up the piano at an early age, *Kind of Blue* was his first inspiration, and by his midteens he was highly active in Norwegian jazz. "In Norway, in Scandanavia, once you reach a certain point, you are encouraged to find your own voice," he says. "As a pianist myself, I was taught early on it's no good copying McCoy Tyner, or Bill Evans, or whoever. There are already hundreds of musicians in America who do that. We want to find our own voice that speaks of where we come from. I haven't grown up in New York, so I see things differently."

Around 1993 to 1994, Wesseltoft was also a pioneer in adapting electronic technology to the rhythms from European club culture as a basis for jazz improvisation. Initially, beat-driven club music was viewed as a tool to keep the dancers on the floor, but gradually musicians in both jazz and popular culture sensed potential and possibilities in the complex rhythmic schemes used in dance music and began experimenting with them by breaking them apart and recombining them, and, in the case of Wesseltoft, working with a DJ to find ways in which they could be adapted to jazz improvisation. Wesseltoft's own *New Conception of Jazz* on his Jazzland label, recorded in 1995 but originally released in Europe in 1998, unexpectedly became a best seller in the European jazz underground. It reached number 40 on the top album chart and received a Norwegian Grammy for Jazz Album of the Year. Wesseltoft comments:

> At the time I recorded it I wanted something new and I was fascinated by the sounds coming out of club culture in Norway, playing these records from Britain. A friend of mine is a DJ and I spent three months going around the clubs checking the music out, trying to figure out a way how I could use it to play my kind of thing.
>
> I like to improvise over a form of soundscapes if you like. I'm fascinated by building rhythmic elements and manipulating sound over time. To me that's more interesting and creative than playing the traditional theme — solo — theme thing.

The New Conception of Jazz was followed by *Sharin'*, a heterogeneous mix of ambient sound washes, techno beats, and jazz improvisation. Jonas Lonna, a DJ who has worked extensively with Wesseltoft, explains his preference for incorporating techno beats: "Lots of the hip-hop stuff that has jazz elements uses old jazz samples that have already been heard and doesn't feel 'fresh.' . . . house and techno have so many more different subdivisions than hip-hop and offers new ways to go."

Fellow Norwegian Nils Petter Molvaer's *Khmer* was an unexpected hit for the ECM label on the European jazz underground in 1997 to 1998. It led to Molvaer's nomination for the prestigious Nordic Council Music Prize 2000 and won several awards, including the annual prize of the German Record Critics (*Preis der Deutschen Schallplattenkritik*), a Norwegian Grammy for Best Jazz Album, and was voted Jazz Record of the Year by the *Los Angeles Times*. Molvaer's music reflects the impact of European House, Techno, and Ambient rhythms on the Oslo jazz underground. "I like the minimalistic grooves of European House, very trancey which you can easily relate to African music," he says. "I work with delays to make the rhythm float, so to speak. Some of the offbeats in rhythms like 7/8 and 9/16 have roots in an old tradition of ethnic musics which I try and relate to the present."

Born in Sula on the northwest coast of Norway in 1960 and the son of a well-known jazz musician, Molvaer played bass, drums, and keyboards before finally deciding to study trumpet. He has performed with Elvin Jones, George Russell, and Gary Peacock, and in 1982 he joined bassist Arlid Andersen's genre-stretching group Masquelero, where he remained for most of the 1980s. "Ever since I started in Masquelero I was listening to a lot of different stuff from Brian Eno to Jon Hassell to Bill Laswell, and when it came time to go out on my own I wanted to mix all these ideas," says Molvaer.

By the time he came to begin work on *Khmer*, Molvaer had already appeared on eight ECM albums, so it was only natural for him to approach Manfred Eicher, the head of the label, with his new project. A genuine road warrior, Molvaer spearheaded the sound of jazz and electronics across Europe while touring his album *Khmer*, his success reinforced by his follow-up album *Solid Ether*.

Guitarist Eivind Aarset was central to the success of Nils Petter Molvaer's group from 1997 to 2002. His debut as a leader in his own right on records came in 1998 with *Electronique Noir*, an album that emerged from a suite of compositions he called "7," originally commissioned by the Norwegian Festival Maijazz 97. At the time it received little attention outside of Norway. Powerful, yet strangely moving tracks such as "Dark Moisture" and "Entrance/U-Bahn" announced a new voice in contemporary jazz, willing to take the music to a level of intensity, depth, and excitement through an incredible range of sounds coaxed out of his guitar through a baffling array of sound-processing devices.

Adopting the name Electronique Noir for his band, the group became the focus for Aarset's questing, experimental style. Along with his most frequent associates, Marius Reksjo on bass and electric bass and Wetle Holte on drums, he developed a musical understanding that allowed his music to evolve and grow. His second album, *Light Extracts* from 2003, continued to refine his unique vision, the track "Between Signal and Noise" reflecting the impact of club culture rhythms. "What drew me to this music was the hypnotic grooves and musical freedom I found," says Aarset. "There's no established rules or tradition in what I am doing, so you make the rules up as you go along. Rhythm is the center of the music, the landscape the soloist travels through. It's fresh territory and I have no idea where this scene will end up, but there's a lot of great sounds and new music being created which makes it such an exciting scene."

The group Wibutee (the title, taken from Sanskrit, means "Holy Ashes") emerged from the Norwegian jazz underground in the late 1990s to receive considerable acclaim across Europe. "For us, jazz is an ever renewing music," says the band's tenor saxophonist Hakon Kornstad. "It has to be. It has to absorb influences from other music styles, like it has always done because it is a mixture of music, a 'bastard music.' We wanted to explore grooves. The group all met in [the Trondheim] music conservatory, and we wanted to implement new ideas into jazz; we liked the idea of being inspired by new things instead of having to be inspired by the old jazz." In live performances, the group's sonic manipulations are impressive; each band member has a laptop and is responsible for his own sound, which is then put through the mixing desk. "All the tools that used to be reserved for the mastering engineer can now — or at least can be if you're that way inclined — become part of the performance. This opens up interesting possibilities," points out producer Leo @ Blu Mar Ten.

The significant point about these European bands was they were communicating with younger audiences and succeeding in demystifying jazz on their own terms. The vibe from the Norwegian group Jaga Jazzist, for example, began in the Oslo jazz underground and went overground with the release of *A Living Room Hush* in 2001. But while their first album made audiences across Europe prick up their ears, their live performances garnered rave reviews wherever they played. "Jaga Jazzist succeed where so many others fail, creating a space where the challenging, chaotic and avant garde join forces with the accessible, beautiful and traditional," said *DJ* magazine. In 2003, during their tour to support their second album, *The Stix,* a line of fans, three and four deep stretching 500 yards around the block, waited to hear them at the Vossa Jazz Festival in Norway. Composed mostly of under-thirty-somethings, the spectators jammed themselves around the bandstand like a rock concert and responded to every solo by waving their arms in the air. After the concert, the band's drummer, cheerleader, and front man Martin Hornveth said that they were receiving similar enthusiastic responses to their performances across Europe.

Formed in 1994 in Tonsberg, a town outside Oslo, Jaga Jazzist developed in the comparative isolation of a small, self-contained music scene. The nucleus of the band is Hornveth, his brother Lars (tenor sax, bass clarinet, and electric guitar) — who was fourteen years old when the band was formed — and their sister Line, who gives the band its backbone with her powerful tuba parts. All ten members of Jaga Jazzist play several instruments, but the basic lineup comprises tuba, vibes, trumpet, saxes, bass clarinet, keyboards, electronics, bass (acoustic and electric), guitar, and acoustic and electronic drums. Six members of the current lineup have been with the band since the beginning, which explains how the band really plays from inside the music.

"The Oslo scene has all types of bands and all this different sounding music," Hornveth says, "that's how we fit in, we're different, because everybody there is different! In our band, everybody doubles, it frees people up for new ideas, rather than just playing saxophone all night. We love the sound of two bass clarinets, we also double up other instruments. It's not just jazz solos or jazz and electronics, we try and get a group sound of our own."

Their convoluted, time-change, rollercoaster arrangements achieved a fascinating balance between acoustic jazz and electronica. On stage for ninety minutes without a break or a page of music in sight, their musical identity is shaped by the unexpectedly sophisticated compositions whose relentless melodicism and avant-garde flourishes unwind in all sorts of unexpected directions. Sitting down and writing for a large ensemble is hard, often thankless work, which is why good, well-realized compositions are rare. That discipline rubs off on the soloists, who don't try and blow each other off the stand but know what to say within the context of the arrangements to make the music work, a communal effort that creates their vivid group identity.

The key cohesive is Martin Hornveth's constant and insinuating percussion presence, both live and on record, using a mixture of kit and drum machine. "I use the Akai MPC2000 live because its very good for live triggering and drum machine playback," he explained. "The large pads make it easy to control the machine and play live drums at the same time. We love playing live and everything we do is approached with that in mind. Maybe you could say we play electronic music with live instruments."

Most of the arrangements came from Lars Hornveth, whose constantly shifting tonal colors, rhythmic shifts, and mood changes avoid collage through fluid juxtaposition and deft writing skills. "We start off with written arrangements then improvise with different sounds and arrangements," says his brother Martin. "We try and write 'too much' music so we can select the best parts and lose the rest. On the albums we try and get that energetic live feel and the cut-up electronics. We're very focussed on the collectivity and the fact we have a unique instrumentation. We like to combine a good melody with unusual orchestration also weird beats and noise. I think people are open for new sounds and complex electronic music. The use of electronics is set to grow fast."

While most of these bands adapted various combinations and recombinations of European techno and house rhythms, another potential direction was inspired by the electronica subgenre known as drum 'n' bass that evolved out of London's jungle scene. The drum 'n' bass style has its roots in reggae (which in turn has its roots in American jazz) and is played in real time but can easily be adapted to technology. "When loops started appearing on the scene I heard immediately the possibilities," says Belden, who utilized drum 'n' bass loops on *Re-Animation: Live*:

> Acid jazz had to get to drum 'n' bass because the tempo of acid jazz was groovy but not Charlie Parker. Drum 'n' bass introduced the "Parker" tempo to the popular subculture. I heard Tony Williams when I heard Roni Size. That's when I knew. Drum 'n' bass adapted this groove to a programmed beat or beats and samples were used as orchestration or an inference of melody.

For the French pianist Laurent de Wilde — author of an acclaimed biography of Thelonious Monk, who has worked on the New York City scene with the likes of saxophonist Greg Osby — drum 'n' bass opened up a new world:

> The drum 'n' bass and the jungle and all that music that comes from London and Europe clubs in general has kind of replaced the acoustic groove with electronic grooves and delivers the same feeling, and the same groove, and it's a great basis for improvisation and composition. The groove can be played many different ways, not only with an acoustic bass and a trap kit, it can be achieved through sampling. . . . I felt pretty bad from being from a generation that didn't witness any revolution in jazz. But all that electronic stuff is a great technological leap forward and is a great chance for my generation and younger to come up with something of value.

Another Frenchman, trumpeter Erik Truffaz, has remained steadfastly acoustic, but as can be heard on his three CDs for Blue Note, he also speaks of how he adapted the flexibility of drum 'n' bass to a jazz context. Truffaz notes, "My album *Bending New Corners* was influenced by bebop and drum 'n' bass, and from then our public changed: we find young people, 15 years to 30, in our audience, which is good."

In Britain, saxophonist Courtney Pine, who in the 1980s established himself as a formidable tradition-based improviser who was invited to join the Jazz Messengers by Art Blakey, found that electronics and rhythms from popular culture — from hip-hop to the drum 'n' bass of Ronnie Size, Squarepusher, and Goldie — opened up new directions for his music. "We all have computers," he told me in 2000. "Everyone in the band has a computer and we're thinking that way. And that really is what sets us aside from the American scene. They have computers but they don't utilize them in their musical outlook where we would use it." On albums such as *Devotion* and *Back in the Day,* Pine mixes powerful, Coltrane-inspired saxophone with contemporary influences. "It seemed that at a certain point we got out playing music for the people," he says:

> But if you go back in the tradition Louis Armstrong and Sidney Bechet, this is what they were doing, every note was for the audience to react to, they played notes that made people want to move, and that's what I'm trying to do. This is what jazz should be, a reflection of life. There is a new scene unfolding so for me I am very happy to be a part of it.

Leeds College of Music graduate Matthew Bourne attracted considerable attention after winning the Perrier Young Jazz Award in 2001. A startlingly inventive pianist, his solo performances have received considerable acclaim across Europe, especially for his creative use of samples, which offset what is very intense, demanding music with passages of humor that draws the audience into his music. "When I entered the Perrier I did it solo," he said. "I wanted to play 'Pure Imagination' from *Willie Wonker and the Chocolate Factory* and I started to transcribe that and thought some of this dialogue [from the film] is quite funny, so I decided to have some dialogue in the background when I was playing the tune. I thought that really works, so I continued [using samples] when I do solo work. I find combinations of dialogue, it's all intuitive it's not like I've gone about it scientifically, more often than not I just put the samples in if they've got emotional resonance." To ensure spontaneity, Bourne never uses the same samples twice.

Parallel to his solo career is his work with small ensembles: The Trio, Metropolis, The Distortion Trio, The Electric Dr M, and Bourne, Davis, Kane. "I think Matthew's approach to performance is refreshing and contains an element of risk-taking that is often lacking on the concert platform," says Dr. Tony Whyton, assistant head of Higher Education at Leeds College of Music in 2003. "This is particularly true for young jazz performers who are keen to establish their reputation and find it difficult to escape the influence of jazz's 'elder statesmen.' This leads to performances which blend new takes on 'Giant Steps' through to political commentary on the Bush administration!"

On his album *The Electric Dr M* (2003), Bourne plays Fender Rhodes piano and an old analogue synthesizer and has developed a remarkable rapport with his group: two drummers, bass, and guitar. Every number is intensely rhythmical, yet spontaneously conceived. "We're all into different types of music," explains Bourne, "each person brings their thing. We don't have an aiming-point like, 'This is going to be a drum 'n' bass groove,' we don't even think about it, we just sit and play." Here was somebody genuinely developing an interesting take on jazz, naturally informed by developments in electronic dance and ambient music, yet subservient to neither.

The mysterious band The Bays, comprising Jamie Odell and/or Simon Richmond on keyboards, Chris Taylor on bass, Andy Gangadeen on drums, and a revolving cast of DJ's on electronics, also produces unbroken sets of totally improvised music that can mutate from ambient, techno, house, to drum 'n' bass. "Absolutely nothing is pre-planned," says Chris Taylor. "The tempo may start at about 90 bpm [hip-hop tempo], but not always, and we often end on some drum 'n' bass, but apart from that nothing is set at all. No keys or themes are ever predetermined even as a kind of safety net or back-up plan and this can make the bigger gigs quite nerve wracking." The band flies in the face of music business norms and have refused major label record deals, instead freely giving away their music from their website on music files; at the Big Chill concert series in England in 2004, they gave away hundreds of CDs of previous gigs from the main concert stage and invited fans to make further copies. "The Bays manifesto of raw improvisation and pure creative synergy is starting to cause major tremors at all levels of the music industry channeling its firmly entrenched and dearly held preconceptions about live performance," said the late John Peel, the BBC radio presenter, "Through their relentless giging schedule and tireless devotion to their art, The Bays have ripped up the rule book and are debunking musical convention wherever they go."

The Bays' totally spontaneous approach to improvisation is also a characteristic of the Australian trio The Necks, comprising Chris Abrahams on piano, Lloyd Swanton on bass, and Tony Buck on drums. Formed in 1988, the band has developed a huge underground following. Albums such as *Hanging Gardens*, *Aether*, or the live four CD set *The Necks* comprising "Athenaeum," "Homebush," "Quay" and "Radio" reveal the diversity of their approach, which has been likened to ambient, minimalism, Gamelan, and Miles Davis's *In a Silent Way*. "Miles Davis's *In a Silent Way* definitely has that spaciousness we aspire to. All of us would agree that's been a big influence," Swanton told *The Guardian*.

The emergence of the UK's Cinematic Orchestra represented a direct result of DJ culture affecting jazz. The brainchild of DJ Jason Swinscoe, The Cinematic Orchestra turned sample culture on its head. The orchestra's debut album from 1999, *Motion*, combined studio technology and live playing to an extent where it was impossible to tell one from the other, an organic sounding whole that was simultaneously raw and refined. Swinscoe's careful arrangements of samples and resamples of both live and prerecorded material were, in effect, an extension of Teo Macero's cut 'n' paste, reel-to-reel editing methods for Miles Davis in the 1970s.

Influenced by film scores (hence the group's name), Swinscoe's technique is to compose pieces through the juxtaposition of samples and then teach his band — which included Tom Chant on saxophones, Phil France on bass, Luke Flowers on drums with Patrick Carpenter on turntables — the composition. The art of bringing his compositions to life, in spite of the heavy reliance on the generally rigid digital tools he uses, lay in the understanding of the musicians to interpret the material with feeling. "Then it would go off with its own life," said Swinscoe, "and the original sample would become redundant."

The Cinematic Orchestra's live performances, a mixture of live and sampled playing, were often a hypnotic blend of the old and new, "What results has grandiose sweep, but the band are actually only a quintet," said *The Guardian*. The track "Night of the Iguana" for example, prompts "I-can't-believe-it's-not-live" cries from even the most technologically literate musicians. Their second album, *Every Day*, from 2002 featured the deep soul vocals of Fontella Bass and the gruff storytelling of Roots Manuva. "The vibe felt just right," said Swinscoe. "I knew that we were about to make something exciting and honest. All we had to do was give Fontella the freedom to express herself."

While Swinscoe's Cinematic Orchestra was a quintet, producer, DJ, and arch conceptualist Matthew Herbert's (aka Wishmountain, Doctor Rockit, and Herbert) Big Band was exactly that, a seventeen-piece orchestra plus electronics. The son of a BBC sound engineer, Herbert's childhood study of piano and violin was complemented by an exposure to electronic composition and music technology. In 2001, he was asked to write three pieces for a big band as part of the score for a French musical *Le Defi*, directed by choreographer Blanca Li. One of these pieces, "Singing in the Rain" incorporated samples of the band, chopping up recordings, looping, splicing, and generally manipulating the raw material to create a new and totally distinct sound. Debuting at the Montreux Jazz Festival, the subsequent album, *Goodbye Swingtime* (2002), was a reaction against a stagnant electronic music scene Matthew perceived as far more conservative than the sounds of Sun Ra and Charles Mingus, who were his guiding lights. "House never surprises me any more," he lamented. "It's very lazy and that's something I don't admire, in music or in life."

Working with arranger Pete Wraight, Herbert deconstructed and reconstructed the big band recordings in an electronic environment. The imminent invasion of Iraq at the time prompted the politically conscious Herbert to use recordings of people dropping their local phone books from various heights. *Downbeat* gave the album three stars; "Electronics permeate the music," said Jon Andrews' review, "sometimes in the form of atmospheric samples, or Herbert's signature glitches." Live, the band aspired to Brecht's idea of epic theatre, albeit with tongue placed firmly in the cheek, with Herbert's compositions bringing to mind maverick Raymond Scott's writing in the 1930s, which occasionally swung, but more often achieved smart effects.

In Belgium, pianist Marc Moulin represented an important link between today's electronic experimentation and its more left-field origins in the early 1970s jazz-rock scene. Beginning as a pianist on the vibrant European jazz scene of the early 1960s, he formed a trio in 1961 and won several prizes at European jazz festivals, as well as accompanying the likes of Nathan Davis and Johnny Griffin. In 1971 he formed the jazz-rock ensemble Placebo and recorded *Ball of Eyes* for CBS Belgium. While it's possible to trace lines of input from the American jazz-rock scene (Herbie Hancock, George Duke, Miles Davis), Placebo's debut album was sonically and compositionally ahead of its time; the drumming on "Humpty Dumpty," for example, could well have been programmed on a MPC3000 or an SP1200 for a contemporary hip-hop track. By 1973, and their second album *1973*, their compositions had become more abstract and experimental. Moulin also had a trio known as Sam Suffy, and his use of synthesized basslines provides another link to contemporary club culture. During the 1980s he led a band called Telex, whose albums are still cited as a major influence on numerous House and Techno producers in the early Chicago and Detroit days; his track "Moscow Discow" was even heard on American dance floors.

In the 1990s, Moulin was an intermittent presence in music (he is also a journalist, producer, playwright, DJ, and critic), but when his work resurfaced on the remix project *I Don't Like Music* by the likes of Carl Craig, Deep Dish, T-Power, and Matthew Herbert, he was invited by Blue Note in Belgium to produce an album reflecting the new dynamic flowing through European jazz. Both *Top Secret* (2001), which includes a sample of his Sam Suffy past on "In My Room," and *Entertainment* (2004) use sampling and club culture rhythms, but seen through the prism of jazz musicians with solos from the likes of guitarist Philip Catherine and trumpeter Bert Joris, leader of the Brussels Jazz Orchestra.

Across Europe, club culture rhythms have provided a new basis from which to underpin jazz improvisation. In Finland, there were bands such as RinneRadio, Nusprirt Helsinki, the Five Corners Quintet, and the free electronic band Gnomus. France spawned bands such as the Metropolitan Jazz Affair, Julien Lourau's ensemble, Ntoumos, Magic Malik, and

Ludovic Navarre's St. Germain (whose live performances are quite different than their huge hit *Tourist*, because of the use of real time soloists over the DJ constructed musical backdrops). The dynamic French group Nojazz, whose eponymous debut album was produced by Teo Macero, had been touring for two years before recording, and the explosive energy of their live performances was captured on tracks such as "Jungle Out" and "Medina." German bands such as Jazzanova and Trancegroove lived on the edge of club culture.

Yet while both popular and DJ culture provided a source of inspiration for many jazz musicians, others were influenced by European classical composers who were deeply involved in electronic music such as Karlheinz Stockhausen, Luigi Nono, Luciano Berio, and György Ligeti, whose highly abstract music cut itself free from traditional musical timbres and narrative, and was driven by electronically generated sounds. The Norwegian group Supersilent took inspiration from the work of Arne Nordheim, a pioneer of electronic music in Norway, thanks to his influential works *Aftonland (Evening Land)* (1956), *Canzona* (1960), and *Epitaffio* (1963). Supersilent was formed in Oslo in 1997, when producer and sound artist Helger Sten approached the free jazz trio Veslefrekk — comprising Arve Henriksen on trumpet, Stale Storkøkken on keyboards, and Jarle Vespestad on drums — with the idea of forming a new quartet. Sten saw the use of electronics as adding a new instrument to the band's lineup. Their first album, a triple CD set called *Supersilent 1-3*, was released in early 1998 yet their names did not appear on the CD, or their subsequent releases, because they wanted to be judged in terms of a group concept where no one's individual personality dominated. Sten believed the use of electronics should be guided by the improviser's impulse. "Today it's very popular to use such technology," he said.

> But you have to apply some rules, as always. You really have to integrate it and make it a great musical experience for yourself and the people who listen to it. I think the meeting [between electronics and jazz] has to be the result of a genuine musical expression, and has to be a genuine musical adventure. You are at the point where you can use sound like an instrument. When you have sound as a tool you can use any pitch in any variation; you can use a lot of color — it's a big, wide spectrum — and it opens up a new universe and it seems very natural to use it inside jazz, because it has been the nature of jazz to experiment and evolve new expressionism. I think jazz really needs to expand anyway, because its been standing quite still for a long time.

Sten's own recordings, under the pseudonym Deathprod, such as *Morals and Dogma* (2004), occupy a position midway between experimental avant-garde jazz and avant-garde classical.

Other groups taking their inspiration from twentieth-century electronic composers included trumpeter Markus Stockhausen's *Karta* (2000) with drummer Patrice Héral providing live electronics in real time and saxophonist Evan Parker's Electro-Acoustic ensemble. On *Drawn Inward* (1999) and *Memory/Vision* (2002), Parker has three and four musicians engaged entirely in sound processing in real time alongside his sidemen. The result, as the *Boston Globe* noted, was, "A bizarre, sometimes creepy, sometimes enchanting vision of improvisation."

Electronics, in all its manifestations, is now being seized upon as a catalyst to trigger change, to reimagine the overall architecture of the music in a way that reflects the world in which we live today. Artistic authority is gained, as Milton Babbitt suggests, by changing the context, and thus altering the discourse of musical meaning. If playful ironic commentary has replaced the 1960s "New Thing" angst, it's an acknowledgment that the artistic experiences of today often end up as consumer products of tomorrow. Maybe this is the price of mixing art and technological media, and breaking down boundaries between high, popular, and mass art styles, so that "innovative" and "new" now replace the term "avant-garde" in the service of creating a "new" future. Ultimately, however, the challenge for jazz musicians still remains to reinvent the music in a way that is relevant to the time frame in which they find themselves. "An important function that jazz musicians have is to reconcile their vision of music with the current state of the universe," says guitarist Pat Metheny. "I think that part of the deal is rarely reflected in the modern jazz of our time and that, to me, is an important part of what we've got to do."

However, evolution — of jazz reinventing itself in the present — is not an exclusionary process. Past styles of jazz will continue to coexist alongside the new, as has happened throughout the music's history; the height of the big band era, for example, saw the emergence of bebop and a New Orleans revival. But the key to any musical renewal emerges from the basic premise that from its very beginnings jazz was a pluralistic music. One of its great practitioners, Ferdinand "Jelly Roll" Morton argued that the music should always include a "Spanish tinge" and the unambiguous *habenera* section in "St. Louis Blues," published by W. C. Handy in 1914, is revealing of jazz's practice of appropriation, an important, if often neglected, feature of a music. The use of appropriation is seldom commented upon, yet it is a recurring theme in the subsequent evolution of the music and reveals a continuing dialogue not only with popular culture but other musical forms to broaden the scope of jazz expressionism.

Mass culture and modernist high culture had been in dialogue since the mid-nineteenth century, modernism appropriating whatever elements it needed for experiment and articulation. Jazz, an exemplary expression of the modernist impulse in American culture, merely continued this practice, including — in perhaps the most controversial moment in contemporary jazz history — the appropriation of the rhythms and tone colors associated with rock music in the late 1960s. Today, the way that jazz musicians are incorporating new technology into their expression is simply a contemporary manifestation of this continuing thread, indicative of how the music has resisted the desire of some, from the moldy figs in the 1930s and 1940s to the moldy figs of the new millennium, to retain the music in some kind of stationary perfection. "Should jazz accept the role of a self-reproducing niche-culture, which was a development of a 20th century society, with nothing to convey to people of the 21st century?" asks Steen Meier, chairman of the Nordic Music Council and Copenhagen's JazzHouse. Because if jazz is the art form its most ardent disciples claim, then the music has to continue to evolve and grow, and that is beyond the control of any narrow interest group and in the hands of creative artists where the ultimate destiny of the music lies.

7
OUT OF SIGHT AND OUT OF MIND: JAZZ IN THE GLOBAL VILLAGE

I think what is going to happen is that we're going to see a broadening of the idea of what jazz is. Jazz is a child of the 20th century, but it has now left home.

Mike Nock, pianist, composer and educator

Globalization: tearing down trade barriers, collapsing distances, spreading information, a world without walls. Every day the business pages are filled with stories of how it continues apace, reaching further and faster month on month, year on year. With the big corporations such as Coca-Cola, McDonalds, Burger King, Levi's, and Ford spending millions developing global brands that transcend their place of origin, marketing departments have come up with concepts like "Salem Cool Planet," IBM's "Solutions for a Small Planet," Reebok's "This Is My Planet," and, of course, wherever you happen to be, you are always home at "My McDonald's." *Sex and the City*, *Will & Grace*, *Friends*, *Seinfeld*, and *The Simpsons* dominate the world's television networks. "The Marlboro Man" may be under siege at home, but across Asia it is impossible to miss him on television, billboards, and in magazines and newspapers. "One worldism" is the buzzword on the lips of politicians, industrialists, and media folk who point to baseball-hatted teenagers around the globe, a shared worldwide television culture, and the power of global pop and computer markets. As American economic power reaches the most remote points on the planet, in its wake follows its cultural power, which replicates itself within local contexts; for example, every day one person in 200 visits one of more than 30,000 McDonald's restaurants in 121 countries.

But what is globalization? According to the British social scientist David Held in his book *Models of Democracy*:

> Globalisation today implies at least two distinct phenomena. First it suggests that many chains of political, economic and social activity are becoming world-wide in scope and, second, it suggests that there has been an intensification of levels of interaction and interconnectedness within and between states and societies.

Globalization operates at many levels, in addition to the economic. It occurs in politics, war, migration, crime, terrorism, the environment, at a cultural level, and in all forms of media. Popular music in particular has seen increasing economic internationalism through the global reach of the four major Anglo-American corporations: Universal-Vivendi, with a 23.9 percent market share, followed by Sony/BMG with 19.4 percent, EMI with 14.4 percent, and Warner Music with 12 percent. Big pop stars of the new millenium, such as Beyoncé, 50 Cent, Justin Timberlake, Eminem, Norah Jones, and Coldplay, were aimed at a worldwide audience and were among globalization's most useful props, projecting a specific set of values: conspicuous consumption, the primacy of the English language, and the implicit acknowledgment that America is best.

While the output of MTV, VH1, and the increasing number of radio stations owned by Clear Channel Communications have been dressed up in pop's customary language of diversity and individualism, the music they offer has become an increasingly standardized and homogenized "product." Initially, MTV was marketed with the empowering slogan, "I want my MTV," but was later changed for the global marketplace to a more sinister, "One planet, one music." Music that was founded in spontaneity and self-expression has ended up at the core of an ever more standardized world, epitomized by the Pepsi advertisements from Michael Jackson to Pink, Beyoncé, and Britney Spears, or the Eurovision Song Contest watched by more than 500 million viewers. Advertisements and events such as these are helping produce a "streamlining" of music across national borders, a lowest common denominator product that can be sold in as many countries as possible. It raises the specter of a global pop village with youth audiences around the world watching the same television programs, adopting the same dress code, and listening to the same music.

It is this threat of a cultural "gray out" through the predominantly one way flow of Anglo-American popular music and cultural products from "the west to the rest" that has given rise to the theory of cultural imperialism. In *Understanding Popular Music*, Roy Shuker discusses this trend:

> Adherents of the thesis tended to dichotomize local culture and its imported counterpart, regarding local culture as somehow more authentic, traditional, and supportive of a conception (however vaguely expressed it may be) of a distinctive national cultural identity. Set against this identity and threatening its continual existence and vitality was the influx of large quantities of slick, highly commercialized media products mainly from the United States.

In many ways this argument represents academic shorthand to describe the "center" — globally dominant Western market forces — dumping their mass-produced products on the "margins," thus threatening to overwhelm local cultural expression. This process has been likened to the spread of "hamburger culture," because the consumerism it embodies — a standardized, mass-produced, packaged brand — has the effect of marginalizing local cuisines, with traditional foods such as pyttipannu in Finland, nasi lamak in Southeast Asia, or faggots and peas in England being swept aside by the Big Mac. McDonald's slogan, "Billions served," points to the goal of proliferation, with a Big Mac in New York tasting exactly the same as a Big Mac in the Red Square. As Professor George Ritzer of Maryland University pointed out in *The McDonaldization of Society*:

> American fast food culture, pop music, films and television infect the cultural body of other nations, co-opting local production of machinery to focus their efforts on mimicry. This pattern of viral replication repeats itself the world over, with American pop cultural norms choking out stifling native flora and fauna.

As our lives and cultures become more and more subject to the disciplines of the global marketplace, globalization has become a formidable engine for change. It is, as David Held and his colleagues say in their book

Global Transformations: Politics, Economics and Culture, a "central driving force behind the rapid . . . changes that are reshaping societies and world order."

Jazz, like any form of cultural capital in the global marketplace, has not been able to escape the effects of globalization and the changes that flow from it. So if globalization is powerful enough to reshape "societies and world order," how is it reshaping jazz?

In terms of mass media and popular culture, the existence of the cultural imperialism thesis has become widely accepted, according to Roy Shuker in *Understanding Popular Music*, "at a common sense level." However, since the 1980s its validity has come under increasing scrutiny. In his article "Disjunction and Difference in the Global Cultural Economy", Arjan Appadurai has argued that the increasingly shifting, haphazard, and disorganized global developments of capitalism and the internationalization of mass media "cannot any longer be understood in terms of existing center-periphery models." He argues that the ongoing interplay between the market forces of global pop and local music cultures and subcultures has resulted in hybridized versions of global pop, in effect a cross-fertilization of local and international sounds, noting that: "As forces from various metropolises are brought into new societies they tend to become indigenized in one or another way: this is true of music and housing styles as much as it is true of science and terrorism, spectacles and constitutions."

This interaction of global pop with local music cultures, what Roger Wallis and Krister Malm call "transculturation" in their book *Big Sounds from Small Peoples*, not only reflects local musical identity but also what Appadurai has called "repatriation of difference," which adapts homogenized musical forms into "heterogeneous dialogues of national sovereignty." Often, "global" pop musicians such as Madonna, Michael Jackson, or Eminem have been invested with different meanings in different countries or "misinterpreted" in creative and idiosyncratic ways. The French Sociologist Pierre Bourdieu has described how cultural texts, practices, and values may be accorded differing values among various social groups, thereby constituting differing forms of cultural capital.

This process of hybridization and transculturation — the reinscription of global pop music with local significance such as national imagery — can often produce distinctive musical features. As Caspar Llewellyn-Smith, author of *Poplife: A Journey by Sofa* and editor of *The Observer Music Monthly*, observes:

> American hip hop stars such as 50 Cent are global icons, but hip hop culture has been appropriated by local acts in myriad ways throughout the world. In Senegal, for example, hip hop is now the dominant urban music form, but the most prominent local act, Daara J, sings in Wolof and French as well as in English, and draws on rumba and Jamaican ragga as well as rap. They are indebted to hip hop culture, but they could only come from Dakar. Or take the example of the excellent group Aiwa: founded by two Iraqi brothers living in Rennes in northern France. They make music that takes its lead from the culture of America's ghettos, but sounds like a true product of its own environment.

The tranculturation of popular music, then, is both fluid and inexact because of the inevitable tensions between the promotion and consumption of global pop and how its significance is interpreted in local markets. While homogenization or "hamburgerization" is inevitable in a shrinking world where dominant economic and cultural forces interact with diverse musical cultures, Wallis and Malm suggest outcomes are by no means predictable. They offer two scenarios that might result: (1) that the interaction of global and local musical practices can become common to an increasing number of musical cultures and so homogeneity will ensue; and (2) that the interaction of global and local musical cultures will increase to the extent that a variety of different types of music might emerge from different locations, adapting traditional musical forms to new environments.

In practice, both outcomes seem to be occurring, with homogeneity ensuing through the dominance in the marketplace of global pop — the so-called globalization process — and hybridity resulting from the interaction of global pop with local musical forms — the so-called glocalization effect. This process has also occurred in jazz where both globalized and glocalized versions of the music coexist alongside each other in the global marketplace. It is this process and its consequences that this chapter seeks to explore.

Ironically, as the flow of communication in the global cultural economy becomes ever faster, the people who are not discussing the effects of globalization on jazz are Americans. While time spent in the United States offers many delights, it is fair to say that news from other countries is not one, as

Jim Dator, professor of Political Science at the University of Hawaii, told authors Ziauddin Sardar and Merryl Wyn Davies: "Even with its gigantic media system operating with state-of-the-art technologies, the US functions as a society closed to information, facts, and opinions of the rest of the world." When it comes to jazz, many fans are unaware of the impact the music has had beyond their shores. Few albums or bands from outside the United States are heard there, although by the early millennium years a handful of musicians from outside the United States who had managed to perform there, such as Martial Solal, Tomasz Stanko, Enrico Rava, Esbjörn Svensson, or Tord Gustavsen, had begun to develop an American following. But in general terms, as Mike Nock, who was musical director of the Naxos Jazz record label from 1996 to 2001, comments: "When Naxos was happening, it was totally disappointing to me that there was no interest in any music we put out on the label that wasn't American."

It is still widely believed in most jazz circles that New York City is "the center of jazz," and that "If it's not happening here, then it's not happening anywhere." Certainly since the late 1920s, New York was at the heart of jazz innovation, a place where most of the significant styles of jazz were either developed or defined in its jazz clubs and after-hours joints. One club, the Village Vanguard in Greenwich Village, which first opened its doors on February 26, 1934, and saw key albums by pace-setting musicians such as John Coltrane and Bill Evans recorded there, is still in business today. New York retains special status because of its role in jazz history and the remarkable number of internationally famous musicians gathered together in a relatively small area. Yet, as the Chicago saxophonist, composer, and bandleader Ken Vandermark, a recipient of a Guggenheim Genius award, notes:

> So much happened in New York that writers tend to focus on New York as a trend setting place. Large record labels like Verve and Blue Note are based there and they still think of New York as the center of things. Jazz writers here in the United States in particular still want to believe New York is the center of things. But it's not. New York is now just one of many places for jazz at this moment in time.

Jazz went global from its very beginning because its birth coincided with the rise of America's industrial and commercial preeminence. In December 1912, when President William Taft declared a new emphasis on "dollar diplomacy," he extended the collaboration between government and business that had underwritten the expansion of the western frontier to the global frontier. By 1917, when a whole generation of Europeans were either dead, wounded, or faint with exhaustion from the brutal fighting of the First World War, America poured two million troops into Europe's battlefields and settled the issue of what was later termed the "war to end all wars" in under two years. American industry, geared to a scale of productivity beyond the comprehension of European industrialists, dispatched arms and material across the Atlantic on a scale impossible to imagine at the time. When the State Department announced that Germany had signed an armistice on Monday, November 11, 1918, Thomas Woodrow Wilson wrote: "Everything for which America has fought has been accomplished. It will now be our fortunate duty to assist by example, by sober, friendly counsel, and by material aid, in the establishment of just democracy throughout the world." His dominant role in the subsequent Versailles treaty, settling the terms of peace, proposed a new world order, and with it emerged a new imperial vision of America's place in the world.

Having brought peace to Europe, America set about "reconstructing humanity's morals" and, in so doing, created unprecedented wealth for itself. In 1923, when Vice President Calvin Coolidge succeeded President Warren Harding, he famously declared "The business of America is business," and very soon America was reveling in Coolidge prosperity. America was the world's creditor nation, its industries were achieving miracles of production on the first giant assembly lines, it had the highest average income of any country, and it was now producing more steel than Europe. By the end of the 1920s, Hollywood films dominated the cinema experience, American agencies dominated the advertising world, the world's popular press copied U.S. tabloid techniques, Henry Ford had revolutionized the production line, and the world of popular music was dominated by Tin Pan Alley. Europe, drained after the Great War, eagerly copied the latest American fads — cocktails, bobbed hair, the Charleston, the Fox Trot and the Quickstep — as signs of a new life.

Wherever the dollar went, American culture and technology followed in its wake, including phonograph records. Significantly, the rise of the phonograph industry coincided with the emergence of jazz, and when the first jazz recording was made in 1917, an aurally transmitted heritage of an otherwise inaccessible milieu was suddenly opened up for global appreciation — and crucially imitation — by recordings that passed unhindered through national borders and political and social barriers around the world. In 1933, when Duke Ellington visited England and met the future king of the then British Empire, he was amazed that Prince Edward had a substantial collection of his records and other leading American bands of the day. It was a decade when the German trumpeter Ady Rosner led the State Jazz Orchestra of the Byelorussian Republic in Stalin's Russia and trumpeter Buck Clayton led a big band in Shanghai.

The phonograph record had provided the means by which jazz quickly became an international musical *lingua franca*. By 1934 Danny Polo, a saxophonist and clarinetist from Toluca, Illinois, was in London, playing in the saxophone section of the Ambrose Orchestra, Britain's top big band of the day; in 1937 Coleman Hawkins and Benny Carter were able to record four jazz classics including "Honeysuckle Rose" and "Crazy Rhythm" in Paris with a Manouche Gypsy resident there, Django Reinhardt, and a band of French musicians; in the spring of 1948, a Swedish clarinetist called Ake "Stan" Hasselgard, who learned his jazz by listening to American 78s, was invited to join Benny Goodman's septet, which included Wardell Gray, Teddy Wilson, and Billy Bauer; in 1956, the King of Thailand, His Majesty Phumiphol Aduljej, was able to sit in and jam with the Benny Goodman sextet in Bankok — an event that was broadcast in the United States on New Year's Day 1957; and in July 1958 a big band comprising jazz musicians from all over the world was assembled under the baton of Marshall Brown to play the Newport Jazz Festival. Unable to speak each other's languages, the band communicated with one another, as Leonard Feather noted, "through the international language of jazz."

The dissemination of jazz around the world, the so-called globalization of the music through recordings, meant that as each "style" of jazz emerged in America, it could be heard months later being imitated by local musicians in London, Paris, and Rome. This effect was reinforced by international tours by American jazz artists (the Original Dixieland Jazz Band was resident in London eighteen months after making the first jazz recordings, for example). The major recording companies of the day, such as Columbia and RCA Victor, and, after World War II, independent labels such as Blue Note, Prestige, Contemporary, and Verve, became, like the film industry, transnational in character, increasing their profitability by turning to the international marketplace through the trade routes of the global economy. The result was the proliferation of jazz to every corner of the globe.

Today, "local" musicians can be found around the world, able to play in the classic hegemonic styles of the music and can be measured by the most exacting standards in jazz. For example, the Swedish trumpet player Bent Persson's acclaimed re-creation of *Louis Armstrong's Fifty Hot Choruses*, a set of Armstrong solos published by Melrose Brothers in 1927, or the English alto saxophonist Peter King's brilliant solos in the bebop tradition aspire to the highest standards of the music. You can find bands dedicated to New Orleans jazz in Bristol, England, and big bands reproducing Ellington, Basie, and Herman charts in Tokyo, Japan. There are hard bop bands in the Art Blakey tradition in South Africa, bands playing Ornette Coleman's music in France, and 1971 Miles Davis jazz-rock–styled groups in Iceland. Adrian Jackson, musical director of the Wangaratta Jazz Festival, points out that in Australia:

> Some musicians are fixated on the past and the golden age in the USA — whether that means, for them, Louis in the 1920s, or Bird in the 1940s, Trane in the 1960s, and so on. These musicians play in the classic styles because that's just the music they want to play; and some do it with undeniable skill, authority and personality. There's nothing uniquely "Australian" about Bob Barnard's trumpet playing, for example, but I doubt you'll hear anyone play that traditional/mainstream style better.

The agents of globalization — the international industrial trade routes and the flow of communication in the global cultural economy — that spread jazz around the world were also responsible for the spread of the English language. Since the seventeenth century, English was spread to a third of the world through British trade and colonialism, and from the end of the nineteenth century, American trade and commerce spread it just about everywhere else. In both instances, an English-speaking economic power was responsible for pushing the English language forward into the world. By the end of the twentieth century, English had become a global *lingua franca*, the language in which most of the world's trade is transacted, the safety of international airlines is regulated, popular culture is communicated, and the Internet is operated.

But with the globalization of the English language, it also took on distinctly local, or "glocal," characteristics that separated it from its "birthplace." Regardless of how English is spoken in England or the United States of America, continentals, for example, have developed their own style of English. The German airline Lufthansa used to request that passengers "switch your handys off." "Handy" was used in lieu of the German word for mobile phone, "Mobiltelefon"; it is an easily understood, short word that is derived from the fact that a mobile phone is usually to hand.

English-speaking passengers knew, presumably, what was being asked of them, Lufthansa successfully transmitted their instructions, and everyone was happy, regardless of the fact that "handy" is not found in any English dictionary as a nickname for "mobile" or "cell phone." English, as a *lingua franca*, does not belong to the British or the Americans; it is the possession of any speech community that uses it, no matter if that community is Lufthansa, the EU parliament, or international university students attending college in Kenya.

Just as the use of English throughout the world does not always mirror the rules of grammar and syntax followed by English speakers in Britain or America — such as "Singlish" in Singapore — there are jazz styles that have evolved outside the United States that do not necessarily follow the way that jazz is played inside the United States. In these examples, jazz behaves as a *lingua franca* the same way that English does, which, as Mary Louise Pratt, former director of the Modern Language Association of America, points out, "break[s] apart into local hybrids." This process of assimilation and appropriation resulting in hybridization or, "tranculturation" as Wallis and Malm call it, produces local, or "glocalized" jazz "dialects," which, like varieties of English, often have no precise counterpart in America at all. "I really believe your environment helps shape what you do as an artist," says the British saxophonist Courtney Pine. "It really has to be out of the musician's natural experience — if you have a classical musician and you ask him to play Bob Marley he's going to sound weird, but if you are going to play something of that musician's natural background that's going to be very natural."

These "glocalized" styles use the basic syntax of the classic and contemporary hegemonic American jazz styles — in this context "hegemony" means "the rules of the game" by which others routinely play — that has been widely disseminated around the world (the globalization process), but are reinscribed with local significance (the glocalization process). Glocalization can involve incorporating elements such as national imagery, folkloric, and cultural concerns that give the music relevance to its "local" musical community. In his essay "Brazilian Jazz and Friction of Musicalities," Professor Acácio Tadeu de Camargo Piedade of the State University of Santa Catarina, says that Brazilian jazz musicians, sensitive to the potentially humiliating effects of cultural imperialism, strive "to avoid contamination from the *bebop* paradigm and seek an expression that is more rooted in Brazil," by drawing on local elements such as the *chorinho*, for example.

In today's pluralistic society, the Italian musicologist Marcello Piras notes that "regional identities may even turn out to be stronger than national ones, maybe even competing with them." As Dr. Elizabeth Peterson, former linguistics lecturer at Indiana University and sociolinguist at the Center for Applied Linguistics in Washington D.C., points out:

> Any community that regularly uses English will work out its own rules of use that suit that particular community. The resulting English will not sound like the English spoken in the U.K., the U.S., or anywhere else, because it will incorporate features from the syntax, morphology, vocabulary, or pronunciation of the native language that is spoken in that area, and then takes on a life of its own as it builds from that foundation.

Yet the people who are reluctant to acknowledge that there is more than one "correct" version of English are, of course, the American and British native speakers of English. They may not even understand some versions of the spoken English that exist in the world, although the speakers of these local versions are, nonetheless, native speakers in their own right, just as much as an American or a British citizen. In the world at large, English and jazz are both viewed as tools for expression, not as something that is "owned" by the Americans or the British. The term "native speaker" — of English or of jazz — becomes expanded beyond traditional recognition because what is used in the world becomes nativized on a case-by-case basis. The result is a creative tension between, on the one hand, a "prescriptivist" view of both English and of jazz, which is enforced by those who are loyal to history and/or economic power, and the "descriptivist" view, whereby a local community has taken something that has come from a global perspective or source, but does not care about the rules or birthright of what gets adopted; it becomes part of their own cultural repertoire.

"In this respect jazz and English show very similar properties in the sense that they both are taken into a given community," says Dr. Elizabeth Peterson:

> But the community that absorbs them and uses them doesn't actually have any sort of reverence for, or need to pay heed to, the way jazz or English are used in their parent cultures; there is no notion of "authenticity." In choosing to use English or play jazz, the adopting culture makes English or jazz all its own, just as we no longer think of pasta as

being Chinese or of the Rubik's cube being Czech. English and jazz are both viewed in the world at large as tools for expression, not as something that is "owned" by anyone. While a farmer's wife in Texas may think that she has some innately endowed ownership of English by virtue of the fact that she was born into it, she has no control over the version of English a university student uses in an internet chat room in Sri Lanka. English, and jazz, is like the wayward child that has flown the coop; it has taken on grandiose proportions that take it outside the realm of those who might think they can lay claim to it by birthright. For both the farmer's wife and the student, the use of English serves the same purpose, which is at the same time both weighted with significance and utterly commonplace: it is simply a tool for expression, a means of both creating and expressing their relationship to the reality around them.

English teachers are especially prone to reject glocalized forms of the language because their very lifeblood depends on adhering to a linguistically imperialist attitude. As Dr. Peterson points out: "Language teachers are actually threatened by the local dialects as it means the English language takes on a life of its own which they cannot do anything about. Teaching the English language may be their bread and butter, but they are unable to enforce the notion of a 'standard prescriptionist English.'" The analogy to jazz is again striking: American traditionalists try to enforce the notion of only one right and true "jazz," otherwise their supposed ownership of jazz is rendered meaningless. However, they are powerless to prevent entirely new forms of jazz evolving around the globe.

Just as in popular music, glocalized styles coexist with globalized ones. While some local musicians choose to play in the globalized styles of jazz that have been transmitted around the world by recordings of the great American masters — be it bebop, big band, New Orleans and so on—other musicians choose to play in a glocal style that incorporates local folkloric, nationalistic, and cultural concerns that are relevant to their own needs and musical community. The British saxophonist Iain Ballamy explains how he moved from performing a globalized jazz style to a glocalized one:

> My first few years as a player were spent learning and absorbing the music of the American jazz masters, but the biggest personal revelation for me was the discovery of the music typified by the ECM label, especially albums like *My Song* with Jan Garbarek and Keith Jarrett, and the

works by British players including Evan Parker, Kenny Wheeler, John Surman and John Taylor. This music — non-blues based, lyrical and occasionally folky — seemed to resonate more strongly with me, being a European. It came to me at the time I was beginning to write my own material and very quickly I discovered that playing one's own tunes in a way that felt right as an "Englishman," rather than in an appropriated genre from another place and time, felt natural and right for me.

Many local musicians play in global hegemonic American styles in some performing situations, and in a hybridized, glocalized form in other situations. The Swedish pianist Bobo Stenson, for example, recorded four albums with American saxophonist Charles Lloyd and frequently toured with him, playing hard-driving, straight-ahead solos. "You can say with Charles this is 'traditional American music,' I think," he explained to me. "It was straight-ahead with Charles, and I put something of that in my playing, too. I felt it and enjoyed it, but with my trio it is different." Formed in 1993, Stenson's trio, with Anders Jormin on bass and Jon Christensen on drums, plays a hybridized form of jazz shaped by Stenson's musical and cultural experiences, which can be heard on recordings such as *Reflections*, *Serenity*, and *War Orphans*. "First of all, Christensen does not play straight-ahead, he's more of a painter, splashes of sound," Stenson observed:

> We don't need to play straight rhythm all the time. It's a very free way of playing, I think. Not free jazz, we play melodies and harmonies and structures, but we have a free flowing approach to it. We play in the language of American jazz but I guess we put other things into the music. We have other traditions here [in Scandinavia], more from classical music and folk music and stuff, and I guess we put that into the thing more than "traditional American jazz." More important, we don't need to play the American way, we can leave that and come back to it. It allows you to take the music in new directions.

"One of the great aspects of jazz is that it's very open," the Norwegian saxophonist Jan Garbarek told *Downbeat* magazine. "It invites all sorts of people of any kind of background to take part. You can apply any personal input, coming from whatever part of the world, and it's possible to find a way that will work in the jazz idiom. That's what I see as the major force of this music. It's been more and more evident the last ten years. We have players from any part of the world now doing their own, shall we say, native version. They find their own direction, influenced by their own culture, but still using the very strong basic elements of jazz."

As the twenty-first century develops, we will see an increasing "multi-dialectism" of jazz, just as we will see the growing use of English. As Mary Louise Pratt pointed out, "The future of English, like that of any *lingua franca*, does not belong to its native speakers." It is like a house being built: you have the foundations, American jazz, as a basic structure is in place, but, as it rises higher and higher, new floors are being added by non-Americans. In the past, it was the Americans who were the leaders in adding new floors to this metaphorical "house of jazz," but now it is the non-Americans who are taking the lead. These are not less authentic subvarieties of an American version of jazz, but new glocal dialects. As critic Gary Booth observed in *BBC Music Magazine*, "America has had a virtual monopoly on calling the changes in jazz music since the music moved out of New Orleans. But that's no longer the case."

In an era of political turmoil and complex negotiations of personal and cultural identity, jazz, more than ever in its history, is being used as a means of asserting cultural identity. Historically, jazz has always been a means of asserting black cultural identity; Wynton Marsalis' legacy for an idealized representation of jazz from its golden years is simply a means of asserting black cultural identity within the predominantly white cultural mainstream of the United States. Today, in the broader forum of the global cultural economy, glocalized jazz styles from outside the United States are now providing a means for musicians around the world to assert *their* cultural identity within the music. "There was a time when we would basically find an icon from America who's current and emulate him, but now we're not happy with that," says Courtney Pine. "So now I feel comfortable enough to present my cultural heritage, so when you see me you know I listened to Bob Marley, you can hear some Caribbean stuff in there, you hear European stuff in there, you can hear some African stuff and you can hear that American thing as well."

As the process of transculturation produces hybridized and often innovative versions of jazz in local and national contexts, these local jazz dialects represent a series of subcultures within the global economy of jazz music. Although "European jazz," for example, is a generalized tag for jazz originating anywhere in Europe, the cross-fertilization of local culture, custom, and practices with American jazz sounds has produced a wide variety of glocal "jazz dialects" across the Continent. There is again a strong analogy to language here, because second-language English users

— L2 speakers — will speak English in their own local way, with the influence of their mother tongues and cultural "conditioning" shaping the way they speak English; as Dr. Elizabeth Peterson notes, "Italians are going to Italianize, Finns are going to Finnisize, and Czechs are going to Czechisize, with all the little idiosyncrasies that fit the speech community therein. Even with the quirks, though, it still qualifies as English due to the overarching features: lexicon, structure, and to a certain extent pronunciation."

Equally, in jazz when non-Americans learn the phonology and syntax of the jazz, local practices and idiosyncrasies, shaped by their cultural backdrop, can produce different "readings" of the music, so that different "pronunciations" of jazz emerge. These can often be as readily identified as the national and regional accents and dialects of second-language English users: a French L2 speaker has a quite different and recognizable way of speaking English than an equally recognizable Italian L2 speaker, for example. In northern Europe, the playing of Norwegian saxophonist Jan Garbarek has been described by Mathias Rüegg, the leader of the Vienna Art Orchestra, as having a style that "remains true to the vast and cool quality of his Nordic origins." Gabarek's playing is quite different from French jazz styles, where native French musicians such as Louis Sclavis, Michel Portal, and Henri Texier have all striven to import elements of their own culture into their music; take, for example, the wonderful Gallic flourishes of the Cartatini Ensemble's masterful deconstruction of Louis Armstrong on *Darling Nellie Gray* (2000). As the Italian musicologist Stefano Zenni pointed out:

> All black music is a continuous process of *signifyin'*, of conversing constantly with elements of the tradition, of turning everything around all the time, playing with music and words, overturning their meaning with all the "voices" that echo in music. When music is produced in Europe, it is logical that its *signifyin'* doesn't draw on blues or spirituals, of course, but on a different cultural heritage that ranges from archaic Nordic tunes to the effervescent Mediterranean cultures, which also have their own particular relationship, in their own particular way, to African-American music (in their case via the Arabic and North African interface), passing through the weighty tradition of classically "educated" music.

Throughout Europe — indeed throughout the world — jazz is being reimagined through the process of transculturation. Musicians seek to make their music connect with their surroundings and want to give it life and vitality that is relevant to their musical situation. The Japanese writer Yui Shôichi (1918 to 1998) called this phenomenon "jazz nationalism." He wrote that contrary to the cultural imperialism thesis, where jazz and/or Western consumer products threaten the vitality and existence of local culture — jazz actually provides a means of rediscovering local tradition. In his essay "Toward a Global History of Jazz", H.E. Taylor Atkins, an associate professor of History at Northern Illinois University, says Shôichi argued this would "create original music that was both part of a universal language called jazz and a singular expression of national or ethnic identity." Atkins quotes Shôichi as saying: "The movement for 'national independence' that surged through each country became the motive power for what must be called jazz nationalism, 'to be free of America.'"

In Europe, with its diversity of nation states and cultures within a relatively small area of the globe, the glocalization of jazz becomes very apparent. As the French saxophonist Julien Lorau observes:

> I think the European scene is more interesting — I don't know, maybe we're more open minded. In France, we know jazz many years, jazz in Paris since the '20s, it's not as heavy as in the States, more easy to blend and to meet with other influences. I think we have more freedom here in Europe now than the States — and especially black musicians [in America] have this particular mission, how can I say? To protect the tradition of jazz, and it's a kind of a mission for them, I think, but not really for me.

In 2001 the legendary French bass player Henri Texier, who has performed with some of the American masters on the Paris jazz scene in the '60s, told me how he thought French jazz acquired its own particular identity:

> Paris was into jazz music very, very early in the '20s, in fact and many intellectuals, people like Picasso, Cocteau — they were very interested and very shocked in a good way by the sounds of this music, and very early it was French musicians starting to play with Afro-American musicians. . . almost from the birth of this music, there was a real commitment

to that music between French musicians and American musicians, and then that music developed. Since, let's say the '50s-'60s, it was a kind of conscience coming to French musicians — and European musicians — that they are not American, they are not black, and they have their own cultural place where many influences come — the classical music, the folk music, and in France also from the colonies, this mixing coming from Africa, North Africa, the Orient like Viet Nam. . . . In the '60s, the French jazz musicians discovered that they have their own material, so they can express themselves.

When I was very young, involved in jazz music of course, I saw Sidney Bechet, who was living in Paris; a lot of Afro-American and American musicians came to Paris and stayed. I was very lucky to have played with giants like Dexter Gordon, Bud Powell, Kenny Clarke, Don Cherry . . . [but in later years] the music was evolving, and with the African influences, Mediterranean influences, south Europe, the Jewish music from southern Europe, and from North Africa, all this makes a special place where we grow maybe a different music. We are also still influenced by American jazz because this music was born over there, but it's very strange it was born also in Louisiana, which was a French-speaking region in those days, and many early jazzmen coming from New Orleans, their names were French names. Bechet is a French name. . . . I know I was influenced first by Afro-American jazz . . . and then I realized I *wasn't* black and I *wasn't* American, and then I started to inte-grate some elements from oriental music, from African music, from North African music. I was respecting that music, I still respect that very much, because I learned this music from great musicians, but then I have been trying — it's not like studying — it was just a feeling, just a sensa-tion, just a sensitive way — in an instinctive way I started to play some-thing different.

When I started playing with those great musicians, we were not studying, it was not like school. It was like life right away, it was a way of life this music, it was no school, no books, no nothing. You had to learn that music by records or speaking with the musicians and trying to get the right harmonies to play. I think especially the young generation in the States, they look to that music in an academic way. In my early years, it was the explosion of the free-jazz period, in my mind there were no barriers, no frontiers no customs! For example, one night I was playing with Dexter Gordon, a giant of the bebop, next day I was playing with Lee Konitz, cool jazz, and the next day I was playing with my own group with young cats — we were playing Ornette Coleman's music! Some-times I hear young musicians they say "I study first the bebop, and when

I will be OK with the bebop I will study the free jazz.: I say don't do that, play everything at the same time! . . .

The MJQ was in town, and John Lewis and Milt Jackson came down and they started to speak together. They were speaking about all these great musicians and they were speaking about *originality*. That was the main word, *originality*. Somehow in my mind this is staying, and I think if you want to be original, you have to be adventurous, too. I think there is a different flavor of jazz in different countries. It may come from very natural things, you know. From the landscape, from the food, maybe things not even coming from the music, coming from mental structures, I don't know. I know here there are many different things. I know why, but to explain it? It is very interesting in a way because there is difference, the differences are nice, because there are different flavors for the audience.

In Italy, compelling examples of the process of transculturation can also be found. For example, the Italian saxophonist Eugenio Colombo plays alto and soprano simultaneously on his recording of "Summertime," creating a sound like the central Italian bagpipes, producing a very "Italian" version of the standard at a very deep level. Equally, Gianluigi Trovesi, composer, for saxophonist and clarinetist, has found a very personal way of unlocking a dialogue between European and African American cultures. "Many years ago, I heard a concert by John Surman with the trio, Barre Phillips and Stu Martin, in my own town of Bergamo," he told me:

> That was the first example I heard of someone playing jazz in a completely different style to the Americans. I always use European elements. Sometimes the dedacaphonic, sometimes from folk, from movies. For me jazz is color and rhythm! We have a very big river and this river is jazz, when you arrive close to the sea, the river becomes delta. The delta is the land where the European musicians install themselves, they use the water from the jazz river and water from the sea, they use jazz and the traditional, historic music of their own country.

In the same way Louis Armstrong's music reflected New Orleans or Duke Ellington's music Harlem, Trovesi reflects the influence of his home town of Bergamo, reimagining jazz in vivid Mediterranean hues, dancing folkloric themes, and bursts of vivid Mediterranean color. He notes:

As a child I listened to many styles of music. I was rich inside because of this: opera, Italian folk music, movies, and jazz. I am a cook, not fantastic, but when I prepare my dinner I use all the elements I like. Same in jazz. I try to organize the dish until I think it is the best I can do, and I hope people like what I cook for them. If we take away one of the elements from the dishes, it is not anymore my story; if you take away the jazz element it is nothing.

Jazz in the United Kingdom had broadly followed the hegemonic American styles until the 1960s. Pianist and educator Michael Garrick, an important voice on the London scene during that decade, whose albums such as *Black Marigolds*, *The Heart Is a Lotus*, *Mr. Smith's Apocalypse*, *Home Stretch Blues*, *Troppo*, and *Cold Mountain* are now regarded as classics of British jazz, notes that:

The 1960s saw an upsurge of originality in British jazz. All the wonders that the great American prototypes so gloriously exhibited were no longer enough. What began to surface and receive delighted attention were those doing something fresh and home grown. Joe Harriott — ironically an immigrant from Jamaica, who scornfully maintained that originality came from "all over the place, not just the USA" — kicked off the decade with his unprecedented free form compositions. But native Brits were at work too; chipping away at this elusive thing called roots, a debate by no means settled in 2002. If we learnt anything, it should be that "soul" is a very fluid commodity.

The big band composer Mike Westbrook — whose albums *Celebration* (1967), *Release* (1968), and *Marching Song* (1969) established him as the foremost British jazz composer of his generation — consciously strove to define a writing style that was individual and not overshadowed by the American hegemonic styles. "It was this body of work," wrote trumpeter Ian Carr in his book *Music Outside*, "that emancipated British jazz from its American slavery." Together with *Metropolis* (1971) and, what Westbrook considers one of his most important works, *Citadel/Room 315* (1974), he created a body of work that is now considered among the finest of all European jazz. However, the problems of sustaining a large ensemble forced Westbrook to diversify. He undertook a remarkable number of projects, often working together with his vocalist wife Kate. They embraced free improvisation, brass band music, jazz-rock, street band music, standards, dance-music-theatre collaborations, jazz-and-poetry, jazz cabaret, opera, music for TV and cinema, and jazz adaptations of everyone from Rossini to the Beatles, earning Westbrook the sobriquet as "the John Bunyan of British jazz."

Despite the critical acclaim that his big band works garnered, Westbrook did not have a regular, working big band during the 1980s. However, in 1991, he decided that he missed working in this context, and made a triumphant return to performing a year later. His new band toured Europe extensively prior to making its British debut at the Royal Albert Hall in the 1992 Henry Wood Promenade Concerts. While it wasn't the first jazz ensemble to appear at the Proms, it was the first to appear as part of the main program. However, once again the financial difficulty of keeping a band of this size together led to the group ending. A good representation of this period can be found on *The Orchestra of Smith's Academy*, recorded live at the Bracknell Jazz Festival in 1992. Westbrook comments, "It has a piece called 'Measure for Measure,' which really is about as far as I have been able to take writing for a large ensemble, very difficult to play, that album has that kind of material on it, 'Viennese Waltz,' more dense, difficult stuff. I really felt I was pushing myself and the band. That was the last time I had a band of that sort of size, again. I tried to keep the band going around London, but it was getting impossible, so I feel the pieces on that album are very personal and couldn't have been done by anyone else, or at any other time."

Big band works such as *London Bridge Is Broken Down* (1987), *Bar Utopia* (1996), and *Chanson Irresponsable* (2002), featuring his wife Kate on vocals, represent Westbrook's continual creativity in reimagining the age-old big band institution in a contemporary context. "I'm very lucky because I have this ability to take on different things," he told me:

> I think the important thing about jazz and what its had to offer throughout its life, is that it's serious contemporary music and that's something people can overlook, or choose to overlook, but its always been avant garde — there's no-one more avant garde than Louis Armstrong, or Jelly Roll Morton. You function within the popular context, there's not been a barrier and this is serious art music, it is art music — you think Ellington, you think Mingus, there's no doubt about it, it's serious and committed art music, but it also works in the street level in the popular environment, we're too segregated between high art and crass entertainment. Great art should be entertaining. So hanging on to the impetus I've got from the American jazz tradition, I've always

wanted to find my own space. I don't know why, but that's the way jazz is, you want your own voice.

Saxophonist John Surman emerged from the ranks of Westbrook's orchestra, appearing on all of his albums from 1967 up to and including 1974's *Citadel/Room 315*, which was written to feature him. Since the 1970s, Surman has projected a British sensibility in his music, particularly his native West Country, which can be heard on such solo projects as *Road to St. Ives* and *A Biography of the Rev. Absalom Dawe*, and with his "English" quartet of John Taylor on piano, Chris Laurence on bass, and John Marshall on drums. "The European model [of jazz] is more flexible," says John Marshall:

> There is more give and take, it comes subconsciously from the European tradition of music which is more elastic, rhythmically. That's what we've all done. It's a much more co-operative approach — a particular case in point would be the Surman quartet, massively talented players, it's all give and take, anybody runs with the ball and we go with it. Everybody trusts everybody else, and that's what it is about. John has spoken about this, he does make this point — he has worked in the European context and the American context, and . . . there is a difference, and he prefers the European context.

In Scotland, the Scots trumpeter Colin Steele, on his 2003 release *The Journey Home*, reflects his Celtic background with swirling folkloric imagery of a Scots reel, "Reel Deal," which is informed by bebop yet expressive of his own cultural identity echoing the way the Scots composer, Hamish McCunn wove the music of the highlands into classical music 100 years earlier.

In Poland, three figures — the highly original trumpeter Tomasz Stanko, alto saxophonist Zbigniew Namyslowski, and self-taught pianist-composer Krzysztof Komeda — have been leaders in creating a glocal jazz style. Komeda became a legend and cult hero after his early death in 1969. He wrote the music for more than forty films, including classics of the Polish cinema by Roman Polanski and Andrej Wajda. While improvisation was used in [a] his cinema writing, he regarded it as a separate activity from his career in jazz. His 1965 album *Astigmatic*, with Namyslowski and Stanko, represents one of the most important contributions in the shaping of a European aesthetic in jazz composition. "He was writing his own music, and he used tradition as material, but his compositions were completely fresh and new," recalled Stanko. "He connected everything in [a] very original way, he was very cunning, maybe from the movies, because film dictates untypical construction; he was a master with this, what he wrote was great for improvisation, was very good for jazz musician. When you play this stuff, it sounds like new."

Stanko continued to have a distinguished career on recordings after Komeda's death. In 1968 he formed a group with Zbigniew Seifert on violin and Janusz Muniak on tenor saxophone, regarded as the finest Polish group of the time. When this group broke up in 1973, he formed a group with the Finnish drummer Edward V, recording *Twet* (1974) and debuting on the ECM label with *Balladyna*. In the 1980s he also collaborated and recorded with pianist Cecil Taylor in what he described as a "difficult time for Poland politically." He "came back to life" in the 1990s; with the political climate changing for the better and with personal problems behind him, his career took off.

A string of critically acclaimed albums followed. Stanko formed a quartet with pianist Bobo Stenson, bassist Anders Jormin, and drummer Tony Oxley. Their first album, *Matka Joanna* (1994), was inspired by the sixties cult movie of the same name, meaning "Mother Joan of Angels." It was a tribute to movie director Jerzy Kawalerowicz, reflecting Stanko's great interest in the cinema (he subsequently wrote several soundtracks himself). Manfred Eicher, the head of Stanko's label, ECM, suggested that he record a tribute to Krzysztof Komeda. The result was the album *Litania*, with a handpicked septet that included Jon Christensen, Terje Rypdal, and Bernt Rosengren, who had worked with Komeda, notably on the soundtrack to the Roman Polanski film *Knife in the Water*. Stanko's imaginative recontextualization of Komeda's music received widespread praise across Europe; in the U.K. newspaper *The Guardian* John Fordham hailed it as "one of the jazz triumphs of 1997."

Following the success of *Litania*, Stanko toured extensively with his group, and European critics discovered what Polish audiences had known for decades: Here was a jazz musician of international stature and one of the most individual trumpet players of contemporary times. The release of 1998's *From the Green Hill* simply served to reinforce his growing international reputation, receiving the coveted German Critics Prize *Deutscher Schallplattenpreis* as Album of the Year in 2000. With an exciting new group of young protégés, comprising Marcin Wasilewski on piano, Slawomir Kurkiewicz on bass and Michal Miskiewicz on drums, who understood and complemented his music, he achieved international acclaim for *Soul of Things* (2002), a balladesque suite, numbered 1 to 13, which brimmed over with Slavic lyricism and melancholy. *Suspended Variations*, from 2004, built on the mood established by the previous album. "I continue the variations [from *Soul of Things*] because I am happy with what I have to say," says Stanko. "I feel like more a poet than a composer. I have to say my compositions are more programs for improvisation, because I am an improviser. . . . The sounds of compositions are always different, [but] everything is related." With *Soul of Things* and *Suspended Variations*, Stanko had two albums that already seemed like classic jazz albums of the new millennium.

Dutch jazz represents yet another quite distinct voice within the European jazz scene. Explored in depth by critic Kevin Whitehead in his book *New Dutch Swing*, it is a scene where, "humor counts more for dead seriousness; where the boundaries between music and theatre blur; where a unique blend of cultural influences, from Surinamese to South African find their way into the mix; and where pranksters Charles Ives and Thelonious Monk are major influences, along with the minimalism of Terry Riley and Holland's Louis Andriessen."

Dutch musicians have a long tradition of adapting the impulse of the jazz improvisation within new and challenging musical environments. Although *Machine Gun* by Peter Brötzman (1968) may not have been the first album by European "free" improvisers who were trying to move away from the American model of jazz and attempt to establish their own identity, it remains the most famous and most memorable, a landmark album that has come to represent a seismic shift in the thinking of the European free movement. But while England, Germany, Denmark, Norway, and Sweden all produced important musicians who contributed valuable recordings in this new style, it was the Dutch jazz scene that came to epitomize the diverse ways in which "freedom" could be managed.

Gaining momentum in the late 1960s, Dutch musicians embraced political issues, blurred the boundary between theatre and music, replaced the seriousness of the American avant-garde with humor and parody, embraced classical influences such as Terry Riley and Charles Ives, and drew on a variety of cultural influences, including elements that reached back into Dutch colonial history. The separateness of the Dutch jazz scene is illuminated in the resolute individuality of players such as Misha Mengelberg (winner of the 1966 Wessel-Ilcksen prize, the Netherlands Jazz Society's annual award, "who initiated the metamorphosis of jazz into improvised music pure and simple)" Willem Breuker, Han Bennink, Maarten Altena (who in 1978 had proclaimed his independence from American jazz), and Peter Kowald (who called his music "Kaputt-play," the main objective of which, as he said in *New Dutch Swing*, was "to do without the musical influence of most Americans")

Drummer Han Bennink emerged as one of the most important figures on the Dutch jazz scene. His first recording was with Eric Dolphy, and in the 1960s, he was the first choice drummer for many touring American musicians, including Sonny Rollins, Dexter Gordon, and Hank Mobley. At the same time, he was immersing himself in the European improvised music scene and was quickly recognized as one of its most original exponents. He was one of the first drummers to assemble a drum kit from all manner of "found" percussion (i.e., almost anything from hubcaps to kitchen pans that could be banged, shaken, or rattled).

During the 1990s, the Clusone Trio (sometimes Clusone 3) was a perfect context in which to feature Bennik's talents and provided a forum that gave vent to his reputation as a "performance" artist. The Clusone Trio brought together Dutch cellist Ernst Reijseger and American saxophonist-clarinetist Michael Moore, a graduate of the New England Conservatory who moved to Holland permanently in 1982. A fluid mixture of prearranged forms and free expression, the Clusone Trio broadened the emotional range of jazz in a way characteristic of the Dutch jazz scene, through humor, parody, and visual theatre.

These elements were not displayed quite so conspicuously in the work of tenor saxophonist Yuri Honing, one of the most influential of the young players in Holland. Artfully deconstructing songs associated with popular culture from the likes of Sting, Abba, Prince, Blondie, and Bjork, Yuri Honing succeeded in disentangling each tune from the memory of the original hit to create something new and subversive, beyond the pop artifact, on albums including *Star Tracks* (1996) and *Sequel* (1999).

Elsewhere on the Continent, the Vienna Art Orchestra under the direction of Mathias Rüegg has, since its formation in 1977, reveled in affectionately disrespectful adaptations of American jazz and has long taken pride in its particular European stance. Rüegg's compositions are often missions into uncharted, in American terms at least, territory for jazz improvisation. Pieces often had beguiling titles like "Nightride of the Lonely Saxophone Player," "The Innocence of Clichés," "Freak Aesthetics," "Concerto for Voice and Silence," and "Blues for Brahms." There is an openness in which Rüegg embraces other musical forms, from classical to folk, Ellington to Erik Satie, which makes the tradition-oriented American jazz of the late 1980s and 1990s seemed narrow and blinkered. Taunting traditions, in America and Europe Rüegg has built a body of work for a large ensemble that is among the finest in European jazz.

As Django Reinhardt revealed, lusty campfire rhythms and Gypsy extemporization is but a small step from jazz. In contemporary times, the work of the Hungarian violin virtuoso Roby Laktos and his ensemble moves convincingly between the two idioms without incongruity. The virtuosic Laktos inhabits the twilight zone between European folk music, classical, and jazz, successfully showing the close interrelationship between all three. His work suggests a continuation of the Gypsy tradition that looked back to both Reinhardt as much as the Gypsy flavors that once colored the music of Haydn, Liszt, and Ravel. The Dresch Quartet also brings these elements more directly into the forum of jazz. Led by Hungarian Dresch Dudás Mihály on tenor and soprano saxophones, with Kovács Ferenc on violin, Szandai Mátyás bass, and Balo Jstvan drums, the leader successfully invokes the spirit of John Coltrane's intensity and spirituality on themes inspired by Hungarian-Gypsy folk songs. The step from Laktos to the Dresch Quartet may be a small one, but as *Riding the Wind* (2000) illustrates, it enriches jazz with exciting tone colors, mid-European rhythms, and folk forms as the basis of profound improvisation.

Similar principles are used by the Yugoslavian pianist and Paris resident Bojan Zulfikarpasic, who combines jazz with ethnic Bosnian and Serbian folk melodies of his homeland. On *Bojan Z Quartet* from 1994, the fusion of these idioms suggested potential rather than a complete realization, but with *Yopla!* from 1995 Zulfikarpasic's well-rounded contemporary piano technique and conceptualization produced moments of genuine musical excitement. It was followed by *Koreni* (1998), featuring "La Petit Gitane," which moved from free jazz to Balkan rhythms to straight-ahead jazz to the sound of an overdriven electric guitar.

In 1948, the Australian bandleader Graeme Bell toured the United Kingdom with his New Orleans style jazz band, giving considerable momentum to the traditional jazz boom in that country during the 1950s. Yet even within the conventions of the New Orleans style, Jim Godbolt points out in *A History of Jazz in Britain, 1919-50* that: "In [the Bell band's] general presentation an Antipodean cockiness was cheerfully and successfully projected." In 2003, I asked Bell, now affectionately regarded as the grandfather of Australian jazz, whether there was an Australian way of playing jazz and if so, what it was. "I think . . . the one thing that comes through with Australian jazz is an openness, a big throatedness because our stuff was spawned in open spaces and sea and sand and not in speakeasies and bordellos and night clubs," he said. "And there is a little bit of Aussie bravado in there too!"

Culture, national attitudes and habits, and even climate can all play a part in forming a glocal dialect, as Paul Grabowsky — pianist, composer, and director of the acclaimed Australian Art Orchestra and a leader of his own groups — observes:

> Australians, because they have been away from the mainstream of the music — we only have American bands visiting here sporadically — don't have that exposure to American music and we have been forced to look to our own scene to find the inspiration we need. To give you an example, one of the main people — arguably the greatest Australian jazz musician — is Bernie McGann, an alto saxophone player. His sound reminds me very much of the Australian landscape. Dry and brittle and almost Coocoboro-like about the way he plays. He spent a lot of time outdoors, he was a postman at one stage, I don't know to what extent he has been influenced by ambient sounds but if Jan Garbaraek is a fjord man, Bernie is the opposite of that, he is dry, witty — he has an almost scatological syntax of bebop — there is always squeals and shrieks and yet he can play sweetly. That is very much an Australian sound, and because of the way he plays he produces a similarly idiosyncratic approach from his rhythm section. He has had a long relationship with John Pochee who doesn't sound like an "American" jazz drummer. He swings in a very unusual way, a kind of roughness.
>
> Australia is a rough place. This is not a place of niceties. This a place where people who love swearing and ridiculing each other and the rest of the world, turn out to be extremely resourceful people — great improvisers. This is why great jazz music does come out of Australia because we are great improvisers, we have to be. We have no choice. Australia is an improvisation. It is an improvised democracy in the middle of South Seas, and now a generation of players have come up, all of whom are extraordinary players who don't sound like anybody else.

Each of these examples of glocal dialects represents a means of expressing identity within the global jazz economy. Yet this notion of asserting "identity" in music, what Yui Shôichi has called "jazz nationalism," is hardly new. A desire to reflect local musical culture had earlier and significantly occurred in the evolution of Western classical music when, in the nineteenth century, many European composers returned to the folk and popular music of their own countries to set them apart from the then prevailing hegemonic "Germanic" style. While not prompted by the agents of globalization, the rise of what became known as Nationalism was marked by an emphasis on literary and linguistic traditions, an interest in folklore, patriotism, and a craving for independence and especially identity. As Steen Meier, Chairman of the Nordic Music Council and the JazzHouse in Copenhagen, notes, "The difference between the rise of the Nationalism in classical music and 'local' styles of jazz is somehow not that big. Jazz, as a musical expression now has almost the same number of national and regional dialects as you find in 'written' classical music. In both cases we could identify influences that come from our native culture, language, history, and folkloric sources, though each is still recognized as either 'classical music' or 'jazz.'"

As the bigger countries in Europe carved out empires for themselves, the smaller ones sought to express their own national identity, either by revolution and uprising or through works of art, especially music. This was especially true of countries under foreign domination, such as Italy and Czechoslovakia, who reasoned that if they could not have political autonomy, at least they could achieve artistic independence. Other countries, such as Scandinavia and Spain, wanted to assert their place in the world, emphasizing aspects of their culture to set them apart from the rulers of the big empires. As composer and conductor Antony Hopkins observed, "Nationalist elements can be traced to different accentuation of languages [as] rhythm tends to be closely associated with words, even in instrumentally conceived music. A tune by Bartók, Janáek, Dvořák, Borodin, or Falla will be easily recognized as having national characteristics both rhythmically and melodically."

Dvořák played a key role in bringing the ideals of Nationalism to the New World. He was enticed to New York to head the National Conservatory of Music, partly in the hope that his presence might help inspire an American nationalistic movement and partly to show how American composers might adapt "local" music into symphonic forms. His ninth and last symphony, called *From the New World*, was composed in 1893 during his three-year visit to the United States. As the country founded its own orchestras, concert halls, and conservatories, a question had been raised with increasing frequency: "Where are the American composers?" Up to this point, those who had wanted to compose sonatas and symphonies, rather than popular melodies, had gone to Europe to bring back to the New World the standards and styles of the old. Composers who emulated European models abounded, like John Knowles Paine, who wrote his *Mass in D* in Berlin, a piece not discernibly "American," and returned to become a professor of music at Harvard.

Louis Moreau Gottschalk, who studied piano in Paris, emerged as the most celebrated American composer of the mid-nineteenth century, particularly among young women who adored his wet-handkerchief pieces such as *The Last Hope*. His New Orleans upbringing, soaking up the singing and dancing of slaves, inspired his historic works, which included elements some believe suggested ragtime and jazz. Yet today, Gottschalk has emerged as a prophet with little honor. "As one of the four scholars who have studied his work in depth, I consider the received wisdom on Gottschalk is greatly unfair," laments the Italian musicologist Marcello Piras:

> He was a veritable genius, and most of the resistance to acknowledging his stature as America's first original and creative voice in music has always come from the kind of musicologists who also dismiss jazz. In fact, Gottschalk wrote potboilers such as *The Last Hope* exactly because he never made money with his masterful Cuban dances, Spanish pieces, and piano meditations, which were far above his contemporaries' ability to understand, and getting a consensus with tear-jerkers was a sort of revenge on the "Brahmins." Also, suggestions of ragtime and jazz, and also tango and *son cubano*, are quite clear in his work, although not always in his syncopated pieces.

Despite Gottschalk's achievements, a contemporary named John C. Griggs, musical director of the Center Church in New Haven, who had pondered the prospects of an "American" voice while studying in the University of Leipzig, concluded: "The very breadth of outlook and the lack of any musical history of importance are two great reasons why American music cannot, for the present, have any distinctive national character." However, working under Griggs in New Haven was a young organ prodigy called Charles Ives, who had been raised on the European classics and American vernacular music through his bandmaster father. Quite possibly he and Griggs talked about developing a "national" voice. When Ives studied at Yale, he wrote a piece covertly based on American gospel tunes at a time when Dvořák had caused a furore with *From the New World*, and declaring, "Inspiration for truly national music might be derived from Negro melodies or Indian chants." But at a time when the dominant culture in America was predominantly derived from Europe, many resisted such ideas, arguing that this devalued the European tradition. Edward MacDowell, in racist outrage, complained, "Masquerading in the so-called nationalism of Negro clothes cut in Bohemia will not help us."

In 1901 or 1902, Ives completed his Second Symphony, which included the introduction of "American" themes evoking gospel music and Stephen Foster ballads. Sounding remarkably like the "Americana" school of thirty years later, it was the first American classical piece with a national voice. The problem, however, was that this music was not heard when it needed to be; it was not premiered until 1951. Even so, Ives, a man of vast mental energy, continued to seize American music of his time, and incorporate various elements of it in a way that made him a precursor of modern American music. The next generation of composers saw the flowering of an American "dialect" within the European classical tradition. Aaron Copland, for example, moved to Paris in 1920 to study with Nadia Boulanger and was fired with the idea of forging a national voice, first turning to jazz and then to western and folk sources before creating his masterpieces *Billy the Kid* and *Appalachian Spring*.

Interestingly, the arguments that originally confronted notions of American nationalism expressed in response to Dvořák's *From the New World* symphony have echoes of those heard in response to the multidialectism of jazz. In both jazz and classical music, resistance to established convention is framed in terms of an idealized past violated by the crass and insensitive pluralism of the present. However, by absorbing elements from other musical cultures, jazz has successfully broadened the basis of its expressionism. Major appropriations in jazz history include drawing on the Broadway show tune toward the end of the 1920s; Mario Bauza's and Dizzy Gillespie's adaptation of Cuban rhythms into jazz; the appropriation of church modes used prior to the seventeenth century by Miles Davis and others in the 1950s ("Milestones," for example, is based on the Dorian and Aeolian modes); and the incorporation of rock rhythms and electric tone colors in the late 1960s. Through the forces of globalization, the transculturation of jazz resulting in hybridized, "glocal" forms of the music is simply a continuation of this process of change; the only difference is that these changes are now predominantly occurring outside the borders of the United States. As the guitarist Pat Metheny points out, "It's no longer 'America's Classical Music' — the globalization of the music is now fully underway and there's opportunities for musicians all over the world to address their own musical issues through the language of jazz."

Today, the arguments against Dvořák's *New World Symphony*, intended as a lesson on how to forge American nationalism in the Western tradition of classical music, have long been discredited as the European classical tradition embraced the great American composers. As T.S. Eliot pointed out, no artist can work "outside" the tradition because the tradition will stretch to accommodate anything artists do. The voices of dissent raised against Dvořák's symphony now seem quaint when seen in the context of such acclaimed composers as Aaron Copland, Samuel Barber, William Grant Still, and Elliot Carter who consciously evoke elements of Americana in their writing, bringing a welcome new dimension to European classical music. Indeed, it can be said that America's classical music *is* classical music, as Bill Kirchner notes in *The Oxford Companion to Jazz*: "Jazz has been called America's classical music — a description I disagree with. America's classical music is classical music: the music of Ives, Copland, Barber, Schuman et al. Western classical music comes from an aesthetic with its own set of ground rules, and America's contributions to it have, for the most part, been created within that framework."

The nationalists in nineteenth-century classical music and the work of American nationalistic classical composers in the twentieth century represent what happens to music when it crosses international borders. The way art evolves has nothing to do with lines drawn on maps — no one today, for example, argues that Bartók, is "inauthentic." Look at the way the Beatles sold back to America a British-ified version of black rhythm and blues, topping the American charts on February 1, 1964, and drawing the largest viewing audience in the history of American television to that point when they appeared on the *Ed Sullivan Show* eight days later. It was the curtain raiser to a remarkable period in popular music history that would transform the music industry, a period that began with what became known as "The British Invasion," when a tidal wave of British beat combos swept through America and the Western world in 1964. The Beatles had absorbed the styles of Elvis Presley, Eddie Cochran, Jerry Lee Lewis, Buddy Holly, and especially Chuck Berry. Their love of black rhythm and blues, which they first heard as youngsters in Liverpool, was immediately apparent in their music. After hearing the Beatles, a whole generation of pop fans began to wonder why they had ignored this music. The Beatles's music, epitomizing what became known as "The Liverpool Sound," represents an exemplary example of the transculturation of pop and was the trigger that prompted a remarkable period of creativity in rock music. Equally, the transculturation of jazz and the emergence of glocal dialects are now proving to be an important step in the evolution of jazz as an art form. As the British saxophonist Iain Ballamy observes: "The future of jazz surely lies with forward thinking musicians making connections globally and putting jazz back where it always was — ahead of its time with an audience catching it up rather than the music functioning as a museum piece trying to recreate itself."

The arguments for multidialectism in jazz are not about challenging the origins of jazz, or how it evolved in the twentieth century, or creating "an alternative order of significance," or of somehow "replacing" American jazz, but of musicians around the world working within the music to find innovative and original ways for it to continue to evolve and broaden the music's expressive resources in the twenty-first century in ways that are relevant to them and their audiences. As E. Taylor Atkins points out in his essay "Toward a Global History of Jazz": "Our understanding of jazz, both as a sociocultural force and as a musical idiom, is significantly impaired by construing it as a narrowly *national* art, expressive of uniquely American experiences and characteristics, and splendidly autonomous from considerations of global politics, cultural power, and national identity."

However, global developments are not something that threaten the traditional hegemonic styles of the music because as has been shown in Holland, the global hegemonic styles coexist *alongside* glocal styles. As Kevin Whitehead wrote in *New Dutch Swing*, "If the Dutch [jazz] scene teaches us anything, it's that jazz conservatives can relax, needn't worry about the harmful effects of cross-breeding jazz and other kinds of music. Because if the stuff that has happened over the last 30 years hasn't killed off mainstream jazz in Holland, it's a hardier growth than the hothouse flower its self-appointed defenders take it for."

The emergence of glocal jazz dialects represents a way that allows the global village to participate in the music, a global village that loves and enjoys American jazz but at the same time seeks to find meaning in its essential spirit of creativity and individuality that is relevant to its own local musical communities. The result is another way of hearing jazz. This is a major evolutionary shift in jazz as the dissemination of glocalized forms and the celebration of new jazz "dialects" around the world are made possible by the exchange of information on the global communications highway. As Gerry Godley, director of the Improvised Music Company in Dublin and the critically acclaimed Dublin Jazz Festival, observes:

When one listens to a musician like French guitarist Nguyen Le and his delicate reworkings of Vietnamese folk opera into a kind of 21st Century jazz fusion, it's patently obvious that the music has moved far beyond its roots, while its first principles remain true. In many ways, jazz is perfectly poised to embrace the potential of globalization, given its enthusiasm, indeed rapacious appetite, for new information — as history has shown us. It is globalization that has created the conduit for that flow of ideas on the information super highway. To push the analogy, jazz will evolve into an open source, more like Linux than Windows.

Walt Whitman heard America singing in all its variety and each voice singing what belonged to that individual and no one else. Outside America, a jazz world is singing in just such a way. As trumpeter Dave Douglas noted in *Downbeat* magazine:

> The voices and communities creating music continue unabated, and the universal is defined in diverse conversations of differing musical communities, each with its own inherent standards of artistic excellence. Relativity in music comes not in all things being equally valuable, but in all things being judged by their own specific and local criteria, with their own discriminating features and principals. We used to have the utopian ideal of a universal culture that would define worldwide cultural movements — the global village. Now it seems the universality accessible to us is a finite, limited universality, one world capable of containing many worlds.

The transculturation of jazz and pop outside America can be seen as symbolic of the way hybridity and difference is being managed in the global cultural economy, an assertion of individuality in an ever-more standardized world of cultural identity: a glocalized response to a global phenomena. When the English language went global, it confronted certain cultural assumptions, and with these assumptions came a particular world-view. How impoverished we are if we believe that there is only one way of looking at life, only one language, or only one way of playing jazz?

8
CELEBRATING THE GLOCAL: THE NORDIC TONE IN JAZZ

Are jazz traditionalists having a difficult time accepting that a music form considered "American" now has more visible international and diverse aspects within it?

Downbeat **June, 2004**

In the previous chapter, we discussed the effects of "transculturation" on a new generation of jazz performers. Forces of globalization (sending the jazz aesthetic around the world) and glocalization (the need to adopt the music to local cultural conditions) have been at work to create new and exciting musical styles. Go to Africa or Brazil and you will hear music that takes American jazz as its starting point, but is shaped, both consciously and unconsciously, by elements from local culture. As the South African Group Tribe point out, "Growing up in South Africa, we are lucky to experience many diverse styles and influences we are not trying to emulate a specific style from a specific place and time. Rather, our music stems from our own experiences in this time." However, the effect of transculturation and the resulting jazz styles that have emerged around the globe continues to be a missing strand in the narrative of jazz history. In his essay "Toward a Global History of Jazz," E. Taylor Atkins, an associate

professor of History at Northern Illinois University, underscores the need
to study:

> those non-American artists who heeded the jazz aesthetic's demand to
> constantly "innovate" and transform the music, those leaders within
> their communities and nations, who approached jazz performance in
> original ways by transcending the hegemonic "influence" of America's
> jazz titans. Collectively they challenge us to consider how the existence
> of such figures might affect common assumptions of an American
> monopoly on creative initiative in jazz. Awareness of these 'local heroes'
> and their music should force future historians of jazz to reconfigure or
> diversify the jazz pantheon. At the very least, it is important that they
> acknowledge that the evolution of jazz as an art did not occur solely
> within the borders of the United States, but rather in a global context.

The extent to which historians have customarily ignored developments
in jazz outside the borders of the United States was institutionalized in the
Ken Burns documentary film *Jazz*, where Europe's role in jazz was portrayed as a place that provided work for American jazz musicians. As
Atkins notes, "Few of Burns's American critics objected to the filmmaker's decision to omit virtually all mention of relevant developments in
other countries: the setting of the jazz history narrative exclusively within
the borders of the United States . . . struck most critics as natural and
unproblematic." In fact, one key area in the growth of jazz outside America has been Europe, whose democracies, entertainment infrastructures,
and social conditions provided similar circumstances to those that allowed
jazz to flourish in the United States.

As a jazz tradition was developing in America, a parallel tradition was
being developed in Europe, shaped by its own aesthetic responses to the
music. While this tradition hungrily absorbed the American vocabulary of
jazz, spurred by the arrival in London in 1919 of the Original Dixieland
Jazz Band (just eighteen months after they cut the first jazz recording),
gradually some musicians sought to modify jazz from a European perspective. Yet today, "European jazz" is a vast catchall that includes "global"
American styles — styles that have been disseminated around the world
through recordings and personal appearances, and imitated and absorbed
wholly or as a composite of several styles, by local musicians — that exist
alongside a variety of hybridized "glocal" approaches to the music.
Perhaps the most influential of all the European glocal styles is the so-
called "Nordic tone," an important, if largely misunderstood voice within

jazz. In fact, it is Scandinavian musicians who now seem to be at the forefront of the global jazz explosion. How then, has the process of transculturation of jazz in Scandinavia occurred in practice to produce this quite distinct glocal dialect?

The Nordic tone, with its "encoding of multiple significances," has its roots in the existentially open, angst-ridden aspects of Scandinavian culture of the past century. A common theme in Nordic art was the struggle to assert individuality, revealed in the writings and paintings of Edvard Munch, for example, and was equally apparent in the writing of Danish philosopher Soren Kierkegaard. In many ways this individuality found voice in what Swedish composer and conductor Wilhelm Stenhammar in 1910 called, a "Nordic chastity and formal simplicity which I find so bracing in these sensually voluptuous times," a phrase that neatly encapsulates the essence and relevance of the Nordic tone in jazz today.

For European artists and thinkers down the years, the Scandinavian north, historically the "pagan north," is a place that mystically beckons, its rural tranquility, majestic scenary and uninhabited interior stretching up to the Arctic Circle appealing to something primal within. Throughout the 19th century, the notion of as a key to the renewal of inner life began to take hold, as much through the landscape and rigorous climate as through the art, literature and music it helped inspire. For example, the Danish composer Per Norgard considered the music of Jean Sibelius was associated with, "the elementary, inmost and quite timeless forces of existence, with nature in its widest sense." The North brings an awareness of the closeness of man to nature, a place where the Danish artist Asger Jorn felt one might defeat the thousand and one distractions of everyday existence and feel life stirring once more in the depths of both oneself and the world. "Nordic art is dangerous," he said. "It compresses all its power *inside* ourselves."

The Nordic tone, equally drawing its power from within, is something that might be best described through analogy to Ingmar Bergman's approach to the cinema. Before Bergman, film was mostly about what could be seen and depicted in the "external" world, such as situation comedy, war, costume dramas, westerns, crime, and the chase. Very little important cinema made visible the internal drama of the self. Bergman found a way of exploring the human psyche, the "the battlefield of the soul," initially through the encouragement of Victor Sjostrom when he was director of Svensk Filmindustri, who taught him about, "The power of the naked face and to be simple, direct, and tell a story."

In the same way that Bergman avoided the external world and the obviousness of the grand movie themes, and instead explored the intensely felt, internalized emotions, the Nordic tone avoids the "external," the patterns, the favorite licks, the quotations, and extroverted technical display of much of contemporary jazz, and instead zooms in close to deeply felt melody, exposing tone, space, and intensity. As saxophonist Jonas Knutsson points out, "Here we have a strong *chanson* tradition, strong melodies and strong folk songs for fiddles. Strong melodies with strong rhythmic and harmonic structure, here we know something about melodies, it would be stupid not to use it in jazz." Equally, bassist Arlid Andersen adds, "The sound is very important, the space in the music is very important, the transparency is important, the dynamic is important, not how clever you can play your instrument, how fast you can play or how impressive you could be but how expressive you are."

With the benefit of hindsight, it is not hard to see why Scandinavia has become a major force in the global jazz explosion. Not only does it have a long history of performing the music, public money is used to provide a high level of free jazz education, a subsidized touring infrastructure, grants and bursaries for artists, and venue subsidy that create an environment where the music has flourished and grown. "The deepest musical education in Europe takes place in Sweden beginning at high school level," observed saxophonist and educator Dave Liebman. "There are many conservatories and programs in jazz as well as the other arts. For the working situation there is even a government sponsored agency which sends groups out to countryside towns for performances as well as an association of nearly 100 jazz clubs country wide. The typical Swedish jazz musician is the best overall equipped craftsman around."

In 1974, governmental support for jazz was instituted in the form of annual grants to music groups and eventually also to concert arrangers. The Swedish Jazz Federation, originally an organization of record collectors, reemerged as a network of over a hundred jazz societies throughout the country that arranged concerts on a regular basis, with some holding annual festivals partially underwritten by public funds. The 1970s also saw the evolution of municipal music schools that offered every child, starting from third grade, the chance to learn a musical instrument free of charge.

These schools have stimulated and broadened musical life in Sweden, offering free lessons for a wide variety of musical instruments and genres, including big band music, rock, classical, folk, and jazz.

Parallel with this development, the Swedish Concert Institute regularly arranged concerts at the nation's schools, thus introducing jazz and other musical genres to young people. By the late 1970s, jazz had also become a recognized subject at the Royal College of Music in Stockholm and other higher education institutions. The club scene also began to enjoy governmental support. In 1977, after many years of arranging concerts at different venues, the Stockholm-based Federation of Swedish Jazz Musicians received municipal and governmental support to operate the club Fasching in the center of Stockholm. Since then, this former discothèque has been a center for jazz activity in the city, presenting both Swedish and international attractions. At about the same time, the club Nefertiti was established in Gothenburg.

Early in the 1970s the Swedish Concert Institute started to present jazz on its subsidized record label, Caprice. In the early 1980s the government began to support independent record companies that focused on jazz and other noncommercial types of music. By the decade's end, about fifty Swedish jazz albums were being released each year, a figure that has since been doubled as a result of increased government subsidy.

But Sweden is not alone among the Scandinavian countries to build a subsidized infrastructure to support the arts, including jazz. Since the 1960s, Norway's Rikskonserterne created and established a national music program that today yields approximately 8,000 concerts per annum, mainly funded by government, of which jazz is a beneficiary. Music festivals — including jazz — have been established in several regions of the country under various auspices, together with support systems (touring, commissions, venue subsidies), which in turn play a part in the cultural job market in Norway. Finland and Denmark both enjoy governmental support for jazz, extending from education through to the bandstand. The result of such long-term strategies has seen the emergence of several major Scandinavian musicians in recent times, with Norwegian and Swedish scenes described by the Edinburgh Jazz and Blues Festival in 2004 as, "One of the most exciting jazz scenes in the world today." The emergence of Scandinavian jazz, and the evolution of a specific glocalized jazz dialect, did not happen overnight. Since the end of the nineteenth century, African American music had been welcomed in Scandinavia; indeed, in either June or July 1899 Sweden can boast making a recording of a Cakewalk. As the Original Dixieland Jazz Band arrived in England in 1919, their records were released in Scandinavia, prompting the Swedish singer Ernst Rolf to record with a "Swedish jazz band." But it was England that had a significant influence on early Swedish jazz, points out jazz historian Lars Westin:

> For many years, Swedish enthusiasts picked up on short-wave or middle-wave radios the dance music broadcasts from Savoy and other venues in London. From 1921 on, there were British bands playing in Sweden, most notably at the Grand Hotel in Stockholm, some with members that were influenced by ODJB and other visitors to London. The British influence was even more significant by way of records. Later on Jack Hylton's orchestra visited Stockholm in 1930, and by the end of the 1930s Nat Gonella had made several visits.

The attraction of jazz in Sweden, says Professor Johan Fornäs of the Linköping University in his essay "Swinging Differences," was "built upon the fact that large groups of musicians and dancing listeners were at the time looking for difference, novelty and surprise and for cultural forms capable of expressing the new sensibilities and values of modern urban life." The acceptance of jazz, he says, was a response to modernity, "jazz was a kind of key metaphor for the modern, the *new* . . . when jazz was mentioned, it was at least in the 1920s and the 1930s, in connection with new trends and lifestyles." It was not long before British and American recordings were supplemented by the real thing: touring American bands.

The roll call of American bands passing through Sweden from the 1920s through the 1950s was remarkable. Early visitors included Sam Wooding and his band in 1927 and 1929. (Wooding's group included Sidney Bechet on his first tour, although nobody seems to have noticed). In October 1933, Louis Armstrong visited and was followed by Coleman Hawkins in 1934. In 1939, Duke Ellington famously celebrated his fortieth birthday in Sweden, an event that prompted his instrumental tribute "Serenade to Sweden" on his return to America.

"I think it is relevant to mention the Quintet of the Hot Club of France made a visit to Stockholm and some other Nordic cities, too in early 1939," points out historian Lars Westin. "By that time their recordings were already well known and their visit also inspired the forming of the Swedish Hot Quintet, which was a studio band only."

In 1933 the jazz magazine *Orkester Journalen* was founded, helping disseminate jazz throughout the country with band competitions, articles on arranging, transcribed solos, record reviews, and features on jazz stars; it still exists today as *OJ*, the oldest regularly produced jazz magazine in the world.

The pace of touring increased after the Second World War. The first American visitor was Don Redman with his orchestra in 1946; the lineup included Don Byas, Peanuts Holland, Billy Taylor, Jr., and Tyree Glenn. They were followed in 1947 by The Harlem Madcaps (including Shad Collins), and this group as well as several musicians from Redman's group gave intimations of the burgeoning bebop movement. Bassist Chubby Jackson, fresh from his stint with Woody Herman's legendary First Herd, also toured the region in 1947, appearing with his "Fifth Dimensional Jazz Group." "We have been treated like royalty," wrote Chubby Jackson in *Metronome* magazine in 1948. "I visited clubs, dance halls and met most of Sweden's top musicians. Younger or old, all wanted to learn the secret of playing bebop. They dig Charlie Parker and Dizzy back! Such interest in bebop I have never seen in America. They face it exactly for what it is — a new phase of jazz."

As Jackson and his group left for America, Dizzy Gillespie and his orchestra arrived in Gothenburg in January 1948, with the likes of Benny Bailey in the trumpet section, George Nicholas and Cecil Payne in the sax section, and a rhythm section of John Lewis on piano, Al McKibbon on bass, and Kenny Clarke on drums plus Chano Pozo Gonzales on conga drum. In 1949 there were visits by James Moody, who appeared as a soloist at one of the dance restaurants, made a couple of broadcasts, and recorded "Moody's Mood for Love" for Metronome. In 1950 American visitors increased with Nat King Cole, Duke Ellington, Benny Goodman (with Zoot Sims and Roy Eldridge), Coleman Hawkins, and most famously Charlie Parker, who toured the country between November 19 and 28. Later, he would record his tribute to Sweden in his original composition entitled "Swedish Schnapps."

Absorbing these influences at first hand, several Swedish musicians began forming their own jazz bands. The 1930s saw Hakan von Eichwald and Arne Hülphers leading the top two big bands in Sweden, followed in the early 1940s by Thire Ehrling and Seymour Österwall. Between 1943 and 1947, the young, up-and-coming Lulle Ellboj's band included Rolf Ericson, Arne Domnérus, and respected arranger and tenor sax soloist Gosta Theselius. Gradually plausible imitation gave way to genuine creative talent. In 1947, two young Swedish musicians moved to America to try their luck: trumpeter Rolf Ericson, who later became a member of Duke Ellington's Orchestra, and Ake "Stan" Hasselgard, a brilliant clarinetist, who quickly became a member of Benny Goodman's Septet. There were other brilliant young players emerging too, including clarinetist Putte Wickman, saxophonist Arne Domnérus, and pianist Bengt Hallberg.

In 1951, 24-year-old saxophonist Stan Getz toured Sweden, employing the 18-year-old Hallberg, who had to get a release from his upper - secondary school to play the tour. On March 23, they recorded a version of an old Swedish folk song called "Ack Värmeland Du Sköna," which would become a jazz standard in the 1950s when, on May 9, 1952, Miles Davis recorded the song as "Dear Old Stockholm." In the eyes of many Swedish musicians, Getz's 1951 recording sanctioned the introduction of Swedish folkloric elements into jazz.

In the mid-1950s, Lars Gullin, who had emerged from Seymour Österwall's band, was the first European to win a jazz poll in the United States, topping *Downbeat* magazine's "New Star" category in 1954. Gullin's childhood and teenage years were spent on the island of Gotland in the Baltic Sea, where he developed a firsthand knowledge of rural and urban Swedish music traditions, providing the inspiration for a tonal vocabulary that evoked the Swedish folk tradition that he applied within the musical conventions of bebop. Inspired by Stan Getz's version of "Ack Värmeland du Sköna" — he was one of the Swedish musicians accompanying Getz at the 1951 session — he developed his own "Swedish" voice by incorporating elements of his own musical culture into jazz. By this time, Gullin was recognized by many as one of the finest baritone saxophonists in jazz.

In 1952, he recorded a version of "Sov du lilla vida ung" ("Sleep, little pussy-willow"). Subsequent compositions such as "First Walk," "Merlin," "Danny's Dream," "Fedja," "Fine Together," "It's True," "Like Grass," and "Castle Waltz" were imbued with a pensive melancholy characteristic of his Swedish folk heritage and of native composers such as Wilhelm Peterson-Berger and Hugo Alfvén. Gullin's pianist from 1964 on, Lars Sjosten, came under Gullin's influence as a composer and instrumentalist, as well as being inspired by the folk music and romantic art music of the Nordic countries.

During the 1950s, recordings by leading Swedish musicians began appearing on U.S. labels, including Lars Gullin, pianist Bengt Hallberg, trumpeter Rolf Ericson, and Arne Domnérus. In 1951, Leonard Feather made recordings in Sweden that were issued on an album titled *Leonard Feather's Swinging Swedes*, while Swedish musicians comprised one-half of a Blue Note release, *New Sounds from the Old World: The Swinging Swedes-The Cool Britons*. Swedish albums featuring visiting American stars also appeared, including the 1953 *Cliff Brown -Art Farmer with the Swedish All Stars*, which featured Ake Persson, Arne Domnérus, Lars Gullin, Bengt Hallberg, Gunnar Johnson, and Jack Norén.

In 1960, pianist and composer Nils Lindberg recorded an album called *Sax Appeal* that contained shimmering allusions to folk culture. A key number was "Curbits," named after an exotic flower that exists in the folklore of Dalecarlia, which was based on the harmonic structure of "Ack Varmeland du Skona." "Surprisingly I did not realize I was influenced by the folk music," Lindberg told me in 2002. "When [*Sax Appeal*] came out in 1960 I thought my arrangements — it was for four saxes and rhythm section with among others Lars Gullin on baritone — I thought I was writing American jazz! West Coast — I didn't know I was influenced by folk music." Although not unaware of his roots, the critical reaction surprised Lindberg, who subsequently wove elements of his own culture into his music. "It came naturally, let's say," he continued. "Then I used it more consciously — when I am writing music it has this touch of folk music."

In contrast, trumpeter Bengt-Arne Wallin consciously drew on Swedish folkloric elements. In 1962, he became a pioneer in combining Nordic music and jazz with *Old Folklore in Swedish Modern*. "When we got to the 1960s I was dead tired of playing American standards," Wallin told me. "Mingus numbers, blues — I was so tired you cannot believe, that's why I started looking for other music, and I found it in my lap. The dialect we're playing comes from that mix up between old Swedish folk music, old accordion music, which is completely different, and jazz."

At the time Wallin was a member of Arne Domnérus's band, whose pianist Jan Johansson was also mixing Swedish folk forms and jazz. In February 1961 Johansson recorded an album under his own name, *8 Bitar Johansson*. (It was later released in America as *Sweden Non-Stop,* and was awarded four and one-half stars by *Downbeat*.) The record was a mix of his own compositions and jazz standards, but it also included an unconventional piece for a jazz record of the time, a Swedish folk melody called 'De salde sina hemman". It garnered a favorable critical response, particularly in Scandinavia, something that encouraged him to record more Swedish folk songs during the course of 1962 to 1963 with bassist Georg

Riedel, which were collected together on the 1964 LP *Jazz pa Svenska*. "The record stands out as probably the most well known and most sold record ever in the realms of Swedish jazz," wrote Erik Kjellberg.

During the postwar years, Scandinavia had readily accepted innovations from the United States from consumer products to social attitudes absorbed through film, theatre, and literature. But by the time of Johansson's premature death in 1968, the Vietnam War was causing a crisis of conscience, prompting a lively debate around nationalism and what constituted the national soul. Johansson's music fitted perfectly into a Scandinavian culture that had become intent on reclaiming its Nordic sensibility; *Jazz pa Svenska* was in perfect synchronicity with the times, assuming the trappings of a "visionary statement," Erik Kjellberg noting it was "a rural symbol of security in a [Scandinavia] marching towards anonymous big city wildernesses."

The carefully nuanced sound of Johansson's piano, the gradation of his touch, the exquisite detail of every note revealed by the meticulous recording quality on *Jazz pa Svenska* captured a unique sound in jazz. "Nordic tonality is in fact a sort of blues, Nordic blues, Scandinavian blues if you will," explained drummer Egil Johansen. "For us jazz musicians it's but a short leap to experience that melancholy as a companion to joy." Sweden's best-selling jazz album to this day, two of its tracks, "Visa fran Utanmyra" and "Emigrantvisa," had wide exposure on Scandinavian radio, especially in Sweden where they are still played, and were seen as a symbol of the Nordic tradition in the midst of an increasingly pluralistic culture.

Johansson was by no means alone in working toward a Nordic voice within jazz. Nonetheless, after *Jazz pa Svenska*, it was Johansson's work that was the most popular, influencing subsequent generations of Scandinavian musicians. For the Norwegian pianist Tord Gustavsen, born in 1970, Johanssen not only represented a key voice in defining the Nordic tone, but also a player who had mastered the American jazz tradition:

> For me, he's very important both as a musician doing Scandinavian folk and jazz and as a funky blues piano player with a lot of subtle finesse — a lot of interesting angles. It's a very natural way of exploring things, a very natural organic way [of] getting yourself into a tradition. He did things with Stan Getz which are in the American jazz tradition, but still I hear something highly original. Although he's a very accomplished player in all aspects of playing — harmonically, rhythmically, melodically — he can still be very childlike, very fresh, almost naïve at some

points. I find that inspirational also. If you loose that somewhat "child-like approach" there's always a danger of the music stiffening and becoming alienated.

Johansson toured and recorded with Stan Getz during the period when the saxophonist was married to Monica Silfverskiod and had settled in Sweden. When they moved to Copenhagen, Johansson also moved to the Danish capital in order to work with Getz, accompanying him on tours all over Scandinavia.

"I played a lot with Jan from 1966 to his death in November 1968 and got to know him well," recalls saxophonist Lennart Aberg, one of the central figures of the contemporary Swedish jazz scene, "Jan was very open minded, the most intelligent person I have ever played with, but the Swedish folk music aspect of his playing is a very small part of his enormous range as a jazz musician. So many after him used Swedish folk music, but I don't think anybody came close to the impact Jan made, which was down to his personality and genius as a player."

At the height of his career, Johansson died in an automobile accident on the way to a church concert in Jönköping on November 9, 1968 at the age of thirty seven. At the time he was writing for Swedish radio and TV and had recorded about twenty albums under his own name.

By this time Sweden could boast several bands of high technical competence that convincingly played in the "global" hegemonic bebop–hard bop styles at a level of many top American bands, from the big band of Harry Arnold to crackling hard bop bands such as Staffan Ableen's Quintet with cornetist Lars Färnlöf as its main composer and soloist. Färnlöf composed "Grandfather's Waltz," which was recorded by Stan Getz, and several other tunes that were inspired by folk music. Other key bands included the Bertril Lövgren–Bosse Wärmell group and the Eje Thelins Kvintett with Bernt Rosengren. Rosengren also figured prominently in his own right with his own quartets and quintets from the 1960s.

A defining moment in the evolution of contemporary Scandinavian jazz came in late 1964, when composer and theorist George Russell moved to Sweden. "He had a great influence on the younger, post–Arne Domnérus generation," recalled Lennart Aberg:

> He raised the standard of Swedish jazz by his demanding modern music, and formed a big band with the best young musicians, playing his now classical "N.Y. Suite," and tunes like "Ezzthetic" and "Stratusphunk." He also had his Swedish-American Sextet, with varying personnel.

I played in the big band and with the Sextet and [at] the Molde Festival
in 1966. Although he gave lectures on his Lydian Concept, his greatest
impact, I think, came from his brilliant music and the standards he
demanded of anybody playing it.

In 1966, Russell's Scandinavian big band recorded *The Essence of George
Russell*, whose personnel included several important emerging young
musicians including the Danish trumpeter Palle Mikkelborg and Norwegians Jan Garbarek on tenor saxophone and Jon Christensen on drums.
By 1967, Garbarek had emerged as a key soloist with Russell, featuring on
Electronic Sonata for Souls Loved by Nature (in a big band that now
included Norwegians Terje Rypdal on guitar and Arlid Andersen on
bass), and was central to Russell's sextet version of the piece from 1969.
Later, Russell described Garbarek as "the most original voice in European
jazz since Django Reinhardt." Prior to the 1967 big band session, they
performed at Stockholm's Gyllene Cirkeln (Golden Circle) for a concert
that was reported at the time as one of the finest ever at the club. There,
the seventeen-piece band was joined by a special guest, trumpeter Don
Cherry, who had also taken up residence in Sweden.

When Russell returned to America in 1969 to join the faculty of the
New England Conservatory, Cherry's influence continued the impetus
Russell had given to Scandinavian jazz. "He brought the avant garde
tradition, but also the inspiration from Indian Raga, African music, Turk-
ish folk music with oriental scales, meters in 5/8, 7/8, 9/8, etc.," recalled
Aberg. This more pluralistic approach to Scandinavian jazz was, as Erik
Kjellberg points out, "symptomatic of those times. In the 1970s . . . groups
like Sevda, Rena Rama, Opposite Corner, and Oriental Wind highlighted
exotic rhythms and world elements." Aberg and pianist Bobo Stenson
were central figures in both Rena Rama and Oriental Wind. "For me
Bobo Stenson is not a 'typical' Swedish pianist, but he is typical Bobo
Stenson," says Aberg. "In the 1990s he began drawing on European
classical influences, and that was a road that Keith Jarrett opened up for
many."

Russell and Cherry had a profound influence on several Scandinavian
musicians including Aberg, Stenson, Jan Garbarek, Terje Rypdal, Jon
Christensen, and Arlid Andersen. Cherry encouraged these musicians to
allow their Nordic background to help shape their musical outlook;
Garbarek in particular cites Cherry as stimulating his interest in exploring
Norwegian folk forms.

In the 1970s, the Nordic tone was given considerable exposure with the formation of pianist Keith Jarrett's Belonging quartet on the ECM label, which took its title from the 1974 album of the same name, with Jan Garbarek on tenor saxophone, Palle Danielsson on bass, and Jon Christensen on drums. The group toured Europe, America, and Japan and recorded two studio and two live albums; it was described by trumpeter and Associate Professor Ian Carr, Jarrett's biographer, as "one of the finest groups in jazz history." It gave considerable exposure to the musical ethics of the three Scandinavian musicians, with Dave Liebman noting, "[They] had a major influence on the jazz scene worldwide as far as setting the *tone* of a style (my italics)."

Garbarek's association with the Munich-based ECM label brought the Nordic tone to a worldwide audience. "I think about the cultural difference," says Manfred Eicher, who founded ECM and has produced the majority of the label's output:

> Even though [Garbarek] was influenced by a lot of American musicians and one could see the influence of Coltrane, Archie Shepp, and Albert Ayler on [his] early recordings — he very often says this in interviews — there was a kind of European "speech" and an idea that this could be something else. The sounds and ideas, what kind of harmonies to choose, that had to do with the surroundings. I just think people who live at that time in Scandinavia, somehow the musicians understood solitude and probably they lived in solitude. They understood transparency and clarity and somehow formulated a certain kind of approach towards music that was entirely different to an American musician living in New York. But that had to do with the sociological context.

Garbarek's music represented an ordered calm in the often frantic world of jazz, projecting the stark imagery of nature in the frozen north. He notes, "I can't say what extent growing up in Norway would influence you, but I imagine deep down it must have some influence. There are very dramatic changes of the seasons and the landscape is also dramatic." Rigorous and highly disciplined, he created an evocative tranquillity strongly rooted in Nordic folk forms that gave prominence to his saxophone *tone* as the main expressive force. On the album *Dis*, he created a context where his haunting saxophone appeared to commune with nature, an effect heightened by his use of a wind harp. His working groups in the early 1980s included Bill Frisell on guitar, Eberhard Weber on bass, and

Michael Pasqua on drums. Later work included his group with pianist
Rainer Brüninghaus, solo recordings against electronic backdrops, and
Officium, a collaboration with The Hilliard Ensemble, which passed
1.4 million sales in 2004.

The Nordic tone can be heard in the playing of musicians from all the
Scandinavian countries. Drummer Edward Vesala emerged as one of the
key musicians in the burgeoning Finnish free jazz scene of the late 1960s
and early 1970s. He came to international attention in 1973 as a member
of Jan Garbarek's trio on *Triptykon*, which stands as the saxophonist's
most abstract statement on record. Subsequently, Vesala toured extensively as a coleader of the Tomasz Stanko–Edward Vesala Quartet, which
ended in 1978 after recording five albums. In addition to his involvement
in free jazz, Vesala also played blues, rock, tango, classical, and film music.

Vesala began his career with two years' study at the Sibelius Academy,
concentrating on music theory and orchestral percussion, which helped
establish him as a drummer, while he was developing a parallel reputation
as a composer in a variety of multimedia projects. His music for theater
included settings of the Finnish national epic *Kalevala*, which drew on
very old folk ballads and his experiences growing up in the remote forests
of eastern Finland, where he became conscious of Finnish folk music's
magical–religious function and the role music and myth played in the lives
of the rural community. In 1974 he recorded *Nan Madol*, which presented
a mixture of brooding Scandinavian melancholia, freely improvised
episodes, and sinister folk dance imagery. It established him as one of a
handful of European jazz composers to make sense of his cultural heritage
alongside the dominant African American ideology of jazz expressionism.

Satu, from 1977, continued Vesala's restless experimentation with a
larger ensemble, this time built around the Vesala–Stanko Quartet with
some impassioned playing from guitarist Terje Rypdal. Vesala entered the
1980s heading his Sound & Fury music workshops, part percussion clinics
and part music school, from which emerged his experimental ensemble
Sound & Fury on the album *Lumi* (1986). As Vesala observed the American jazz renaissance during the 1980s, he became disturbed at what he saw
as glib revivalism, whose surface slickness, he believed, masked the music's
loss of faith. His opposition to this perceived emotional sterility was voiced
most forthrightly on his next album, *Ode to the Death of Jazz*, recorded in
1989, a denouncement of the status quo that he felt had come to prevail in
jazz. "This music is first of all about feeling and the transmission of *feeling*,"
he wrote in the liner notes. "This empty echoing of old styles — I think it's

tragic. If that is what the jazz tradition has become then what about the tradition of creativity, innovation, individuality, and personality?"

Although an integral part of Scandinavia, Denmark has a jazz scene that is perhaps less in tune with the tundra wastelands, pine forests, and dramatic scenery of its Nordic sister states, more in tune with the urban intensity of American jazz. "Denmark does not have a strong folk music tradition like its Scandinavian neighbors Sweden, Norway and Finland," says Cim Meyer, editor of Denmark's leading jazz magazine *Jazz Special*:

> Denmark's geographical position on top of Germany has made us more continentally oriented than the rest of Scandinavia and also more cosmopolitan. Historically the German occupation during World War II had a huge effect, a period that's called "The Golden Swing Era of Danish Jazz," when Danish jazz music was isolated and the public interest became a way of showing resistance. Danish jazz today is often more influenced by [the] US than our neighbors, that is less ethereal and more hard swinging. Projects across borders are also happening more and more, so you could say the present Danish jazz music scene is an amalgamation of the "Nordic Tone" with the more energetic, powerful American style — something distinct in its own right that cannot be pigeonholed.

In the postwar years, the influence of American jazz on the flourishing Danish jazz scene was reinforced by several important American jazz musicians taking up residence in and around Copenhagen, including Dexter Gordon, Ben Webster, Ella Fitzgerald, Stan Getz, and others. Their inspiration helps produce several world-class Danish jazz musicians, including Niels-Henning Ørsted Pedersen, Alex Riel, and Jesper Thilo fluent in American styles; indeed Pedersen, who as a young man had played with Bud Powell, was for several years Oscar Peterson's bassist.

In 2001, the then-Danish Prime Minister, Poul Nyrup Rasmussen, wrote that, "The Danish jazz scene is still vigorous; there is a fine environment with many foreign musicians, a young talented generation and a dedicated audience." In the new millennium years, a number of distinctive musicians and groups have emerged, including Thomas Clausen, who has worked for years with Brazilian music; Erling Kroner, who has worked with tango music (after years focused on Mingus); and a whole generation of young musicians who are devoted to the music of Paul Motian.

"Danish jazz has tended in the past to emulate American models," says Cim Meyer:

But it now has a number of established artists with a distinctive and different voice: Pierre Dørge's New Jungle Orchestra tours all over the world as does Palle Mikkelborg and Marilyn Mazur in various constellations. New voices push Danish music in many different directions — electric, bluesy jazz, Balkan-music, and a host of other permutations. Much has a high energy level, such as Jakob Dinesen, Fredrik Lundin, Thomas Agergaard, Josefine Cronholm (Swedish but living in Copenhagen with husband and kids), Hans Ulrik, Carsten Dahl and upcoming artists such as as Søren Siegumfeldt Eriksen's String Swing, drummer and organizer Kresten Osgood, keyboard player Jacob Anderskov, and the groups MS4 and Ibrahim Electric.

In Norway in the 1980s, Arild Andersen's Masqualero (named after the Wayne Shorter composition of the same name from the Miles Davis album *Sorcerer*) emerged as a key Scandinavian band in a Nordic style, with Jon Balke on piano, Jon Christensen on drums, Nils Petter Molvaer on trumpet, and Tore Brunborg on saxophones. "When I came to Oslo, real young, I was playing in the National Theatre of Norway with Jon Balke," recalled Nils Petter Molvaer:

> He said "We're going to have a gig with a trio, do you want to join in? It's a gig in Kongsburg." I said yes, we looked at some notes and stuff and played the first gig there, and then we got together for 13 years. For me to play with these older guys — especially to play with Jon Christensen, the process of reacting to him — was very, very learning experience, and it was like you had to stand on your own two feet, you can't lean on anyone, you know? Sometimes it's like someone grabs you from behind and lifts you up, so sometimes I could experience this, and sometimes he didn't play and then there you were, hanging there! You just had to deal with these things. And for me this was incredible, very, very important part of my career and my musical training.

Their debut album *Band A Part* was followed by *Aero* with guitarist Frode Alnaes replacing Balke. "The idea was we were a group of people and everybody had full responsibility for the music, everybody has the freedom to do what they want. If you have a band like that then you can really play the moment. That for me was Masqualero in a nutshell, the freedom of doing things," said Andersen. Their third album *Re-Enter* saw them incorporating to a greater extent folkloric elements, including two traditional songs "Lill Lisa" and "Heiemo Gardsjenta" arranged by Andersen. "We went into that folk thing at the end of the 1980s," said

Molvaer. "It was basically Arlid, who started to collaborate with this singer called Sidsel Endressen, and he had some themes and we really liked them and we improvised from there totally. It was more like instead of playing blues we played Norwegian folk music, sort of messed it up a bit [laughs], playing around with it is what we did!"

Andersen had increasingly become interested in integrating Scandinavian folkloric elements into his music, often working with folk musicians to reach a deeper understanding of his cultural heritage. "I became increasingly aware that this music was very much a part of who I am as a musician. I began to seek simplicity and meaning," he said. For the 1990 Vossa Jazz Festival, he adapted compositions of Edvard Grieg, resulting in the album *Sagn*. "I then had a commission to write music in the folkish idiom with a band of improvising musicians," said Andersen. With Kirsten Bräten Berg, voice and Munnharpe, Nana Vasconcelos on percussion, Bendik Hofseth on tenor saxophone and voice, Bugge Wesseltoft, keyboards, and Eivind Aarset on guitar, they recorded *Arv* in 1993, a brilliant conceptualization of folk and jazz. "Looking back on that band, the development of Bugge Wesseltoft was incredible," recalls Andersen. "He was coming on so strongly. And this was true of Nils Petter [Molvaer] with Masqualero. He had that energy and personality that you could see him develop as a musician."

In the 1990s, the folk singer Lena Willemark formed the pioneering Swedish folk-jazz group Enteli, which, as Erik Kjellberg has pointed out, "placed the Swedish folk tone in new surroundings." With saxophonist Jonas Knutsson, keyboard player Johan Söderqvist, bouzouki player Ale Möller, and percussionist Bengt Berger, they explore medieval ballads and folk songs within a contemporary jazz setting. Willemark studied at the music conservatory in Stockholm and used her studies to find ways in which her folk music background could be combined with more progressive ideas. "I played quite a lot with jazz musicians and sang jazz standards and my own material," she says. Collaborations with Ale Möller resulted in two key albums that unified this concept, *Nordan* (1994) and *Agram* (1996), which combined various jazz and folk musicians, including bassist Palle Danielsson.

Jonas Knutsson was key to both of these projects. "I found it more interesting to make music out of our own blues, which is special, and original," says Knutsson:

> You cannot find this music in any other place in the world, so that's why
> I started to get into the Swedish "tradition." Jazz is a fantastic vehicle for

doing things like this because the tradition in jazz is that you sound like yourself. It's a fantastic music and quite unique because of that.

I don't recall when I wanted to make my own music, but it had partly to do with working with musicians from different cultures. I went to Italy when I was 18 and discovered Italian musicians have their own way of approaching jazz, they were influenced by American jazz, but they wanted to do their own thing. I was also very inspired by the music that was released on ECM, all that concept, I found it fascinating to make music that way. It was not traditional American style. I had started to play along with records, tried to copy solos of Phil Woods because I love his music so much. I then went to the conservatory in Stockholm, and got to thinking deeply about art, what is originality in art in this country, because what is interesting to the rest of the world is what is original. If I wanted to keep on in Phil Woods style, I did not want to be a bad version of Phil Woods, because Phil Woods is so great. So I got interested in mixing Swedish music and jazz, and that is how it began.

In 2003, Stenson and Aberg, who had recorded with Cherry during his Swedish residency, collaborated on an album of duets. *Bobo Stenson/Lennart Aberg* was a mixture of originals and jazz standards by Monk, Kenny Wheeler, Lars Gullin, and an excellent version of "Nature Boy," which opened the album. Stenson's reflective "Bengali Blue" continued the mood of quiet introspection, with Lennart reaching into the very heart of the music to create a solo that fits into the song's architecture perfectly. His own original "Lisas Piano" is revealing of his past musical associations with Cherry, Kenny Wheeler, and Jan Johansson in its questing, questioning mood. Together, Aberg and Stenson created music of great depth, not content to play through the compositions, but always trying to unearth new meanings, their lyricism imbued with the particular melancholy of the Nordic tone.

In the early millennium years, Scandinavia had acquired a reputation as a jazz "hot spot" across Europe, with genuine curiosity and interest in its unique jazz scene. In addition to Jan Garbarek, Jon Christensen, Palle Danielsson, Arlid Andersen, Bobo Stenson, Terje Rypdal, Lennart Aberg, and Per Henrik Wallin who had established themselves on the European circuit, an exciting generation of young Scandinavian musicians were emerging who were beginning to make a reputation for themselves across Europe, each in their own way reflecting a distinct Nordic tonality in their music. Musicians such as Nils Petter Molvaer and Bugge Wesseltoft enjoyed best-selling albums mixing jazz and rhythms from club culture and considerable success on the European jazz circuit. As Wesseltoft observed:

> I realized there was a certain identity of Norwegian jazz which was important, of course. The roots come from America, but still we were able to transform or transport it into a certain Norwegian way of playing jazz, which is more mellow maybe. I mean, you can like or you can dislike it, but it's something on its own. Being aware of that I was proud of it, and the fact that for instance Jan Garbarek and Jon Christensen and these musicians were world famous, was a very important point for me when I decided to go out on my own with a first solo project. I did not really want to copy their style, because I think there's enough bands already in Norway trying to play the same style, just not that good as the originals somehow, which is of course is always like that — you are never as good as the original. I wanted to do something different but still hopefully at least keep the tradition from what I had experienced with from playing with people like Jon Christensen. I was into electronic stuff which was not so common in the Norwegian jazz at that time, and also I have always been beat orientated somehow — so what I tried to do was a mixture of groovy music, but still of course hopefully trying to keep the atmosphere from the Nordic jazz thing.

Acoustic artists were also making considerable impressions throughout Europe. Leading acoustic acts include the group Atomic (with a Swedish front line and a Norwegian rhythm section); Norwegian pianist Havard Wiik, and bassist Terje Gewelt; Swedish saxophonists Mats Gustafson, Jonas Kullhammar, and Magnus Lindgren (also a composer-arranger), and pianist Jan Lungdren; and, from Finland, the brilliant saxophonist Jouni Jarvela, the U-Street All Stars, the Ilmillikki Quartet; and pianist Jarmo Savolainen.

In 2004, the West Norway Jazz Centre, the Norwegian Jazz Forum, the Rikskonsertene, and the Norwegian Ministry of Foreign Affairs combined to create a fund of NOK 900,000 to promote two Norwegian musicians across Europe between 2004 and 2006. The fund was intended to pay for the travel expenses of both musicians and their groups so they could tour their music across Europe and build their reputation to an extent they would no longer need subsidy. It was an ambitious undertaking, reflecting on the importance Norway attaches to the jazz scene.

The first recipients of this award were the Norwegian trumpeter Arve Henriksen and the drummer Paal Nilssen-Love. Henriksen was already one of Norway's most in-demand jazz musicians. His distinctive trumpet sound can be found on a wide range of albums, as well as several releases under his own name, including *Sakuteiki* (2001) and *Chiaroscuro* (2004). Henriksen's trumpet playing is influenced by Japanese *shakuhatchi* flute playing, a solo art developed by Buddhist monks, introduced to him by Nils Petter Molvaer. It became the basis of his solo concerts, which he has performed all over Europe:

> I had the idea of doing a solo trumpet improvisation inspired by the *shakuhatchi* tradition and also bringing in some electronics, and the first solo concert I did was actually in my own village, just wanted try it and see if I could dare to go onstage alone! I played my first real concert in 1998 in Bergen, and from that point I have been doing some solo concerts, and I remain quite nervous about it. It is interesting to see how much courage you have, how much energy, and where are the limits for your own musicality and with a solo project you also have to communicate with the audience.

Henriksen attended the University of Trondheim's jazz course during 1987 to 1991. While in Trondheim, he met the founding members of what would become the band Supersilent: keyboard player Stale Storløkken on keyboards and Jarle Vespestad on drums. Hendriksen recalls:

> We met in my second year and . . . that was the most important thing that happened to me, in my career. We rehearsed several hours every day, worked three years rehearsing and then started to play some concerts. Electronics helped me be "in" the music all the time. This old tradition with the quintet with Miles, they play the melody, solos, melody, is over. I wanted to be more "in" the music, electronics helped me be there.
>
> We called the trio Effect, we made a CD in 1994, we played together for some years and then one year when we didn't do anything. Then the idea of Supersilent came up to bring in Helger Sten [on electronics], and then we played this concert in 1997 in Bergen. At that point this fantastic man Rune Storsve, who formed the Rune Grammophon label, wanted us to be the first band on his label. So from that point we just continued to play together as a quartet, and we found it so interesting, it was extreme in every way, the music at that point was noisy, loud and aggressive and it was new to me. But we had an idea that we had found something that was very new, very fresh for us and we continued. And now we have done 6 albums [by 2004].

Henriksen has also recorded with the Christian Wallumrod Ensemble and various groups led by saxophonist Trygve Seim

Pianist Anders Widmark studied at the Royal Academy of Music in Stockholm where he met Bob Brookmeyer, who was so impressed with his playing he wrote the suite *Dreams* for him, a turning point in the young pianist's life. He subsequently recorded the suite with Brookmeyer and the Stockholm Jazz Orchestra in 1989. Among Scandinavia's finest young musicians, Widmark is an accomplished pianist in the hegemonic styles of the Cannonball Adderley groups, Erroll Garner, and Ramsey Lewis, as he demonstrated on *Soul Piano* (2004) recorded live at the Fasching Club in Stockholm. The album was in effect one voice raised in protest to those who have asserted that Europeans cannot play "the blues." However, he is also very conscious of his own cultural background. In 1998 he recorded *Hymns* with his trio, taking sacred Swedish chorales, ranging from a hymn from the fourth century composed by Ambrosius, hymn writer, saint, and Bishop of Milan, to a twelve-tone hymn written in 1959 by the Swedish composer Sven-Erk Bäck, and adapting them to jazz. "It is important to me to reflect my place in the world, where I come from, something of my own culture in what I play," he said. "So yes, there maybe is a Nordic blues that reflects where we are in the world."

In 2003 to 2004 the debut album of a young, unknown Norwegian pianist Tord Gustavsen, *Changing Places,* sold a remarkable 60,000 copies in its first year of release. Gustavsen, a pianist of poetic cast, is an exceptionally lucid soloist with a sure sense of melodic structure and lyrical imagination. Together with bassist Harald Johnsen and drummer Jarle Vespestad, who followed the precise contours of his compositions with unflappable taste, they produced an album rich with inner meaning and nuance. Inhabiting mainly slow and medium tempos, they probed deep into the heart of Gustavsen's twelve original compositions. The trio's scrupulous use of dynamics gave shape and definition to each piece; drummer Vespestad often reducing his playing to pointillistic pings, shimmering cymbal backdrops, rhythms tapped out by his fingers on the snare head or using two cardboard tubes (of the sort that might be supplied with kitchen towels) instead of drumsticks to gently shade the music.

Gustavsen studied sociology, psychology, and the history of religions at the University of Oslo, attaining a B.A., and in 1993 he applied to the jazz department of the Conservatory of Music in Trondheim, and graduated three years later. Returning to Oslo he continued his career as a freelance musician while continuing his academic studies at the University of Oslo, graduating with a degree in musicology. During this time he was involved in several musical projects, saying the interaction of playing with musicians is as important to his musical development as his solo work with his trio. With the Nymark Collective, a band that explores rip-roaring New Orleans grooves on *First Meeting*, their debut album from 2000, Gustavsen plays in an exuberant, funky style on numbers like "Blues Tonic" or "Jubilee Sunday," a style far removed from the one he plays with his trio, yet clearly his piano playing emerges from this tradition.

In 2000 he joined singer Silje Nergaard, one of Scandinavia's leading jazz vocalists, on her 2000 album *Port of Call*. "After playing a lot with Silje, touring and recording with her, the trio emerged out of that," says Gustavsen. "We started feeling this chemistry, this sound we make when we play, very focussed, very minimalist; something we felt we should develop as a setting in its own respect." As part of Nergaard's band, they recorded two further albums, *At First Sight* (2001) and *Nightwatch* (2003). Gustaven continued to tour extensively with her, including an appearance at Jazz at Lincoln Center in 2004.

Gustavsen had a religious upbringing; he played piano in church while studying the instrument formally in classical studies. "These inspirations are crucial," he says. "What I am doing is combining my classical studies with the fact I've studied a lot of cool jazz — Lennie Tristano and Lee Konitz, for example — and the fact that I've played a lot in churches playing gospel music." Gustavsen also cites the influence of Keith Jarrett and Bill Evans on his playing. "I am also indebted to Wayne Shorter for his melodic thinking and composing. Then there are two Scandinavian pianists, Norway's Jon Balke and Sweden's Jan Johansson, who make up the cornerstone of my Scandinavian influences. Balke has a basic lyricism, and a rhythmic strength that has been a tremendous inspiration."

Gustavsen's playing reflects the Nordic tone in its spare, pensive themes. "I would think a lot of this is really unconscious because you are shaped by the culture you are brought up in," says Gustavsen:

> Even though we live in a very globalized world and Norway is very much a part of that, it is still shapes me differently than it would living in New York or London. I wouldn't be the one to know exactly what happened there because I haven't experienced anything else. But some of it is on a conscious level. I hear phrases from *Setesdal* [traditional Norwegian music] for example. It's a long answer but . . . its an example of the interplay between the unconscious and the conscious — the melancholy and

reflective moods, associated with Nordic music. This terms "spacious open music" have been connected with the term Nordic so this mixture of things that are in my musical self will come forward whether I want it too or not.

The Finnish pianist Alexi Tuomarila emerged in the early millennium years as a musician of enormous ability and imagination. Tuomarila studied classical piano at the Espoo Music Institute in Finland, but came to jazz through his father's record collection. He went on to study at the Royal Conservatory in Brussels, Belgium, where he graduated with a Master of Music degree in 1999. Tuomarila has won several prizes and awards, including the trophy for best band at the International Jazz Hoeilaart competition in Belgium, and best soloist, in 1999; in 2001, he won first prize in the international jazz soloist competition in Monaco, the Newcomer of the Year Award in Belgium's Django d'Or awards, and, with his quartet, the international jazz band competition in Avignon, France.

Pianist Brad Mehldau celebrated Tuomarila's achievement in the liner notes to his debut album *O2* (2003):

> What struck me first was his sound on the instrument. He gets a clear tone out of the piano that makes you focus on what he's playing. His playing "cuts through" the other instruments, demanding your attention, and never gets ambiguous or unclear. Even when he's playing only single note melodies, they have an authority to them that draws you in as a listener. That authority also comes from Alexi's strong, innate rhythmic sense. He's not just playing lines when he is soloing, but is really concerned with phrasing. You can hear sentences with a beginning and an end, punctuated by rhythmic accents pull on the drummer's groove. Those sentences form paragraphs, and Alexi has a strong compositional sense to his soloing as well, allowing ideas to develop organically, taking his time, building a solo with patience. That kind of maturity in a musician is really more the exception than the rule and it's always a real pleasure when you hear a player who's addressing several things at once — melodic phrasing, compositional storytelling, a strong rhythmic dynamic and a concern for the sound of the instrument.

This is, in many ways, a wonderful description of the so-called Nordic tone. Tuomarila's playing, a rich, expansive vocabulary that is never flaunted but put to compositional ends within the framework of his improvisations, has a very Scandinavian feel to it: a lyrical intensity that

eschews prolixity, and a folk song–like flavor, such as on the track
"Noáidi," mixed with a touch of the profound melodicism of Sibelius, as
on "Sacrament."

In 2004, it was announced that the Esbjörn Svenssön Trio, or E.S.T. as
they like to be known, were the winners of the European Jazz Award,
voted by twenty-one industry professionals across Europe. The prize,
which has a substantial bursary, is awarded to celebrate "outstanding
musical achievement in the field of jazz." It was a fitting climax to an
incredible few years that had seen the group — Svenssön on piano with
Dan Berglund on bass and Magnus Öström on drums — pick up just
about every jazz award in Europe (including a BBC Jazz Award in 2003)
and become one of the top attractions on the European jazz circuit. Their
rise has been so strong that it even caused consternation among the top
American agents, anxious that their prime market was coming under pressure from the homegrown product.

After almost fifteen years of constant touring, E.S.T. had become, in
European jazz terms at least, regarded as something of a supergroup.
Born in 1964, Esbjörn's single-mindedness was apparent even as a child
when he refused piano lessons, preferring to find his own way. His
mother was a pianist who played Chopin, Liszt, and Bach, and his
father was a jazz fan who played records by Ellington, Monk, and
Parker. At sixteen he decided to study in music college, and at eighteen,
he was asking for a jazz teacher. "I was assigned Jerzy Lisewski in '82-
'83," he recalls:

> He was a piano player, a Polish teacher, and he knew everything — the
> classical field and also the jazz, the improvised field, an extremely good
> piano player, he learned a lot to me. I mean, I was working very hard with
> myself practicing, trying to develop, trying to compose and play in different
> moods. He was very keen on that as well, which for me was fantastic,
> things I was already doing but somebody was looking at them, with some
> critical ideas about it. I only had him for one year because then I moved to
> Stockholm, to music university. There I had another piano teacher, sup-
> posed to be a jazz teacher, but that really sucked, it was so bad I just told the
> headmaster of the school "This is not working," so he gave me a classical
> piano teacher instead. So I then played classical piano in music university
> — I was there to play jazz but there was no teacher to teach that! So there-
> fore Jerzy is the only piano teacher in jazz I had, and he was really good.

One of his first jobs after university was with a hard bop band:

I got a chance to play tours, like playing two weeks in a row, a gig every night, that was great, quintet jazz — piano trio and saxophone, trumpet. From that I really got a chance to play jazz, that was really "jazz," no doubt about it. When we were playing gigs everyone had a great sound, the saxophone player the trumpet player, the drummer, the bass everything, but where is the sound of the band? They weren't thinking of how does it sound out there to the audience. It was more or less acoustic, I always thought the drummer played too hard, you couldn't hear yourself, and I was trying so hard to have a nice sound on the piano but it was no use. Wait a minute, is this what I want to do?

By now Svensson had established himself on the Swedish jazz scene and had discovered Keith Jarrett's *Facing You*, an important influence, but surprised everyone by leaving jazz to work with some of Sweden's pop elite:

I started playing a lot of pop, playing synthesizers and composing pop songs, singing and playing with pop artists and not improvising at all, just playing what they wanted me to play, having the right sound, and then again I felt like I was lost. I went back to the piano more and more and I started to play with Magnus [Öström] again, we had played together when we were younger. I had this feeling, probably around 1990, so I got back to the piano and started to practice more and really felt like I really wanted to play the piano, I like what I am doing on the piano, I missed jazz, I missed the sound. That's how it started, that's what we're working with in the trio since we started, the "sound" of the band.

Getting enough work to support his trio took time, and in the meantime he worked with various other jazz groups. Gradually, however, he got his trio project off the ground. "We had been trying hard for many years before it really started to happen," he recalls.

First we traveled without a record company, without a booking agent, that was really tough, because I did all the booking myself to get enough gigs so I could keep Dan and Magnus, make them stay in the band. . . . The playing and the composing was the fun part, but to sit on the phone and tell everyone how great you are, you should really book us, that wasn't too fun. . . . But then Ziggy Loch signed us for the ACT label, and also at the same time we found Hopper Management, they are both based in Munich. So suddenly we had a fantastic weapon to conquer Europe! Because a great record company and a great booking agency is the kind of combination you need. We had to come up with the music, of course! But, then when that is done, we had a great company promoting the album and you have tours and everybody can see there's something happening. That's very useful and a common concept but it's not often done.

The knowledge he had gained in working in the pop field — basically how to tell the world you exist and how to present the music — proved invaluable in establishing the group. Where possible, they toured with a sound engineer and a lighting designer because of the emphasis they placed on presentation. The trio points out that while they love jazz, they also grew up in one of the most creative periods in pop music. "I listen to rock music all my life, I grew up with pop music and hard rock in the 1970s, Black Sabbath and Rush and I still listen to them a lot," says bassist Berglund. "I used to say my biggest hero is Richie Blackmore [of Deep Purple], I love to hear him!"

It is this openness to contemporary music of all kinds that allows them to sound the way they do. "I think when we were 14 or 15 years old, or something, all our interests were in pop," says drummer Öström. "Later on we were always open to different kind of musics and that helps create our group sound, because we put these influences into this group. We couldn't sound like we do if we didn't have those interests, if we just listened to bebop." By keeping their lines of musical input open, taking in new ideas and passing then through the "creative filter" of their own musical experiences, they have kept their music fresh and moving forward. By taking inspiration from popular culture and groups like Radiohead and Wilco, they are thinking outside the loop of the tradition-based jazz orthodoxy.

"In all music there is a certain attitude," says Svenssön:

It's like religions — "We have the answers, what you doing is wrong, we're doing the right thing!" . . . That's not something I like at all, I don't like religions at all, because it comes from people being scared. As soon as somebody does something you don't recognize, they say, "That's dangerous, you should do it this way, because this is the way I know." It's about control, I don't like it. If people try and be open there's so much to explore, to do, and to create. We grew up with rock n'roll — that was our music, and of course I was singing rock, wanting to be a rock star. We listen to a lot to new music that is not jazz, more pop. Singer songwriters. Might be anything, just try and find new music, someone who is creating something, someone who is doing something new. We want to hear stuff that bites us, we try to find that music. It's not a question that the only good music you can find is classical music or jazz, the problem is to find it and hear music and get inspired. I don't know how it works really, the creative filter or whatever, but it's fun.

Just as in language, however, Scandinavians are going Scandinavian-ize, whether consciously or not. "A lot of people talk about [the Nordic tone]," says Svensson. "When I am in Germany, they talk a lot about it, in France, in Italy. Here we don't talk about it at all. If there is a Nordic tone, we are the Nordic tone! So we don't think about [it], but I think when I compare in general Nordic music to European music, there is some kind of difference, I don't really know what it is, maybe it has something to do with the folk music, or the light, or the less of light, but there is definitely something, there *is* something!"

The influence the Nordic tone is being felt in the rest of the Europe, and even on the U.S. jazz scene. It can be heard in the work of the Scots saxophonist Tommy Smith and the English saxophonist Andy Sheppard. In 2001, tenor saxophone virtuoso Michael Brecker told me he was greatly attracted to the "mountain jazz" style of Jan Garbarek, whose unhurried, intense lyricism and exploitation of the saxophone tone influenced his playing on *Ballad Book* (released in 2001). In 2001, pianist Herbie Hancock told the British magazine *Jazzwise* how, during the recording of his album *Future2Future*, he was listening to the work of Norwegian trumpeter Nils Petter Molvaer during the recording sessions: "Chuck Mitchell, who had been the president of Polygram's jazz division sent over a bunch of discs for me to listen to by Nils Petter Molvaer and some other musicians . . . and suddenly it clicked, and I said to myself, 'Oh, I see!'"

Such examples of a glocal jazz style feeding back into global American jazz styles is similar to the way in which glocalized versions of pop music have fed back into international or global rock, such as on Paul Simon's *Graceland*. Regardless of what jazz used to be, it is now subject to the disciplines of the global cultural economy, and, as is every art form, inter-acting with other cultural forms, a process that is age old. No culture goes untouched by the world, and as cultures become increasingly subject to the disciplines and pressures of the global marketplace, change becomes more and more inevitable. Yet historically the purest cultural values are often products of complex strands of interaction; in jazz, cultural interac-tion (transculturation) has been a recurring theme in the evolution of the music outside the United States, revealing a continuing dialogue with other musical forms to broaden the scope of jazz expressionism.

Today, the different glocal styles around the world hold the key to the future of jazz as they interact with the global American styles. As musicians adapt aspects of these glocal styles that they feel might work for them, various concepts and approaches are tried and either rejected or adapted in the constant quest to produce new contexts that broaden the expressive potential of the music. Where once the dynamic for this change and evolution in jazz came from within America, it is now shifting to its glocal communities around the world. As just one example, the Nordic tone's "chastity and formal simplicity" offers a different approach to playing and hearing jazz, its rural lucidity and folkloric allusions providing a contrast to the intensity of urban, big city life.

9

A QUESTION OF
SURVIVAL: MARKETPLACE
OR SUBSIDY

If we take a look at jazz in the USA now it exists only as a historical niche culture. Musicians can hardly make a living in a society which offers no subsidies in this musical genre.

**Steen Meier, Chairman of The Nordic Music Council
and Copenhagen's famous JazzHouse.**

The social and cultural forces that helped shape American jazz in the past are largely absent today, and have been replaced by the homogenizing effect of the market place. Many small jazz clubs economically unfeasible to maintain have been replaced by large "performing arts centers" that book only the biggest names — at the highest fees. Jazz is fighting to be heard among a huge choice of leisure activities competing for the entertainment dollar that were unheard of in Duke Ellington and Charlie Parker's day: not least the huge popularity of ring tones and multitask cell phones, DVDs, video games, and cable television. Multinational entertainment conglomerates promote their culture products through the multiple strategies of pop music, television, and style magazines on a global scale, creating a monoculture that threatens to trample local and more diverse cultural expressions. The American cultural critic, Frederic Jameson, argues that it is no longer credible to see culture as an ideological representation since we are not only witnessing the collpase of the distinction between high culture and popular culture but the collpase of the distinction between culture itself and economic activity.

Of the hundred largest economies in the world, more than half are not countries at all, but corporations, bringing the notion of the nation state in question. As a result, a growing number of countries have tried to resist the homogenizing effect of the market by protecting their indigenous cultures through state intervention. "Governments have a duty to make available the widest range of cultural activity. We must not let the market alone decide. Without that balance we face the homogenization of culture," said Tessa Jowell, Minister of Culture in Tony Blair's government, in 2005. France, Canada, South Korea, China, and Australia — to name just a few — have all passed laws to help protect native arts and to encourage local producers to be competitive with the multinational companies. Measures to protect "local" cultures from the inevitable effects of commodification and homogenization in the global marketplace have proved largely successful. Could it be that state intervention and funding might provide the means by which jazz could be protected from the tensions of the marketplace and aid its survival?

While the globalization of jazz in the early years of the twentieth century owed much to the fast expanding record industry, it also plugged into a leisure revolution that was global in scope. When the first American jazz recordings reached Europe, there was already a sophisticated production and distribution network in place to take advantage of the Jazz boom. Even before the jazz and dance craze had taken hold, the Victor Talking Machine Company's worldwide sales in the early 1910s was 50 million, of which 10 million were from Britain and an equal number from Germany, with 300,000 sales in Sweden for the year 1913 alone. The Victor Company's representative in Europe, the Gramophone Company, made at least 200,000 different recordings between 1898 and 1921. Together with its main competitors, Columbia, Pathé, and Lindström, that number more than doubled.

Equally, the leisure revolution that had spread through the Western world spawned a similar entertainment infrastructure in Europe to that which existed in most large urban American centers: a burgeoning radio industry, dance halls, cinemas, stage shows, clubs, cabarets, restaurants, and bars, all catering to mass audiences enjoying a level of prosperity unknown during the previous century. As in America, it was precisely the kind of environment in which jazz thrived. Together with the established chains of production and distribution of the recording industry, jazz quickly became embedded in the social and cultural life of many European countries, where it was welcomed as an expression of engagement with modern life. Post–World War II, one of the most useful tools of the globalization of jazz were the short wave broadcasts of Willis Conover's *Music USA* on Voice of America, particularly in countries under the Soviet sphere of influence. As author Gene Lees has pointed out in *Friends Along the Way*, "Conover did more than any other human being to make jazz an international musical language."

Broadcasting eight times a week, Conover was heard by an estimated 100 million people. One of those who followed his broadcasts was the Polish trumpeter Tomasz Stanko: "I started to learn classical music from 7 years old to 14, I started piano and changed to violin, then I had a break with the music, that was my darkness in my life. I was in the middle of school — Junior High — and as a sixteen-seventeen year old boy I heard jazz, Willis Conover, I heard the programs, and then I decide to come back to music. I would play on trumpet and my father's friend was a teacher on trumpet. With the trumpet I became a jazz musician."

To audiences in the Soviet bloc, "jazz was like freedom, it meant freedom for us," Stanko asserts. Dubbed America's "Secret Sonic Weapon" in a famous *New York Times* headline in 1955, several musicians, such as Louis Armstrong, Duke Ellington, Benny Goodman, Earl Hines, Dizzy Gillespie, and Dave Brubeck, were sent on State Department–sponsored tours. "At the height of the Cold War, a belief in the music's inherent democratizing potential motivated the State Department to deputize jazz musicians as counterrevolutionary agents and cultural ambassadors to non-aligned or democratizing countries," wrote E. Taylor Atkins in his essay *Toward a Global History of Jazz*. The U.S. government sponsored jazz to project an image of how America wished to be seen in the world, using the music to represent American values such as democracy, individualism, social mobility, and inventiveness. With this kind of cachet attached to it, jazz, whether it liked it or not, was now part of the cultural capital of the United States.

As jazz history evolved inside America, it was also acquiring other histories in countries beyond its borders, countries that had embraced it as either an engagement with modernity or as a symbol of freedom. In some countries, jazz has been a part of their social life for almost as long as it has in the United States and had been absorbed into their cultural norms, symbolic meanings, and contextual rules (collectively referred to as cultural capital). In the years following World War II, many European countries increasingly came to acknowledge that jazz contributed to their cultural diversity, and along with other performing arts — classical, opera, dance — the music began to enjoy a degree of governmental subsidy that effectively protected it from the vicissitudes of market economics. Increasingly, some countries recognized the glocalization process of transculturation provided the means by which their own local identity could be asserted within the overarching hegemonic styles of the music. As E. Taylor Atkins has pointed out, jazz "enabled a rediscovery, redefinition or renewed appreciation of local traditions which were then marshaled to broaden and transform the music's expressive capacities." Thus the value of jazz's cultural capital in these countries (especially Holland, Norway, Sweden, Finland, and France, for example) was correspondingly enhanced.

Today, Europe's nation states, with their history of left-of-center governments that have supported the concept of a public realm and the underwriting of public science, public transport, public art, public health, public broadcasting, and the wider public interest, have helped preserve the unique character of European culture. As author Will Hutton points out:

> For Europeans, the state and government cannot be so easily portrayed as enemies of the people as they can in the US . . . they are seen rather as upholders of, and means of expressing, public values. Europeans expect the state to finance scientific research or, by owning television and radio companies, to serve a notion of public service broadcasting, just as they expect the state to tax and spend to provide public goods like defense and education.

European countries have made an investment in an arts and culture infrastructure of which jazz has been a beneficiary. While it is certainly the case it has had to stand in line behind classical music, opera, and ballet, jazz nevertheless enjoys governmental subsidy, to a greater or lesser degree, in most European countries. "I think funding and support by the government for the arts is actually one of their responsibilities," says tenor saxophonist Yuri Honing, one of the Holland's leading young jazz musicians. "If you look at history, the church was originally the main financier of most of the arts and later on royalty took on that role as the most important promoter of art. So it is quite logical that as church and royalty no longer support the arts, the government is responsible."

In the United Kingdom, the Arts Council formed Jazz Services to promote the growth and development of jazz throughout the United Kingdom. Although in 1991 to 1992 jazz received less than one-tenth of the subsidy given to opera, in more recent times the funding for the music has steadily increased. "We have seen our funding lines increase during the last few years from both the Arts Council and National Lottery," says Chris Hodgkins, director of Jazz Services. "It has enabled us to organize tours, concerts and live events and through the National Touring Support Scheme help British musicians in reaching new audiences."

Funding of the arts in the Netherlands operates mainly through the Ministry of Education, Culture and Sciences on a four year rolling cycle. "The Ministry has roughly made a division between the supply side and the demand side," says Paul Gompes of the Dutch Jazz Connection, wholly funded by government to further the international recognition of Dutch jazz.

> There are two organizations. One is called the Fund for the Performing Arts, the other is called the Fund for the Podium Programming. So if you've got a group you can apply to the Fund for the Performing Arts for Project Funding. From the same fund you can apply for funding if you want to go on tour. All jazz groups can apply for Structural Funding, and they do. It varies from 49,000 Euros for the smallest group to 227,000 Euros for the largest group on an annual basis over a four year cycle. There are approximately 18 jazz and improvised music groups "structurally funded" at the moment. Then there is a fund for venues, the Fund for the Podium Programming, so if a venue wants to do a program with jazz musicians and thinks it will cost more than they will earn at the door, then they can apply through this fund in order to get money. Then there are subsidized venues, the three main ones are in Amsterdam, Rotterdam, Utrecht and Tilburg, and they are all funded nationally as well as locally by the city council. And there are also 30 smaller jazz venues funded by the Fund for the Podium Programming and they receive a regular annual amount to support their activities and they are also structurally funded.

In many European countries, jazz enjoys a high degree of subsidy. In Norway, for example, music educators devised a strategy for what they thought the musical life of the nation ought to be by maximizing the wealth of talent to be found in Norway's children, a policy formulated in the 1960s and called "The Vision." This long-term project started from the premise that the job market for musicians should be subsidized by taxes, if necessary, both within the education system and in the market-place as a whole. Since then, Rikskonserterne, a state agency, has developed a nationwide music program that now yields over 8,000 concerts a year, funded mainly by the government. Festivals of music, including jazz, have been established around the country, together with a subsidized touring infrastructure to enable musicians to play in community centers, churches, schools, and other venues. It has meant live music, including jazz, has been brought into the community, so audiences do not have to live in a big city to hear it; music is available on, say, a Saturday morning for adults and children at their local school or community center, where they can take in an hour-long concert on the way to the shops. School children are regularly exposed to concerts of classical, folk, rock, and jazz throughout school life as professional musicians from each genre, including jazz, are paid to perform concerts for children from kindergarten to high school, again creating more jobs in the cultural market.

Norwegian audiences are thus exposed to a broad range of music from a young age, and by adulthood are often extremely knowledgeable about music, which creates future audiences for jazz, classical, folkloric forms, and rock. In addition to touring grants, venue subsidies, commissions, bursaries for composition, and recording subsidies, there are even grants to assist in developing an ensemble by funding rehearsal time. The level of subsidy that is available includes supporting tours abroad; when the Tord Gustavsen Trio made its first U.S. tour in 2004, it was with the help of government funds. "The tour we did involved some co-operation with the Norwegian Council in New York," he said. "They helped with some costs, the bookings were done in America and it was financed through a combination of fees [for the gigs] and grants from Norway."

This support for the arts has helped create an extremely vibrant music scene, with Oslo a nexus for an extraordinary synergy of musical activities that exploded across Europe in the late 1990s and early millennium years, with musically informed audiences open to new ideas, which provided an ideal environment for experimentation. "It's a very interesting scene," says trumpeter Nils Petter Molvaer:

There are so many things happening. It's not so hooked up to main-stream jazz like our close neighbors Sweden and Denmark. In Norway it's a different tradition. It started out with Manfred Eicher of ECM records developing the careers of people like Jan Garbarek, Terje Rypdal, Jon Christensen, Arlid Andersen. So these people are our starting point, musicians who are known to experiment — so our base is a different one to the rest of Europe.

The leading jazz club in Norway, the Club Blå in Oslo, which was given a "6 out of 6" rating by *Dagbladet*, Norway's biggest daily newspa-per, was managed in 2004 by Erice Horpestad Berthelsen, a twenty-six year old who is effectively an arts administrator with responsibility for the concert productions, artist booking, and ten employees. She pointed out that the club could not exist without funding lines from government and municipal sources:

> To run Blå we get 500,000 NOK [krone; 1 krone equals approx. $6.50 in US dollars as of March 2005, making this amount approx. $86,000] a year from the government, 100,000 NOK a year from the community [Oslo], plus approximately 70,000 NOK to run jazz-concert-series throughout the year from Fond For Utøvende Kunstenere. In addition to this we get 60,000 NOK from Norsk Jazzforum in "club support," and for the last two years, we have been getting around 400,000 NOK from the project Nasjonal Scene for Jazz. For jazz musicians in Norway, this means they have an excellent venue to play where they get decent fees and they also have the opportunity to see, hear, and meet other musicians.

This kind of support from central government, local government, and cul-tural funds, unheard of in the United States, has been crucial for sustaining jazz as part of the cultural life of the city and building an audience for the music. The Club Blå also plays an important role in supporting lesser-known jazz artists because with governmental subsidy its programs are not driven by bottom-line economics. "Jazz attracts people from 18 to 60, the average age of the audience at Blå is something like 26," says Berthelsen:

> Over the last five years or so, this genre has become really "hip" and we have to turn away a lot of people because we're sold out. But this is also about building up a genre; in the early years of Blå we could have 20 peo-ple coming to hear Atomic [an acoustic free-bop group], now it's never less than 150. So, being persistent in what you believe in music-wise pays

off after a while; the [young] audience has now come to agree that this genre is worth listening to. This is thanks to musicians, clubs, and schools like Trondheim [Conservatory] never giving up on the genre and constantly renewing it and redefining the music.

Governmental subsidy, regional subsidy, and lottery money has allowed the music to flourish in Europe, to the extent there are very few towns and cities that do not have some form of jazz activity with an audience to support it, which is why it is such an attractive market for American jazz musicians. Indeed, some countries have harnessed jazz to project an image of how they see themselves in the world: as upbeat, modern, and cosmopolitan. In short, they seek to portray themselves as the sort of place in the global economy that would be attractive to inward investment, an agreeable environment to transact business, and a vibrant and exciting place to live. As Erling Askdal, head of the jazz course at Trondheim Conservatory in Norway, points out, "Jazz is much bigger in Norway than the size of the audience indicates."

In these countries, jazz is perceived as an exciting, evolving contemporary art form, projecting an image of cultural excellence with positive connotations that can be harnessed for what Ferdinand Dorsman, past deputy head of the Department of International Cultural Policy of the Dutch Ministry of Foreign Affairs, called "cultural diplomacy." "Usually foreign ministries consider their tools of diplomacy are such that they serve particular purposes, such as giving a good impression or image of their country," he explained to me in 2004:

> If they have thought this through, they want a particular image, should it be an image of peace, a high tech image, or whatever. So public diplomacy, which is to say diplomacy aimed at the public, incorporates cultural diplomacy. Holland has developed a policy that is set up with the Cultural Ministry, and the aim of that is to export and engage in cultural co-operation with other countries so that the best of Dutch culture would be seen abroad. As all the other disciplines, dance, contemporary classical, and other performing arts and visual arts, jazz is an instrument that really links people, and as such jazz has proved very useful in achieving this. The sort of things people associate with the Dutch are liberty, tolerance, a certain playfulness, not liking everything within set limits or following the rules, and I think jazz is a very good example of illustrating this image. . . . The Willem Breuker Kollektief [an internationally famous Dutch jazz ensemble] — they've been working for decades for us

and have built their reputation on this "playfulness" side, I'd say. When I worked in the Embassy in Mexico and they came along for a performance in Mexico City, they really set Holland apart from the rest of the performances there!

As Dr. Wolfram Knauer, director of the Jazzinstitut Darmstadt and a recipient of the Hessischer Jazz Preis 2002 for his achievements in establishing the institute as an internationally acclaimed information and documentation center on jazz, observes:

> Jazz is now used as a cultural tool in Holland, because the Dutch government realizes that jazz, more than other music, is a "multinational language" which is able to cross borders. They also realize that the Dutch jazz scene has somehow developed its own identity. The same too in France who have a "French Music Export Office," a state-funded organization with an economical aim: "to help French record companies to promote their artists abroad." This is also the case in the Scandinavian countries. The British Council helps stage concerts with British musicians and a similar program exists in Germany where the Goethe Institut stages concerts and tours with contemporary jazz musicians around the world. On a smaller scale my institute is a municipal institute totally funded by the city of Darmstadt which I see, besides its cultural implications, as a public relations measure to identify the name of the city with something positive. And that, after all, is what PR is all about. Spread the word, make the name of a goods into a word with positive connotations. So the city is proud of the name the Institut has made for itself — and, thus, for the city.

It is a curious paradox that the American government no longer harnesses jazz as a tool of cultural diplomacy as it did in the 1950s with State Department tours, which in turn could play an effective role in the cultural job market for American jazz musicians. The absence of state subsidy and a coherent jazz infrastructure has meant the music is exposed to the homogenizing effect of a very competitive marketplace. This is perhaps best illustrated by the major recording companies' commitment to jazz during the 1990s. Instead of searching out jazz that was unique or innovative, the majors opted to promote a well-established style that they considered had the broadest appeal — jazz within the hard bop continuum — a style that was perpetuated for over a decade in a sort of pre-Nietzschean notion of eternal recurrence, so artificially re-centering the music around virtuostic recapitulation.

This conservative approach was largely dictated by financial considerations. With costs running at $20,000 to $30,000 to record a small jazz
group for a major label, mastering costing another $3,000, plus a modest
promotional budget of around $5,000, an instrumental jazz record would
have to sell in excess of 5,000 copies just to break even and make a small
profit. Typically, the average sales for a name jazz instrumentalist was
running at 3,000; sales of 10,000 was considered good, and sales of 25,000
or more made it, in jazz terms at least, a hit record. As the profitability of
jazz came under increasing scrutiny by the majors, accountants asked hard
questions about sales potential of a potential artist before signing. Who
was the music aimed at? How big was the potential audience? What were
the anticipated sales territory by territory? What development did the
artist offer over a three- to five-year period? Decisions were made in committee, and reaching a consensus about the musical direction and commercial viability of a potential signing frequently resulted in the lowest
common denominator position of eliminating risk. Consequently, some
major's back catalogs were more adventurous than their current batch of
signings, exemplified by a Blue Note double-page advertisement in the
major jazz magazines in 2003 that on the left offered its current crop of
signings, albums by singers Van Morrison and Al Green, and on the right
a previously unreleased album from the late 1960s by Andrew Hill and
reissues by Sam Rivers, Hank Mobley, Lee Morgan, and Larry Young. As
recording engineer David Baker told the *Boston Globe*, "You've got an ultra
conservative industry right now and that's unfortunate. Safe bets have
never been the world in which jazz has flourished in."

As the major's interest in "traditional jazz" signings began to wane, they
claimed instrumental jazz did not sell, or when it did, it did not generate
the kind of returns that were attractive to them. "As an industry we continually try to promote instrumental jazz artists," Glen Barros, president
of Concord records, told *Jazz Times* in 2003. "But I have to say that it's
pretty alarming there have been so few successes — particularly with
traditional jazz records — despite their being some pretty aggressive
campaigns behind them."

It never occurred to the major recording companies A&R departments
that while one particular style of jazz did not sell, others might do so. Yes,
there was experimental jazz at the margins, but the majors were reluctant
to become involved in this music because this was a hard sell, and in any
event, they believed it could not be commodified for mainstream
consumption. In effect, the major recording companies were guilty of

underestimating the record-buying public. As Dave King of the trio The Bad Plus pointed out to me in 2003, "I look out at an audience I'm playing at, half the number of people are in my eyes under 18 — what you would think of as people 'not getting it.' The music can get really complicated and atonal at times. The idea that 'the public' in some way is 'not able to understand jazz' is ridiculous!"

Although the Bad Plus were signed by a major, they were a stark exception to the safety-first policy of Sony/Columbia Records whose presence in the jazz marketplace by the end of the 1990s was a shadow of its former glory days when it once had on its books the likes of Louis Armstrong, Duke Ellington, Miles Davis, Dave Brubeck, Charles Mingus, Thelonious Monk, Don Ellis, the Mahavishnu Orchestra, and Weather Report. Like all the majors, it had simply lost its way with its jazz signings in the 1990s. Elsewhere, the instrumental jazz artists who were yielding sales were, like the Bad Plus, artists who did not play in the conservative styles favored by the major's A&R departments. "I think when you *do* hear a great new instrumental artist, someone that stands out and really has something to say, the most obvious one [in 2004] is the Esbjörn Svenssön Trio, people buy into it because there's a very good reason to — because it's good! It's *not just down to marketing*," said Adam Seiff, Sony's Head of Jazz for UK and Europe in 2004. "The Bad Plus are another group that are not only original, but they play with great sincerity. It's fundamental, it's exciting, and instrumental jazz over the last decade or so frankly hasn't been that."

Both Esbjörn Svenssön with *Seven Days of Falling* (ACT) and the Bad Plus with *These Are the Vistas* (Columbia) achieved sales of more than 60,000 worldwide by the end of 2004. But they were far from alone. Tord Gustavsen's 2003 album debut, *Changing Places* (ECM), for example, approached 60,000 sales worldwide in the first year of release and received laudatory reviews across Europe and the United States, where it was voted among *Stereophile* magazine's "80 Records To Die For" — all this from a musician whom hardly anyone had heard of outside his native Norway before the album was released. It suggests instrumental jazz can sell in significant numbers, but when it does, it is usually by artists and producers with an awareness of art, which involves uniqueness.

The way the majors marketed jazz, in the main sticking to a tried and tested product, and the homogenizing effect it had on the mainstream of jazz that ensued, reflected the way jazz itself has been marketed. The effect of market economics on any commodity, goods, or services is that it inevitably has to conform to majority tastes to increase sales potential and thus homogenization ensues — a cliché of business studies courses from Harvard to Cambridge, but, because it is rarely mentioned in jazz discourse, warrants some exploration. In the case of marketing jazz, many key United States artist agencies stuck largely to a post–hard bop agenda because (1) it was easier to sell, and (2) it promised higher returns on their overhead. An easier sell meant that when pitching player A to a promoter, there was a common understanding in terms of style, whereas an adventurous player B was a harder sell involving subjective description, sending out CDs and press packs, and therefore slowing down the sales process. Equally, there is a general perception in the market that adventurous players do not generate the same box office returns as artists in more mainstream realms, and thus do not command higher fees — a disincentive to the sales process. Playing, then, in a specific hegemonic style — be it post–hard bop or fusion — aids the sales process because there is a mutual understanding of style, allowing discussion to move on to "how good" a player is — for example, citing audience size in comparable venues or ratings by industry magazines like *Downbeat* — thus establishing the basis for the fee.

Several major European promoters have explained to me how the jazz industry in America is in the hands of just a few agencies who effectively decide musicians' careers: who is in and who is out, who is on the up and who is going down. Between them, they have very close links with the European scene, "Whatever band they try to sell you they will start at $20-$25 thousand for lesser known, and $40-$50-$60-$70 thousand for the more well known bands," said Bo Grønningsaeter, one of Europe's leading figures in jazz and arts promotion and former director of the Molde Jazz Festival and the Nattjazz Festival and presently director of the West Norway Jazz Center and General Secretary of the Europe Jazz Network:

> Then you add the cost of transportation, accommodation, meals and you have an expensive package with all the risks borne by the promoter. With jazz in the United States being a business, often it is quite cynical, because the concept and the artists are promoted by agents who are, as Frank Zappa would have put it, are "only in it for the money." If you look at rosters from different agents you will often see the same musicians from four or five different agents and at the end there is a bidding war for who will pay them the most.

The "business of jazz" often meant that bands were assembled for the European and other circuits with a focus on maximizing profit, rather than developing artistry, such as "All Star" ensembles formed to celebrate the music of this-or-that deceased giant. The Swedish saxophonist Jonas Knutsson sees this as evidence of how the "jazz business" is having a homogenizing effect on the music. "It's so stupid to reduce music to something you can buy and sell," he said.

> If you are playing music that is a business idea you will seldom create art. What is your message, what do you want to say? You can think too much of how to make a living out of jazz — that's important — in the States you have a lot of people who have lost their compass and direction. A lot of European musicians that play the festivals like myself, we see a lot of these American projects. I would say a lot of them are not organic or have an interesting musical concept — artistic concept — it's more like "We can't get gigs here, let's sell some package to Europe. Some tribute to Miles Davis or whoever." I've seen endless tribute concerts and the music is just not happening. That can't be good for jazz.

Other promoters have described how "the business of jazz" saw some agents who did not seem to be working in the best interests of their clients, demanding fees that were unrealistic for a breaking or new artist. "An artist may have made one or two CDs and had a review in *Jazz Times* and they want top dollar right away. There is no thought of coming in at a lower price and building an audience for their work and raising the fees over time. It means that some artists are losing out on work," one said. Once again, "the business of jazz" was creating a situation where jazz and the jazz musicians were the losers. This was illustrated by an incident in 2004 described by Bo Grønningsaeter: "We offered [Oscar Peterson] $60,000, the going fee which was agreed, but when the agent found out our hall seated more people, then he demanded $75,000, so we said goodbye."

Another key area of jazz activity is the jazz festival circuit. Once again, broadly speaking, there can be key differences in how programs are put together in the United States and Europe. In the United States, many festivals (but not all) are put together for the purposes of profit, where the need is to maximize ticket sales by appealing to the broadest constituency. This lowest common denominator approach has a homogenizing effect on the music: a roster of big names and safe bets governed by profit considerations, at the expense of more challenging artists or up and coming talent. It is in contrast to most (but not all) European festivals. Here the greater majority enjoy a level of subsidy (often a combination of central government and regional subsidy) that means the profit and loss account does not dictate artistic choices, as Bo Grønningsaeter explains:

> There's more idealism among European organizers and also they have public funding . . . so they have a fixed salary. You're not in it for the money. If you have a successful festival you don't get a huge bonus, your pay is exactly the same, but of course you have the satisfaction of creating something audiences want to see. It's not like "the festival makes a lot of money, you make a lot of money"; it's a different perspective. So you relate to jazz differently than a profit-orientated businessman. It's not a question of maximum profit, it's a question of making a good program and being able to make the wheels go round, financially, so to speak. We're not in the business of making money, but we have to make the books balance. There is an opportunity to aspire to an aesthetic balance in the composition of the program because you're not in it for personal profit, you're actually doing it because you're interested in it, even though you're getting paid maybe less than you would in another job!

The result is often a broader-based program than one constructed with a profit motive, which presents the opportunity to put on artists that audiences may never have heard of, so helping the audience for the music to grow.

The way the "business" of jazz is structured in the United States without governmental subsidy has meant that many jazz musicians have come to rely on markets outside the borders of America for a significant portion of their income. The most important market is the subsidized jazz circuits of Europe. Promoter and pianist George Wein, who was involved in the organization of several international festivals, such as the Grande Parade du Jazz in Nice from 1974, once famously said, "No Europe, no jazz" after seeing firsthand the extent to which American jazz musicians had come to rely on work in Europe. In 2004, he explained this remark in an interview for the Norwegian jazz magazine *Jazznytt*, saying: "The fact is that so much of the [American] musician's salary came from touring Europe. It was the main reason why some musicians could live a better life. Without Europe they would have lost a lot of money."

In August 1992, a major feature on the European scene in *Billboard* called "Wealth of Jazz in Europe" pointed out, "European tours by major American artists are a year round activity — indeed, without them, U.S. jazzmen's incomes would be 50 percent lower in many cases." Four years later, in July 1996, the *New York Times* arts pages opened with a feature headlined, "For U.S. Jazz Players, Europe Is the Place to Be," noting: "A musician, especially one with a following in Europe, can earn up to 80 percent of his annual income during a summer tour. It is not unusual for a headliner to make $100,000 or more in a month of concerts." And in 2003, the industry journal *Music & Media* carried a feature headlined, "Jazz Players Head East For Eden — Europe has replaced America as the land of opportunity for jazz music and jazz musicians." "I think the big market is still Europe," guitarist John Abercrombie told me in 2004:

> At least it is for me. Japan is sort of in and out, whereas Europe seems to be consistent. I am always able to work in France and Germany and Italy and Southern Spain and Scandinavia, a little bit in the UK, so there always seems to be a certain amount of work. That's my market and some of the younger players I meet when they do get to Europe, they see what I mean. They see that this is the place where you get more appreciation, you get bigger audiences, there's more work available, and the money is better. So if you are actually able to make several trips a year and between that and some teaching and whatever else — recording — you are able to make a living.

As the Italian pianist Enrico Pieranunzi told *Music & Media*, "I would say that at this historical moment the European scene supports more jazz than the U.S." But how long could American jazz artists continue to rely on Europe for a large slice of their income? As Steen Meier, Chairman of The Nordic Music Council and Copenhagen's famous JazzHouse, points out: "Ironically, American jazz musicians only make real money when they come to Europe and play for exorbitant wages. These demands have not yet become impossible to meet, but one could well imagine that they will become so in the near future." The reason was that the jazz marketplace in Europe was undergoing a seismic shift. Audience tastes were beginning to increasingly embrace the more experimental approach of homegrown musicians. Michael Moore, the American saxophonist now resident in Amsterdam in the Netherlands, contrasts the homogenizing effect of the marketplace in the United States to that in Europe:

> In America, there's more pressure to be conformist, and players who were once pioneers of new music can work a lot more if they play tunes in a traditional way. In Europe, there's a larger audience that grew up

listening to [experimental jazz] over a 25 year period and they appreciate
not hearing the same thing every time . . . [the jazz] tradition can be a
burden as well as a blessing.

The expectation in Europe is that jazz should continue to evolve and
broaden its expressive resources; audiences are tiring of a tradition-based
synthesis of earlier styles and are turning to more experimental European
artists. In his role as general secretary of the Europe Jazz Odyssey, Bo
Grønningsaeter is ideally placed to see the tensions in the jazz business.
The Europe Jazz Odyssey was formed with financial support from the
European Commission under the aegis of its "Culture 2000" program and
is a platform for cultural cooperation involving over fifteen European
countries to further European jazz. In 2004, there were almost forty major
European festival directors and animators involved from across Europe,
including festivals and venues as diverse as the Berlin Jazz Festival, the
London Jazz Festival, Banlieues Bleues Festival in France, Clusone Jazz
Festival in Italy, the Jazz Kaar Festival in Estonia, the Bimhuis in Amsterdam, the JazzHouse in Copenhagen, and the Stadtgarten JazzHaus in
Germany. These were the people who experienced change in audience
tastes first, since it is reflected in their box office takings, as Grønningsaeter explained:

> The way [the scene] is changing is that more European acts are used,
> our collaborators in the European Jazz Network have become less and
> less interested in paying big fees and are finding audiences want what
> they see as "more interesting" European acts. It's better to offer more
> concerts of high quality than a few concerts at high prices. Ten years ago
> a number of American artists would sell very well, all of a sudden you
> can't sell any tickets anymore because the audiences have passed on to
> something else. They want to listen to newer and more fresher material
> and other ways of approaching the music than the post-bop, or jazz-rock
> orientated stuff, playing the standards or recreating the jazz from the
> 1960s. I think a number of American musicians who really haven't
> developed that much during the last ten or fifteen years, will have
> increasing difficulties in the years to come finding these well paid gigs in
> Europe. Also because they have greedy agents who ask for too much
> money. There is much less focus now on American musicians than was
> the case ten or fifteen years ago. You can put together a commercially
> viable program without American stars — in Norway, we have experi-
> enced that. Our festival in Bergen, which is 35 years old, for the first
> time this year [2004] we had a program without any American artists at

all. This was not an act of faith, or an act of protest, it just happened that way. And the festival was a success, the audience loved it.

Gerry Godley, director of the Improvised Music Company in Dublin, funded by the Irish government to provide festival programming, concert promotion, touring, recording, education, and audience development, plus the promotion of the critically acclaimed Dublin Jazz Festival, sees these changes in the jazz marketplace as a continuum of the tensions that have always run through jazz and that helped shape the music in the past. The only difference is that today jazz is a global music and the tensions that are now shaping the music are occurring outside its land of origin within the broader global jazz community:

> One could look at the music's zeitgeist in previous epochs and broadly cat-
> egorize it as one of conflict, which is to say Swing versus Bebop, Free ver-
> sus Structure, Fusion versus "Acoustic," and so on. Today, the same
> maxim applies, albeit that the conflict plays itself out along geographical
> rather than stylistic lines. In the Star Spangled corner — the U.S. view —
> as promoted by its jazz ideologues, is that the music is now a fixed culture,
> one of consolidation rather than experimentation — although it is naive to
> assume consensus on this in the American music community. In the
> opposite corner resides everyone else, largely unthreatened by the idea of
> jazz as a "fixed culture," witnessing the music constantly renewing and
> enriching itself from other sources — an example of how globalization can
> empower. These two opposing *modus operandi* are in themselves a reflec-
> tion of the political times we live in, as evidenced by the dissonance
> between the US and Europe in 2002–4 on issues such as the Middle East,
> trade, and the environment. That state of flux equally applies to the econ-
> omy that drives the music and supports its practitioners and audiences.
> Take the major European festivals for example, where there's a palpable
> sense of change as the US orientated star system, now past its sell-by date
> in terms of driving ticket revenues, is being unceremoniously discarded in
> favor of a new paradigm that harnesses the potential of artists with a
> strong regional identity, be they Mediterranean, Scandinavian or Balkan.

We are, then at a key moment in jazz history. The music is being reshaped and reimagined beyond the borders of the United States through the process of glocalization and transculturation with increasing authority by voices asserting their own cultural identity on the music. Non-Ameri-can musicians want to connect with their own surroundings and want to give the music life and vitality that is relevant to their own socio-musical situation, so they are broadening the expressive base of the music in ways over which American jazz has no control. Key to these developments in Europe is that they are not a response to commercial logic. Sheltered by subsidy from the homogenizing effect of this marketplace, the music has been able to grow and develop in ways musicians want, rather than conforming to the expectations of the marketplace or shaped by the conventions of previous practice.

Herein lies a fascinating paradox. At the turn of the twentieth century, many European artists blamed "the tradition" for stifling creativity, particularly in classical music. The arrival of jazz was seen as a breath of fresh air, whose vitality and exuberance brought something new to European art. Georges Auric, Louis Durey, Arthur Honegger, Darius Milhaud, Francis Poulenc, Germaine Tailleferre, and their unofficial and mischievous "godfather," Erik Satie—all shared a fascination with jazz, which in turn provided them with a source of inspiration in their own works. They claimed that they "fused art and modern life," thus challenging Impressionism in the hope of invoking a new art music based on popular sources: for example, Auric's suggestion of "blue notes" in "Huit Poémes"; Satie paraphrasing Irving Berlin's "That Mysterious Rag" in his own "Steamship Ragtime" from *Parade* that mocked the loftiness of Romanticism; or Milhaud's 1923 ballet *La Création du Monde,* which was hailed for its jazz influences. These members of "Les Nouveaux Jeunes," or as they later became known, "Les Six," believed that art should continue to evolve and broaden its expressive resources and that music must be true to itself. Just under a century later, jazz musicians in Europe were also looking beyond a tradition whose overpowering legacy was similarly freezing current practice in search of a new vitality and exuberance.

But what impact will this fast-changing European scene have on American jazz if any? Initially the effect is going to be felt financially. Money, as Cyndi Lauper once famously sang, changes everything. Europe has historically been a key market for American jazz in album sales, in its extensive festival circuit, and in year-round gigs. Of course, there will always be a market in Europe for jazz's top headliners –a Herbie Hancock, a Wayne Shorter, a Pat Metheny, a Chick Corea, a Keith Jarrett and so on –but subsequent generations of jazz musicians, especially young musicians establishing their reputations, are finding less job opportunities in Europe as European musicians move into the space once occupied by American musicians. Less job opportunities in Europe poses the question of whether the fragile American jazz economy will be able to provide additional employment opportunities to enable musicians to maintain their income stream without governmental subsidy in a country where its culture is overwhelmingly popular culture and where the music is in danger of sliding into high-art marginality.

Aspiring to greater cultural enrichment should be the goal of any society, particularly in a world that is growing ever more conservative in its values through events on a global stage that engulf us all. The Cold War, a period when jazz thrived, was a world that we all knew — some countries supported one set of political beliefs, others set another agenda — and the historical narratives of the left and right allowed us to make sense of the world. But the old world has been superseded by a new, post–9/11 world that is inchoate and chaotic, whose rules we no longer know, whose future seems complex and indeterminate. So we turn away from the unfamiliar, yearning for a return to a golden age that never was. Societies are retreating into themselves and in the United States, jazz too has seen the cool winds of conservatism blow through it while its destiny is increasingly shaped by the tensions of the marketplace, a marketplace very different from that which helped shape the music in its golden years, whose homogenizing tendencies are now at odds with the music's inherent complexity. The survival of jazz in America has to be seen in the context of today's increasingly complex infrastructure of profit-maximizing multinationals, and a conservative government loathe to support the arts. The chance of American jazz musicians receiving state subsidy appears remote at the very time it is needed most. While governmental subsidy cannot and should not prescribe aesthetics, it can secure freedom from the homogenizing tendencies of the market. That is why Tessa Jowell's rallying cry at the beginning of the chapter to protect culture should be fought for, and urgently. The future of jazz as a growing, developing art form in America may depend on it.

REFERENCE BIBLIOGRAPHY

Appadurai, Arjun. "Disjuncture and Difference in the Global Cultural Economy." *Public Culture* 2, no. 1, 1990.

Asthana, Anushka. "Kiss My Chuddies! (Welcome to the Queen's Hinglish)." *The Observer*, 25 April 2004.

Atkins, E. Taylor. "Toward a Global History of Jazz" in *Jazz Planet*, ed. E. Taylor Atkins. Jackson, Mississippi: University Press of Mississippi, 2003.

Bakari, Imruh. "Exploding Silence" in *Living Through Pop*, ed. Andrew Blake. London: Routledge, 1999.

Balliett, Whitney. *Collected Works: A Journal of Jazz, 1954–2000*. New York: St. Martins Press, 2001.

Barzun, Jacques. "Introductory Remarks to a Program of Works at the Columbia-Princetown Music Center" in *Audio Culture: Readings in Modern Music*, ed. Christoph Cox and Daniel Warner. London: Continuum, 2004.

Beale, Charles. "Jazz Education" in *The Oxford Companion to Jazz*, ed. Bill Kirchner. New York: Oxford University Press, 2000.

Berger, Monroe, Ed Berger, and James Patrick. *Benny Carter: A Life in American Music*. Metuchen, New Jersey: Scarecrow Press, 1982.

Berne, Terry. "Jazz Players Head East For Eden." *Music & Media*, March 29, 2003.

"Biography: Wynton Marsalis." New York: Sony Music Entertainment, June 1996.

Birnbaum, Larry. "Review: *Blood on the Fields.*" *Downbeat*, September 1997.

Birnbaum, Larry. "Young Lions: Have They Delivered?" *Downbeat*, June 1992.

Blumenfeld, Larry. "Citizen Wynton." *Jazziz*, December 1999.

Bourdieu, Pierre. Distinction: *A Social Critique of the Judgement of Taste*. Translated by Richard Nice. Cambridge, MA: Harvard University Press, 1984.

Bourne, Michael. "Jan Garbarek: Scandinavian Design." *Downbeat*, July 1986.

Booth, Gary. "Shifting Sounds." *BBC Music Magazine*, June 2003.

Boyuton, Robert S. "The Professor of Connection" *New Yorker*, November 6, 1995.

Bronson, Fred. "The Year in Charts." *Billboard*, 29 December 2001.

Broughton, Frank. "The Original Spin Doctor." *The Guardian*, January 26, 2002.

Brown, John Robert. "Euro Jazz." *Music Teacher*, July 2004

Burns, Ken, dir. *Jazz: A History of America's Music*. Washington, DC: PBS, 2001.

Byrnes, Sholto. "The Controversial King of Jazz." *The Independent*, March 15, 2003.

Carr, Ian. *Music Outside: Contemporary Jazz in Britain*. London: Quartet, 1973

Cascone, Kim. "The Aesthetics of Failure: 'Post Digital' Tendencies in Contemporary Computer Music" in *Audio Culture: Readings in Modern Music*, ed. Christoph Cox and Daniel Warner. London: Continuum, 2004.

Cassy, John. "Old School Earners: Sanctuary Proves Safe in Global Music Downturn." *The Guardian* 21 January 2003.

Chinen, Nate. "Pardon the Musical Interruption: The Annual IAJE Conference Takes on Manhattan." *Jazz Times* May 2004.

Cohen, Aaron. "Tortoise: New Formula." *Downbeat*, June 2004.

Coker, Jerry, Jimmy Casale, Gary Campbell, and Jerry Greene. *Patterns for Jazz*. New York: Warner Bros. Music Publ., 1970.

Conrad, Thomas. "Reviews: Dave Douglas: *Strange Liberation*/Wynton Marsalis: *The Magic Hour*." *Jazz Times* April 2004,

Cook, Richard. "Wynton Marsalis: Diligence." *The Wire*, April 1987.

Corbett, John. "Fanfare for the Working Band," *Downbeat* March 1997.

Crouch, Stanley. "Liner Notes." *Marsalis Standard Time Vol. 1*. New York: Columbia 451039–2.

Crouch, Stanley. "Liner Notes." *The Magic Hour*. New York: Blue Note 91717.

Crouch, Stanley. "Putting the White Man in Charge." *Jazz Times* April 2003.

Crouch, Stanley. "The Negro Aesthetic of Jazz." *Jazz Times*, October 2002.

Crouch, Stanley. "The Place of the Bass." *Jazz Times*, April 2002.

Crouch, Stanley. "The Tradition is Not Innovation." *Jazz Times*, January/February 2002.

Crouch, Stanley. "Whose Blood, Whose Fields" (liner notes). *Blood on the Fields*. New York: Columbia CXK 57694.

Crouch, Stanley. "Wynton Marsalis 1987." *Downbeat*, November 1987.

Culshaw, Peter. "A Talent for Making Music and Enemies." *The Daily Telegraph*, January 20, 2003.

Davis, Clive. "Sour Notes in New York." *The Sunday Times* (London), August 14 1994.

Davis, Francis, Adrian Jackson, and Steve Klawans. "Letters," *Jazz Times*, May 2003

Davis, Francis. *Bebop and Nothingness*. New York: Schirmer Books, 1996.

Davis, Francis. *Like Young*. New York: Da Capo, 2001.

Davis, Francis. "The Right Stuff" in *In the Moment*. New York: Oxford University Press, 1986.

Davis, Miles, with Quincy Troupe. *Miles: The Autobiography*. New York: Simon & Schuster, 1990.

de Barros, Paul. "Southern Swing: A Week on the Road with the Lincoln Center Jazz Orchestra." *Downbeat*, October 2000.

Dellar, Fred. "The Shape of Jazz to Come?" *Mojo*, March 2004.

DeVeaux, Scott. "Constructing the Jazz Tradition" in *The Jazz Cadence of American Culture*, ed. Robert G. O'Meally. New York: Columbia University Press, 1998.

Douglas, Dave. "Roswell and Relativity." *Downbeat*, March 2004.

Dyer, Geoff. "Cherry Picking." *The Observer Review*, 12 July 1998.

Eisenberg, Evan. *The Recording Angel*. London: Picador, 1988.

Ellison, Ralph. *Living with Music: Ralph Ellison's Jazz Writings* ed. Robert G. O'Meally. New York: The Modern Library, 2002.

Elmes, Simon. *The Routes of English, Vol. 4*. London: BBC Books, 2001.

Elwood, Philip. "Racial Tension Blights Jazz." *San Francisco Examiner*, March 15 1995

Erickson, Paul. "Black and White, Black and Blue: The Controversy over the Jazz Series at Lincoln Center." *Jazz and American Culture* 2, Summer 1997.

Farber, Jim. "Pop's Smooth Operators: New Wave of Singers Strikes a Soothing Chord With Older Listeners" *Daily News*, 17 March 2003.

Feather, Leonard. *The New Edition of the Encyclopaedia of Jazz*. New York: Horizon, 1960.

Fordham, John. "This Man Is Killing Jazz. Or Is He?" *The Guardian*, June 23 1999.

Fornäs, Johan. "Swinging Differences" in *Jazz Planet*, ed. E. Taylor Atkins. Jackson, Mississippi: University Press of Mississippi, 2003.

Frith, Simon. *Performing Rites: On the Value of Popular Music*. London: Oxford University Press, 1996.

Galper, Hal. From http://www.halgalper.com, with permission.

Garrick, Michael. "Liner Notes: *Impressed* with Gilles Peterson." Universal 064 749 2.

Garrity, Brian. "For Music Biz: No End to the Blues." *Billboard*, December 28, 2002.

George, Nelson. *The Death of Rhythm and Blues*. New York: Pantheon Books, 1988.

Gerard, Charley. "Battling the Black Music Ideology" in *Riffs & Choruses: A New Jazz Anthology* ed. Andrew Clark. London: Continuum, 2001).

Giddins, Gary. *Rhythm-a-Ning*. New York: Oxford University Press, 1985.

Giddins, Gary. "Shackling Surprise." *The Village Voice*, October 12, 1993.

Giddins, Gary. *Visions of Jazz: The First Century*. New York: Oxford University Press, 1998.

Gillett, Charlie. "Sufi, So Good." *Observer Music Monthly*, July 2004.

Gioia, Dana, Press release, Washington, D.C. NEA Jazz Masters, 2004.

Godbolt, Jim. *A History of Jazz in Britain, 1919–50*. London: Quartet, 1984.

Goffin, Robert. *Jazz from Congo to Swing*. London: Musicians Press, 1946.

Gould, Glenn. "The Prospects of Recording." *High Fi Magazine*, April 1966.

Green, Madeleine, and Michael Baer. "Global Learning in a New Age." *The Chronicle of Higher Education*, November 9, 2001.

Greenlee, Steve. "Jazz Electronica: The New Fusion adds fresh ingredients to the original melting pot." *Boston Globe*, February 17, 2002.

Guttridge, Len. "The First Man to Bring Jazz to Britain." *Melody Maker*, 14 July 1956

Hahn, Steve. "An Open Letter to Stanley Crouch—A Fantasy." http://www.birdlives.com/crouch.hmtl

Hajdu, David. "Wynton's Blues." *The Atlantic Monthly*, March 2003.

Heble, Ajay. *Landing on the Wrong Note: Jazz, Dissonance and Critical Practice*. New York: Routledge, 2000.

Heidkamp, Konrad. "The End of Jazz As We Knew It (And I Feel Fine)" in *Grenzüberschreitungen (Trespassing Borders)*. Frankfurt, Germany: Between the Lines, 2001.

Held, David. *Models of Democracy*. Cambridge, UK: Polity Press, 1999.

Held, David, David Goldblatt, Jonathan Pearson, and Anthony McGrew. *Global Transformations: Politics, Economics and Culture*. Cambridge, UK: Polity Press, 1999.

Hendrickson, Tad. "Band on the Run: Bad Plus Gives as Good as it Gets." *Jazz Times* April 2004.

Hendrickson, Tad. "The Bad Plus Good, Bad or Even a Plus?" *Jazz Times*, April 2004.

Hennessey, Mike. "Wealth of Jazz In Europe." *Billboard*, August 1, 1992.

Hobsbawm, Eric. *On History*. London: Abbacus, 1997.

Hobsbawm, Eric. *Uncommon People: Resistance, Rebellion, and Jazz*. London: Abbacus, 1999.

Hopkins, Antony. *Understanding Music*. London: J. M. Dent & Sons, 1979.

Hutton, Will. *The World We're In*. London: Little, Brown, 2002.

Jackson, Anthony. "The New Dark Age." *Bass Player*, March–April 1991.

Jaggi, Maya. "Blowing up a Storm." *The Guardian Review*, January 25th 2003.

Jameson, Frederick. "Postmodernism or the Cultural Logic of Late Capitalism." New Left Review, no. 146,

Jarrett, Keith. "Letters." *The New York Times*, June 11, 2000.

Jazz at Lincoln Center. "Return of Organization Exempt from Income Tax, for year July 1st, 1998 to June 30, 1999."

Jenkins, Willard. "Wynton Bites Back: Addresses his Critics." *National Jazz Service Organization Jazz Journal* 5, no. 1, ca. April 1994.

Johnson, Martin. "Acid Jazz." *Downbeat*, April 1997.

Jolly, James. "*Gramophone* Questions Whether The 21st Century Should Be The Era Of The Composer Rather Than the Performer," *Gramophone*, 12 April 2000.

Jones, Alan. "Single and Album Sales See Boost." *Datafile*, 6 March 2004.

Jorn, Ager in Michael Tucker. Jan Garbarek: *Deep Song*. Hull, U.K.: Eastnote, 1998.

Jost, Ekkehard. Sozialgeschichte des Jazz. Frankfurt: Mai 2003.

Jung, Fred "In Words... A conversation with Dave Liebman. Jazz USA. http://jazzusa.com/stories/davidwebman interview.asp

Kallevig, Margaret. "Mr. Jazz." *Jazznytt* September/October 2004.

Kaplan, Fred. "With Sales Flat, the Jazz Industry Has Lost It's Groove." *The Boston Globe*, 24 September 2002.

Kart, Larry. *Jazz in Search of Itself.* New Haven, Connecticut: Yale University Press, 2004.

Keepnews, Peter. "Jazz Since 1968" in *The Oxford Companion to Jazz*, ed. Bill Kirchner. New York: Oxford University Press, 2000.

Kernfield, Barry, ed. *The New Grove Dictionary of Jazz*, 2nd ed. Macmillan Press London, 1988.

Kirchner, Bill, ed. *The Oxford Companion To Jazz.* New York: Oxford University Press, 2000.

Kjelberg, Erik. "Swedish Folk Tone in Jazz" in *Jazz Facts Sweden 1998*, ed. Odd Sneeggen. Stockholm: Swedish Music Information Center, 1998

Kjellberg, Erik. *Jan Johansson.* Stockholm: Svensk Musik, 1998.

Kohn, Alfie. "The Dangerous Myth of Grade Inflation." *The Chronicle of Higher Education*, November 8, 2002

Koransky, Jason. "First Take: And Now for Something Completely Different." *Downbeat*, May 2004.

Kozinn, Alan. "Marsalis Officiates As Classical Weds Jazz." *The New York Times*, May 9, 1995.

Laban, Craig, and K. Leander Williams. "Taylor Holds Recital on Lincoln Center Turf." *Downbeat*, June 1994.

Lambert, Constant. *Music Ho!* London: Faber & Faber, 1937.

Lees, Gene. *Cats of Any Color.* New York: Oxford University Press, 1994.

Lees, Gene. *Friends Along the Way.* New Haven, Connecticut: Yale University Press, 2003.

Levine, Lawrence W. *Black Culture and Black Consciousness.* New York: Oxford University Press, 1977.

Levine, Mark. *The Jazz Theory Book.* Petaluma, California:, Sher Music, 1995.

Levy, Steve. "Courthouse Rock." *Newsweek,* 22 September 2003.

Lewis, John. "Norse Code." *Time Out London,* October 9–16, 2002.

Liebman, Dave. *Self-Portrait of a Jazz Artist.* Rottenburg, Germany: Advance Music, 1988.

Liebman, David. "Europe: It's Role In Jazz." http://upbeat.com/lieb/Feature_Articles/europe.htm.

Llewellyn-Smith, Caspar. *Poplife: A Journey by Sofa.* London: Sceptre, 2002.

Macero, Teo. "Interview" in Modulations: A History of Electronic Music: Throbbing Words on Sound, ed. Peter Shapiro. Ca: Pirhna, New York, 2000.

MacFarlane, Alan. *Letters to Lily.* London: Profile Books, Ltd., 2005.

Mansfield, Harvey C. "How Harvard Compromised Its Virtue." *The Chronicle of Higher Education,* February 21, 2003.

Marsalis, Wynton. "What Jazz Is And Isn't" *The New York Times*, July 31, 1988.

Marsalis, Wynton, and The Lincoln Center Jazz Orchestra. *Publicity material.* London: Royal Albert Hall, 27 July 2002, concert.

Marsalis, Wynton, and Frank Stewart. *Sweet Swing Blues on the Road.* New York: W. W. Norton, 1994.

Masland, Tom. "Between Lions and Legends." *Newsweek*, February 24, 1992.

Mehldau, Brad. Liner notes to Alexi Tuomarila Quartet 02, Finlandia Records 0927–49148–2.

Meyer, Leonard B., ed. *Style and Music: Theory, History and Ideology. Studies in the Criticism and Theory of Music.* Philadelphia, Pennsylvania: University of Pennsylvania Press, 1989.

Milkowski, Bill. *Rockers, Jazzbos & Visionaries.* New York: Billboard, 1998.

Miller, Paul D. "Algorithms: Erasures and the Art of Memory" in *Audio Culture: Readings in Modern Music*, ed. Christoph Cox and Daniel Warner. London: Continuum, 2004.

Mitchell, Tony. *Popular Music and Local Identity: Rock, Pop and Rap in Europe and Oceania.* London: Leicester University Press, 1996.

Moore, Michael. Press release to accompany release of Clusone Trio, *I Am An Indian.* Rykodisc GCD 79505.

Murph, John. "A New Mix." *Downbeat,* September 2003.

Murray, Albert. *Stomping the Blues.* New York: Vintage Books, 1976.

Murray, Albert. "The Function of the Heroic Image" in *The Jazz Cadence of American Culture*, ed. Robert G. O'Meally. New York: Columbia University Press, 1998.

Murray, Albert. *The Omni-Americans: Some Alternatives to the Folklore of White Supremacy.* New York: Da Capo Press, 1990.

Neill, Ben. "Breakthrough Beats and the Aesthetics of Contemporary Electric Music" in *Audio Culture: Readings in Modern Music,* ed. Christoph Cox and Daniel Warner. London: Continuum, 2004.

Nicholson, Stuart. *Jazz: The 1980s Resurgence.* New York: Da Capo Press, 1995.

Nicholson, Stuart. *Jazz-Rock: A History.* New York: Schirmer Books, 1998.

Nisenson, Eric. *Blue: The Murder of Jazz.* New York: Da Capo Press, 2000.

Nixson, Viv. "The Trouble With Jazz" (letter to the editor). *The Guardian,* 14 March 2003.

Nüchtern, Klaus. "I Am Increasingly Going for the Heart: Interview with Franz Koglmann" in *Grenzüberschreitungen (Trespassing Borders).* Frankfurt, Germany: Between the Lines, 2001.

O'Meally, Robert G. "Introduction: Jazz Shapes" in *Living with Music*: Ralph Ellison's Jazz Writings ed. Robert G. O'Meally. New York: The Modern Library, 2002.

Orgill, Roxanne. "Fewer gigs mean fewer jazz bands." *The New York Times,* August 6, 1995,

Ouellette, Dan. "The Question Is . . . Should Jazz Labels Release Pop Music?" *Downbeat,* February 2004.

Ouellette, Dan. "Young Woman's Club." *Downbeat,* December 2004.

Pareles, Jon. "Eclectic Benefit for Downtown Club." *The New York Times,* Nov 1987.

Pareles, Jon. "Kathleen Battle, Jazz Headliner." *The New York Times,* 14 September, 1995.

Parris, Matthew. *Chance Witness.* London: Penguin Books, 2003.

Payton, Nicholas. Press Release for *Soniz Tranee.* Warner Brothers Records, 2003.

Pécseli, Benedicat, ed. *Spontaneous Combustion.* Copenhagen: Jazz House, 2001.

Pellegrinelli, Lara. "Dig Boy Dig." *The Village Voice,* November 9–14, 2000.

Pellegrinelli, Lara. "Singing for Our Supper: Are Vocalists Saving the Jazz Industry?" *Jazz Times,* December 2003.

Peretti, Burton W. "Epilogue: Jazz as American History" in *Riffs & Choruses: A New Jazz Anthology.* ed. Andrew Clark. London: Continuum, 2001.

Peterson, Lloyd. "Esbjörn Svenssön Trio: Bored With Tradition." *Downbeat,* June 2004.

Petridis, Alexis. "New Romantics." *The Guardian* 19 December 2003

Petridis, Alexis. "Reviews: Jamie Cullum." *The Guardian* 1 March 2004,.

Piedade, Acácio Tadeu de Camargo. "Brazilian Jazz and Friction of Musicalities" in *Jazz Planet,* ed. E. Taylor Atkins. Jackson, Mississippi: University Press of Mississippi, 2003.

Porter, Christopher. "The Bad Plus, One Bad McBride and Bad Taste." *Jazz Times,* April 2003.

Porter, Eric. "The Majesty of the Blues: Wynton Marsalis's Jazz Canon" in *What Is This Thing Called Jazz?* Berkeley, California: University of California Press, 2002.

Porter, Lewis, ed. *Jazz: A Century of Change: Readings and New Essays.* New York: Schirmer Books, 1997.

"Press Release." Washington, DC: NEA Jazz Masters, 2004.

Pritchett, V.S. "V.S. Prichett as Critic" in *United States Essays* 1952–1992 by Gore Vidal. New York: Broadway Books, 2001.

Purcell, Simon. *Musical Patchwork: The Threads of Teaching and Learning in a Conservatoire.* London: Guildhall School of Music and Drama, 2002.

Ratliff, Ben. "Jazz Innovator During His Late, Funky Phase" *The New York Times,* 3 August 1997.

Reich, Howard. "Wynton's Decade" *Downbeat,* December 1992.

Rhodes, Frank H. T. "A Battle Plan for Professors to Recapture the Curriculum." *The Chronicle of Higher Education,* September 14, 2001.

Ritzer, George. *The McDonaldization of Society.* Thousand Oaks, California: Pine Oak Press, 1993.

Russell, George. Liner notes by Burt Korall (1960): *Jazz in the Space Age*: George Russell and his Orchestra.

Sancton, Thomas. "Horns of Plenty." *Time,* October 22, 1990.

Sandall, Robert. "Parky the Hit-Maker." *The Daily Telegraph,* 18 December 2003.

Santoro, Gene. "All That Jazz." *The Nation,* January 8–15 1996.

Santoro, Gene. *Dancing in Your Head.* New York: Oxford University Press, 1994.

Santoro, Gene. "Young Man with a Horn." *The Nation*, March 1, 1993

Sardar, Ziauddin, and Merryl Wyn Davies *Why Do People Hate America?* Cambridge, UK: Icon, 2002.

Schuller, Gunther. *The Swing Era.* New York: Oxford University Press, 1989.

Scofield, John. "Interview with John Scofield." *The Wire*, September 1991.

Segal, David. "To Music Marketers, Oldies Are Goldies" *Washington Post*, 3 February 2003.

Seidel, Mitchell. "Wynton Marsalis." *Downbeat*, January 1982.

Shatz, Adam. "Music 70's Redux: Notes from the Jazz Underground." *The New York Times*, October 29, 2000.

Shatz, Adam. "Music: Organized Sound from Chicago's Jazz Underground." *The New York Times*, March 18, 2001.

Shipton, Alyn. "Back To The Future." *Jazzwise* October 2001.

Showstack-Sasson, Anne, ed., *Approaches to Gramsci. London*: Writers and Readers, 1982.

Shuker, Roy. *Understanding Popular Music.* London: Routledge, 1994.

Sidran, Ben. *Talking Jazz: An Illustrated Oral History.* San Francisco, California: Pomegranate, 1992.

Solomon, Andrew. "The Jazz Martyr." *The New York Times Magazine*, 9th February 1997.

Spencer, Neil. "Keeping Up with the Jones." *The Observer Review*, 18th January 2004.

Stenhammer, W. Ihelm. in Michael Tucker, *Jan Garbarek: Deep Song.* Hull, UK: Eastnote, 1998.

Swafford, Jim. "Inventing America." *The Guardian*, 26th September 2003.

Sweeting, Adam. "After the Storm." *The Guardian*, 26th September 2002.

Sweeting, Adam. "No Strings." *The Guardian*, February 28, 2002.

Swenson, John. "Jazz Condition" *The Washington Times*, May 21 2003.

Taylor, Billy. *Jazz Piano: A Jazz History.* Dubuque, Iowa: W. C. Brown, 1982.

Taylor, Chris. Interview The Bays on http://www.bbc.co.uk/dna/collective A1137638.

Taylor, Yuval, ed. *The Future of Jazz.* Chicago: A Cappella, 2002.

Teachout, Terry. "The Color of Jazz." *Commentary*, September 1995.

The Necks Big Thing." *The Guardian*, January 9, 2004.

The Shape of Jazz and What's To Come." *The Atlantic Monthly*, 4 December 1997.

The Young Lions. *Liner notes.* New York: Elektra Musician 96–0196–1.

Toop, David. "Replicant: On Dub" in *Audio Culture: Readings in Modern Music*, ed. Christoph Cox and Daniel Warner. London: Continuum, 2004.

Tribe. Linear notes. *Johnie Walker Jazz Impressions at the Gree Dolphin Volume 1.* Sheer Sound SLCD04–8.

Tucker, Michael. *Jan Garbarek: Deep Song.* Hull, UK: Eastnote, 1998.

Vesala, Edward. Liner notes: Ode to the Death of Jazz, ECM 843 196–2.

Waddell, Ray. "The Top Tours of 2002." *Billboard*, 28 December 2002.

Wallis, Roger, and Krister Malm. *Big Sounds From Small Peoples.* London: Constable, 1984.

Walters, John L. "The United States of Jazz." *The Guardian*, April 30th 2004.

Watrous, Peter. "For US Jazz Players, Europe Is The Place To Be." *The New York Times*, July 31, 1996.

Watrous, Peter. "Jazz, Classical, Art, Business: A Series Wraps into One." *The New York Times*, August 2, 1994.

Watrous, Peter. "Lincoln Center Elevates Status of Jazz" *The New York Times*, December 19, 1995.

Watrous, Peter. "Polishing the Image of Louis Armstrong." *The New York Times*, December 14, 1994.

Watson, Phillip. "Southern Blue Soul Brother Number One." *The Wire*, New Year 1992.

Wavell, Stuart. "Life, As Advertised, Ends At 50." *The Sunday Times* (London), 16 May 2004.

Werner, Kenny. *Effortless Mastery.* New Albany: Jamey Abersold Jazz, 1996.

Westin, Lars. "Liner notes: *Bebop Enters Sweden 1947–49.*" Dragon DRCD 318.

Westin, Lars. "Liner notes: *Harry Arnold 1964–65.*" Dragon DGCD 379.

Whitehead, Kevin. "It's Jazz, Stupid." *The Village Voice*, November 23, 1993.

Whitehead, Kevin. "Jazz Rebels." *Downbeat*, August 1993.
Whitehead, Kevin. *New Dutch Swing*. New York: Billboard Books, 1998.
Williams, Richard. "Jazz: The Obituary." *The Guardian Review* May 25, 2001.
Williams, Richard. "Spontaneous combustion". *The Guardian*, provenance unknown.
Withers, Glen. "Boy Wonder" *City*, March 2004.
Woideck, Carl. *Charlie Parker: His Music and Life* Ann Arbor, Michigan: University of Michigan Press, 1996.
Woodward, Richard B. "Jazz Wars: A Tale of Age, Rage and Hash Brownies." *The Village Voice* August 9, 1994.
Woodward, Richard B. "Kind of Blue." *The Village Voice*, January 10–16, 2001.
"Wynton Marsalis Signs with Blue Note." Blue Note press release, Summer 2003.
"Wynton Marsalis: Swinging Into the 21st Century," Sony Jazz press release, 1999.
Zenni, Stefano. "Liner Notes: *Round About A Midsummer's Dream*," Gianluigi Trovesi Nonet Enja ENJ 9384–2.

Author Interviews and Emails

Eivind Aarset, 2001, 2002
John Abercrombie, 2004
Lennart Aberg, 2004
Erling Aksdal, many conversations and e-mails, 2003 and 2004
Arlid Andersen, 1999, 2004
Reid Anderson, 2002
Larry Appelbaum, 2003
Iain Ballamy, 2004
Bill Bauer, 2004
Yves Beauvais, 2002
Bob Belden, 2001
Graeme Bell, 2003
Ola Bengtsson, e-mails 2004
Erice Horpestad Berthelsen, 2004
Matthew Bourne, 2003
Michael Brecker, 2001
Bob Brookmeyer, 2004, e-mail 2004
Guillermo E. Brown, e-mail 2002
Sholto Byrnes, 2004
Don Byron, 2000
Jon Christensen, 1999
John Coxon, 2002, 2003
Laurent de Wilde, 2002, 2003
Ferdinand Dorsman, 2004
Dave Douglas, e-mail 2003, 2004
Manfred Eicher, 1999
Jon Faddis, 1993
Orjan Fahlstrom, e-mails 2004
Ingebrigt Haker Flaten, e-mail 2002
Jan Garbarek, 2004
Adrian Gibson, 2002
Rob Gibson, 2000, 2003
Gerry Godley, 2004
Paul Gompes, 2005
Paul Grabowsky, 2003
Nathan Grave, 2003, 2004

Frank Griffith, 2004
Bo Grønningsaeter, 2004, 2005
Tord Gustavsen, 2004
Heorbie Hancock, 2005
Duncan Heining, e-mail 2004
Arve Henriksen, 2004
Christopher Hodgkins, 2005
Yuri Honing, 2005.
Martin Hornveth, 2003
Adrian Jackson, 2003, 2004
Marty Khan, e-mail 2004
Dave King, 2002, 2003
Bill Kirchner, e-mail 2003
Wolfram Knauer, 2004
Jonas Knutsson, 2002, 2003
Hakon Kornstad, 2000, 2001
Bill Laswell, 1998
Leo @ Blu Mar Ten, 2004
Dave Liebman, e-mail 2005
Nils Lindberg, 2002
Gunnar Lindgren, e-mail 2004
Caspar Llewellyn-Smith, 2004
Jonas Lonna, 2002
Julien Lorau, 2001
Steve Marcus, 2003
Peter Margasak, e-mail 2004
Branford Marsalis, 2002
Wynton Marsalis, 1991, 2000
John Marshall, 2003
Masters at Work, e-mail 2002
Christian McBride, 2002
John Medeski, 2002
Gianluigi Trovesi, e-mail 2003
Brad Mehlldau, e-mails 2002, 2003, 2004
Steen Meier, 2002, 2004, e-mails 2004
Pat Metheny, 2002, 2004
Cim Meyer, e-mail 2005

Nils Petter Molvaer, 2001, 2004
David Murray, 1999.
Silje Nergaard, 2001
Jon Newey, 2004
Mike Nock, 2003
Eivind Opsvik, 2003
Dr. Elizabeth Peterson, 2003, 2004
Courtney Pine, 2000, 2003
Marcello Piras, 2004, e-mails 2004
Dr. Lewis Porter, e-mail 2004
Bobby Previte, 2003.
Jack Reilly, 2002, e-mail 2004
Tim Richards, e-mail 2004
Paul Rinzler, e-mail 2004
Mighty Mo Rogers, 2002
Randy Sandke, e-mail, 2004
Gene Santoro, e-mail 2003
Jarmo Savolainen, e-mails 2004
Adam Seiff, 2004
Matthew Shipp, e-mail 2003
Solvieg Slettahjell, 2004

Odd Sneeggen, 2002
Tomasz Stanko, 2001, 2002, 2004
Helger Sten, 2002
Bobo Stenson, 1998
Esbjörn Svenssön, 2001, 2004
Henri Texier, 2001
Mikko Toivanen, e-mails 2004
Erik Truffaz, 1999
Wouter Turkenburg, e-mails 2004
Ken Vandermark, 2001
Bengt-Arne Wallin, 2002
Bugge Wesseltoft, 2000, 2002
Mike Westbrook, 2005
Lars Westin, 2004
Dr. Tony Whyton, e-mail 2003, 2004
Anders Widmark, 2002
Cassandra Wilson, 1992
Paul Wilson, 2003 & 2004
Per Zanussi, e-mail 2004
Joe Zawinul, 2002, 2004

INDEX